Race and Popular Fantasy Literature

This book illuminates the racialized nature of twenty-first century Western popular culture by exploring how discourses of race circulate in the Fantasy genre. It examines not only major texts in the genre, but also the impact of franchises, industry, editorial and authorial practices, and fan engagements on race and representation. Approaching Fantasy as a significant element of popular culture, it visits the struggles over race, racism, and white privilege that are enacted within creative works across media and the communities which revolve around them. While scholars of Science Fiction have explored the genre's racialized constructs of possible futures, this book is the first examination of Fantasy to take up the topic of race in depth. The book's interdisciplinary approach, drawing on Literary, Cultural, Fan, and Whiteness Studies, offers a cultural history of the anxieties which haunt Western popular culture in a century eager to declare itself post-race. The beginnings of the Fantasy genre's habits of Whiteness in the twentieth century are examined, with an exploration of the continuing impact of older problematic works through franchising, adaptation, and imitation. Young also discusses the major twenty-first-century sub-genres which both re-use and subvert Fantasy conventions. The final chapter explores debates and anti-racist praxis in authorial and fan communities. With its multi-pronged approach and innovative methodology, this book is an important and original contribution to studies of race, Fantasy, and twenty-first-century popular culture.

Helen Young is an Honorary Associate of the Department of English at the University of Sydney, Australia.

D1570368

Routledge Interdisciplinary Perspectives on Literature

Race and Popular Fantasy Literature

Habits of Whiteness

Helen Young

Routledge
Taylor & Francis Group

NEW YORK AND LONDON

First published 2016
by Routledge
711 Third Avenue, New York, NY 10017

and by Routledge
2 Park Square, Milton Park, Abingdon, Oxon OX14 4RN

First issued in paperback 2018

Routledge is an imprint of the Taylor & Francis Group, an informa business

Library of Congress Cataloging in Publication Data

Young, Helen Victoria.
Race and popular fantasy literature : habits of whiteness / Helen Young.
   pages cm. — (Routledge Interdisciplinary Perspectives on Literature ; 51)
Includes bibliographical references and index.
   1. Fantasy fiction, English—History and criticism. 2. Fantasy fiction, American—History and criticism. 3. Fantasy fiction—History and criticism. 4. Whites in literature. 5. Race in literature. 6. Popular culture and literature—Great Britain—History. 7. Popular culture and literature—United States—History. I. Title.
PR830.F3Y68 2015
823'.0876609—dc23   2015011573

ISBN 13: 978-1-138-54770-4 (pbk)
ISBN 13: 978-1-138-85023-1 (hbk)

Typeset in Sabon
by codeMantra

For Steph

Contents

Contents

List of Figure

Acknowledgments

This work was funded by an Australian Research Council Discovery Early Career Research Award, and I thank the anonymous reviewers of the scheme and Professor Annamarie Jagose, then Head of the School of Letters, Art, and Media at the University of Sydney, for supporting the project in its infancy. I would also like to thank Professor Carole Cusack, and Associate Professor Carol Reid for their support in the years leading up to this project, and throughout it.

Dr Kieryn McKay, Lydia Saleh Rofail, and Timothy Steains provided excellent and invaluable assistance throughout the course of the research, for which I thank them. I am also deeply grateful to the authors who shared their time and thoughts: Aliette de Bodard, Ambelin Kwaymullina, Kij Johnson, Daniel Heath Justice, Kevin Rigathi, and Mary Anne Mohanraj. Thank you also to Dr Gillian Polack for knowing almost everyone working in speculative fiction. The staff of the Eaton Collection at the University of California, Riverside, were generous with their time and materials, as were the members of the International Association for the Fantastic in the Arts mailing list, and the Pulp Studies mailing list hosted by the University of the Sciences.

Multiple people have supported me in multiple ways throughout this project, including: Assistant Professor Carol Robinson, Professor John Frow, Professor Clare Bradford, Professor Richard Utz, and Professor Louise D'Arcens. Members of the Early Career Researcher writing groups at the University of Sydney and the University of Melbourne provided excellent feedback on early drafts of chapters, as did my mother Dr Ann Young on the entire manuscript. My father, Dr Robert Young, started the whole thing by reading me *The Hobbit* before I was old enough to read it for myself. I am also very grateful to the many friends and colleagues whose excellent company and ideas have sustained me throughout, some of whom are named here already and others who are too many to list. All errors are my own.

Thank you, finally, to my partner Steph, without whom this book would not exist, for many things, including her willingness to deconstruct the racial politics of favourite books and television programs and to play *Lego The Lord of the Rings* with me, excellent editing skills, and tea.

Introduction

RE-THINKING GENRE, THINKING ABOUT RACE

Fantasy is one of the most prominent genres in twenty-first-century Western popular culture. From blockbuster movies such as Peter Jackson's *The Lord of the Rings* trilogy (2001–2003) based on the novels of J. R. R. Tolkien, to the Harry Potter franchise (1997–2007), George R. R. Martin's *A Song of Ice and Fire*, HBO's television spin-off *Game of Thrones*, and video-games like *World of Warcraft*, Fantasy is phenomenally successful. Fantasy has a reputation for being a eurocentric genre, that is, one which is by, for, and about White people; in this volume I explore the ways in which the foundations of that reputation were established and how they are now being both attacked and defended. In doing so, it seeks to shed light on much broader cultural and social debates around race and difference, inclusion and exclusion, which are currently taking place in local, national, and global arenas.

The Whiteness which characterised much of the Fantasy genre throughout the twentieth century, and which still has significant influence, reflects the social and cultural milieu in which Fantasy was produced. Richard Dyer argues that "the invisibility of whiteness as a racial position in white (which is to say dominant) discourse is of a piece with its ubiquity;"[1] Whiteness as default setting is as much a feature of the Fantasy genre as it is of western culture and society. This book takes Fantasy as a microcosm of popular culture to investigate the discourses around race and racial difference which circulate in the Anglophone world. What is said about race and ethnicity? How are the concepts conceived? Whose voices ask and answer?

The past decade has seen a number of works explore Science Fiction and race, particular within American popular culture.[2] There has been, to date, however, no book-length work devoted to race and Fantasy. The work which does is exist is often framed within volumes dedicated to the fantastic mode rather than the Fantasy genre, such as in the themed volume 21 of the *Journal of the Fantastic in the Arts* and Elisabeth Anne Leonard's important *Into Darkness Peering: Race and Color in the Fantastic*.[3] It is generally focused on a single work or series,[4] or on a particular medium – video-games are increasingly of interest.[5] A relatively small body of work explores adaptations,[6] while fandoms have also drawn some recent attention.[7] This volume moves beyond studies which are the norm, to offer a comprehensive account of the ways in which discourses of race and difference circulate within the Fantasy genre-culture.

Fantasy is a useful sub-set through which to explore popular culture not only because of its prominent position at the present historical moment, but because its inherently non-mimetic nature creates a space which is at least nominally not "the real world" and is therefore safer for cultural work around fraught issues such as – although by no means limited to – race. This is not to suggest that the imagined worlds of Fantasy are separate from reality, but rather that the inclusion of an impossible element – magic, dragons, and the like – constructs rhetorical distance between one and the other. That rhetorical distance can be merely escapist and allow a work to *not* overtly engage with difficult questions, but, like other speculative genres – Science Fiction and Horror – Fantasy has the potential to make us look at our world in new ways, to reconsider attitudes and assumptions. This volume explores Fantasy which both does and does not overtly engage with discourses around race and difference, taking an approach inspired by critical race theory by considering Whiteness as race and racial habit.

FANTASY AS A GENRE

Scholarly engagements with the Fantasy genre tend to come largely from literary perspectives and to focus on genre as a body of texts, usually written. Definitions, as a result, are generally concerned with how to delineate its boundaries – which texts are in and which are out? Brian Attebery's delineation of "fantasy-as-mode" and "fantasy-as-formula" from the Fantasy genre continues to be one of the most influential and useful approaches to that project. The "fantastic mode" encompasses "all literary manifestations of the imagination's" ability to soar above the merely possible, that is, non-mimetic writing.[8] Formulaic fantasy is "essentially a commercial product," the success of which "depends on consistency and predictability."[9] It is not necessarily bad, but is rooted in "the opposite extreme" of the "potential anarchy of the fantastic."[10] Attebery proposes the still widely used "fuzzy set" model of genre. A "fuzzy set" has "a clear center but boundaries that shade off imperceptibly, so that a book on the fringes may be considered as belonging or not."[11] One of the key questions suggested by to this model, albeit one which often goes undiscussed is: whose opinion counts? The "fuzzy set" is necessarily open to interpretation at its edges, but its centre must also come from somewhere.

In their introduction to *The Cambridge Companion to Fantasy Literature*, Edward James and Farah Mendlesohn observe that scholars tend to "generate definitions of fantasy which include the texts that they value and exclude most of what general readers think of as fantasy."[12] Scholarly work tends to be more concerned with placing Fantasy as a genre within the broader "fantastic mode." Classic works like Ann Swinfen's aptly titled *Defence of Fantasy* (1984) and Rosemary Jackson's *Fantasy: the Literature of Subversion* (1981) worked against both popular and academic prejudices which saw Fantasy as juvenile, generic, and unworthy of attention.[13] The desire of more recent historians of Fantasy literature to trace its roots back to at least medieval times is suggestive of a continued desire to represent Fantasy as a literary mode of writing which can be validated by locating its antecedents in the canon.

One of the underlying problems when it comes to defining Fantasy, as James and Mendlesohn imply, is that scholarship by and large – Cultural Studies is a major exception – values works deemed to have artistic merit. Art – literary or otherwise – is deemed to be, as Pierre Bourdieu terms it, "autonomous," created for its own sake and without consideration of the desires or needs of the potential audience; the opposing system of value is the "heteronomous" which operates throughout society, particularly "in the economic field."[14] The artistic value of a work is commonly framed in opposition to its market value: "because it is a good measure of the degree of autonomy, and therefore of *presumed* adherence to the disinterested values which constitute the specific law of the field [of art] the degree of public success is … the main differentiating factor."[15] Twenty-first century Western culture is still deeply steeped in the belief that a work which has commercial success and mass appeal is not good art, although I do not subscribe to the idea in this book. Defining Fantasy in artistic – Literary – terms is not *necessarily* at odds with considering it as what Bourdieu terms a "field of large-scale production," but the two systems of value are always in tension and are not easy to reconcile.[16]

James and Mendlesohn's volume attempts to do so in its approach nonetheless. It "endeavours to take the body of genre fantasy as a multiplicity of terms that recognizes academic, reader and commercial understandings of fantasy as equally valuable."[17] They include, for example, chapters written by authors of creative works as well as scholars. Their collection and Mendlesohn's earlier *Rhetorics of Fantasy*[18] mark important shifts in criticism by breaking down boundaries between general and theoretical definitions of Fantasy, and moving beyond work which seeks mainly to define what the genre is and where its limits lie. It is perhaps inevitable that a slim volume attempting to do so much would be critiqued for not being sufficiently comprehensive. Author Steven Erikson took James and Mendlesohn's volume as synecdoche for contemporary scholarship on Fantasy, arguing that it is concerned too much with the edges of the genre and that "academic discussion of the fantastic" has "a gaping hole in the middle."[19] My approach to texts in this work is suggested by James and Mendlesohn, as well as Erikson: I am interested in those which lie at the centre of the "fuzzy set" – considered Fantasy by authors, academics, publishers, fans, general readers, and critics alike, and sit within Bourdieu's "field of large-scale production," that is, popular genres.

Popular fiction, Ken Gelder suggests, is: "open to mass audiences and necessarily caught up in the logic of the marketplace, which means it remains *conscious* of its viewers/readers … It values conventions over originality ... [and has] usually ... a potentially immediate, broad-based distribution."[20] I do not invoke this categorisation to suggest that either writers or readers of Fantasy consider it to be merely a commercial enterprise, or to dismiss the artistic merit of any works within the genre. Rather, I use this description of "popular fiction" as a starting point for both my general approach and selection of texts. That is to say, I am principally interested in works which are published with a potential mass audience in mind, and which engage with genre conventions. I am, moreover, interested in the ways in which the practices and logics of industry, and the increasingly active role of audiences in shaping production and publication.

Fantasy as Genre-Culture Network

Recent work on Science Fiction has engaged in detailed ways with the processes involved in creating genre. Mark Bould and Sherryl Vint, discussing science fiction and drawing on Rick Altman's work on film, have argued that:

> genres are never, as frequently perceived, objects which already exist in the world and which are subsequently studied by genre critics, but fluid and tenuous constructions made by the interactions of various claims and practices by writers, producers, distributors, marketers, readers, fans, critics and other discursive agents.[21]

Deciding whether a work is considered Fantasy by all these "discursive agents" is, in practical terms, impossible – not least because of the different views which might be held even within those broad groups. So, in deciding whether a work is Fantasy or not for the purposes of this research I have looked at two key areas: the ways it is presented to the public both by its author(s) and publisher, and the way it is read and received by critics, fans, and general readers. This applies not only literary works, but to the other media which have become increasingly important during the twenty-first century: video-games, film, television, and comics.

In this volume I am, however, not interested just in texts, nor in the ways in which Bould and Vint's "discursive agents" talk about them and assign them – or do not – to genre. Rather, I take an approach suggested by recent work in studies of popular music, and on connections between culture and society and include discursive agents, creative texts, and the mass of material in which agents talk about texts under the more inclusive term genre-culture. Chris Atton gives the following useful account:

> genre culture in popular music places musical practices within a wider set of social processes that include not only norms of musical performance, but the behaviours of musicians and audiences, the ideological arguments that circulate around the music and the meaning and location of music within a political economy.[22]

With simple substitutions this becomes a coherent account of the how Fantasy as a genre can be usefully conceived: genre culture in popular fantasy places textual practices within a wider set of social processes that include not only Fantasy conventions, but the behaviours of authors and audiences, the ideological arguments that circulate around the texts, and the meaning and location of Fantasy within a political economy. By hyphenating genre-culture, I wish to draw attention to how firmly texts and "discursive agents" are tied to each other; neither would exist without the other.[23]

If genre is expanded to genre-culture, how then to account for the nature of those ties and the networks of influence which flow back and forth along them, how they act on each other? Texts – the books, films, games and so on that are read, watched, played, and created – must be taken into account, but so must the people who make and engage with them in many different ways. My approach to genre-culture is influenced by flat ontologies which do not privilege human perspectives, particularly Actor Network Theory (ANT), as described principally in the work of Bruno Latour as it allows ways to account for the agencies of what would traditionally be considered textual objects and human subjects. ANT is a method through which to explore material-semiotic systems, that is, networks which include both material "things" and semiotic "concepts." The network of ANT is itself "a concept, not a thing out there,"[24] just as a genre is a concept as well as a community, not simply a pre-given set of creative works.

I use ANT more as an exploratory heuristic tool than a methodology, considering the entities which exist within the network of Fantasy genre-culture. How are often competing discourses of race and diversity translated through the network? An ANT-style approach allows this work to consider the multiple roles that different entities might encompass simultaneously, and also to consider not only human agents but the non-human, material and otherwise. So, an individual has a body, and that body for a person of colour is likely to be particularly visible in the commonly, although not invariably White, communities of Fantasy. The same individual might identify as a fan and as an author at different times and in different places, and have different meanings to others and the person themselves accordingly, meanings which are sometimes related to their physical being and sometimes not.

Conventions and Habits

Taking genre as a complex network which encompasses more than just creative works requires an expanded understanding of genre conventions. Conventions are invariably textual – characters, events, settings and the like – which in the case of Fantasy, as I detail in the first chapter of this book details, traditionally are inspired in European culture and history, particularly that of the Middle Ages. The culture aspect of Fantasy, however, has its own conventions, notably around its racial and gender composition which is stereotypically – if increasingly inaccurately – White, middle-class, and male. While there is considerable evidence to suggest that this is a great over-simplification, it is unarguably true that the loudest voices – authorial and audience alike – were those of White men for much of the genre's history. Referring simply to "convention" where I mean more than textual features is likely to not only cause confusion, but to down play the human aspects of Fantasy as genre-culture, so I have preferred "habit" throughout, unless I am referring only to textual material, in which case I have used convention.

Bennett et al. give an account of the intellectual history of habit as a concept which resonates with changing approaches to genre conventions, particular in a genre like Fantasy which is strongly aligned with the formulaic. They argue that post-Foucaldian accounts of habit draw ultimately on the thought of Immanuel Kant, who understood habit as "automatic, unthinking repetition."[25] In the Kantian tradition, habit "served as the key marker of the boundary line separating nature from culture as the historically accumulating realm of free human agency." In many literary approaches to Fantasy, convention takes on a mantle resembling Kantian habit by tending too much towards the formulaic and away from the fantastic mode; the mode inspires newness and change to the (potential) extent of anarchy, while the formulaic is merely safe, conservative, unthinking acceptance of existing order.[26] Marxist critiques of Fantasy in particular tend towards such a reading.[27]

Drawing on film criticism, Jason Toynbee argued that genre should be seen "as a process in which the tension between repetition and difference fundamental to all symbolic forms is regulated."[28] Conventions exist not merely to be repeated but to be departed from, and, perhaps, altered. His account of genre, which he approaches as genre-culture, anticipates concepts of habit inspired by Giles Deleuze's *Difference and Repetition*.[29] Bennett et al. describe this approach: "it is through habit that the past is accumulated and stabilized, providing a point of anchorage for action in the present through which processes of open-ended becoming are perpetuated."[30] I prefer this to the Kantian approach not only because it recognises that habit/convention/genre is not static, but because it allows space to recognise that even a choice made without conscious thought is still a choice; acts of change *and* repetition require agency. Using a genre convention which inscribes Whiteness into a creative work or imagined world is as much about race as rejecting or subverting that same convention.

RACE

Defining race is equally if not more difficult than defining Fantasy; both are discursive formations, shaped by social and cultural forces contingent on time and place. This study does not seek to outline definitive borders for either. It rather offers insights into how, and why, ideas attached to "race" are meaningful in twenty-first-century popular culture through the microcosm of Fantasy, and into what those meanings are and who is involved in producing them. The ultimate foundation of the present study is that race is a social construct which assigns non-necessary meanings to common phenotypical features of humanity in order to distinguish groups and assign hierarchical value to them. There is no genetic basis for race as a concept of human difference, as Patrick Sussman states:

> There is no biological reality to human race. There are no major complex behaviors that directly correlate with what might be considered human "racial" characteristics. There is no inherent relationship between intelligence, law-abidingness, of economic practices and race, just as there is no relationship between nose size, height, height, blood group, or skin color and any set of complex human behaviors.[31]

Individuals are born with the ability to learn any language or culture.[32] This is a critical work as much as a descriptive one which seeks to offer foundation for further explorations of race – as well as racism and anti-racism – in Fantasy, popular culture, and the globalized societies which produce them.

The taxonomist of nature Carl Linnaeus included humanity as part of the natural world – as opposed to divinely distinct from it – for the first time in his *Systema Naturae*, first published in 1735. The Enlightenment drive for both rationality and classification led him to divide humanity into four groups: *Homo europaeus*, *Homo asiaticus*, *Homo africanus*, and *Homo americanus* – or Europeans, Asians, Africans, and Americans. As Justin Smith observes, divisions between human groups "would remain very difficult to specify with any precision or clarity, even though a great number of 18th century thinkers were actively devoted to the project."[33] No agreement could even be reached as to how many races existed, let alone what they were. Skin colour as a marker of racial difference was codified in the 1795 third edition of J. F. Blumenbach's *On the Natural Variety of Mankind*;[34] prior to this skull shape and size were considered the most important factors in the delineation of race, and remained very significant into the twentieth century.

Modern concepts of race were formulated as a "widely shared theory of biologically determined, physical, intellectual and moral differences between human groups."[35] Hannah Augstein identifies three key elements in nineteenth century race-thinking: that humanity can be divided into races "whose characteristics are fixed and defy the modifying influences of external circumstances;" that these racial groupings have different "intellectual and moral capacities;" and "that mental endowments are bound up with certain physiognomical specifications [… which] reveal the inward nature of the individual or population in question."[36] Race was variously taken to be both marked and determined by blood, skin colour, and language use. Racial logics thus link physical traits with the non-physical, and understand both as biologically heritable. The first chapter in this book offers an account of those specific features of race theory which most profoundly influence Fantasy's habits of Whiteness – philology, Anglo-Saxonism, evolution and polygenesis – linking the writings of foundational authors, Robert E. Howard and J. R. R. Tolkien, to those constructs.

None of the methods of differentiating races hold up under scrutiny, and were often based on extremely unscientific methods, such as using a single skull to represent the characteristics of an entire race. The physical and philological factors which were used to taxonomize humanity were, without exception, structured so as to show the superiority of Europeans; they were linked to the supposed mental and moral capabilities of each constructed race. Arthur de Gobineau wrote in his now infamous 1854 *The Inequality of the Human Races* that "the language of a race is strictly bound up with its intelligence."[37] One key purpose of race theory, particularly in the nineteenth century was to simultaneously explain and justify European imperialism around the globe; the British Empire was particularly successful, but was not the only one. European whites may have been the best, but the English appeared to be the best of the best on the basis of their imperial and colonial successes, even if the American colonies had thrown off the yoke and begun their own expansionist projects. As this book focuses on Anglophone Fantasy, the British, colonial, and American contexts are of particular interest.

Race and Discourse

In 1998 Matthew Frye Jacobson began his important work *Whiteness of a Different Color* thus:

> We tend to think of race as being indisputable, *real*. It frames our notions of kinship and descent and influences our movements in the social world; we see it plainly on one another's faces. It seems like a product not of the social imagination, but of biology ... however, scholars in several disciplines have recently shaken faith in this biological certainty.[38]

A decade and a half later at the time of writing for this book, genetic science has demonstrated conclusively that the notion of biological race, developed throughout the eighteenth and nineteenth century, has no scientific basis. Science, having made race in modern terms, has disowned its creation. The American Anthropological Association, for example, stated in 1998 that "human populations are not unambiguous, clearly demarcated, biologically distinct groups" as had once been thought, and that "physical variations in the human species have no meaning except the social ones that humans put on them."[39] Races, to use Jacobson's terms, "are invented categories" the boundaries of which shift according to socio-cultural context.[40] Race has never been a purely scientific or value-neutral concept.

If race has no biological, genetic basis and cannot be fixed by scientific definitions, what then does it mean? What is race? Sally Haslanger critiques both descriptivist and externalist philosophic approaches to explorations of the meaning of race. She characterises descriptivism as giving priority to thought, and externalism as prioritising "things in the world … we communicate, according to the externalist, by talking about the same things; according to the descriptivist, by expressing the same thoughts."[41] In this book I follow Haslanger in preferring the former approach because, as she argues, it "provides better access to the process of creating meanings."[42] The semantic meanings of "race" are multiple; the *Oxford English Dictionary* offers "a group of people, animals, or plants, connected by common descent or origin" as the first of eight possible variants on this concept.[43] This book is concerned with the cultural and social significances of "race," rather than codified semantic meanings; it asks not so much what race is, but how it is made, and by whom.

In *The Philosophy of Race*, Albert Atkin argues that concepts of race create "labels, badges and particular racial identities that … are deeply powerful and impacting" even though they lack scientific basis.[44] He highlights the socio-historical elements which structure contemporary concepts of race, and argues that the most philosophically fruitful approach to race is to consider "how the race concepts we would like to see in the future might be best realized in the social and political presents we can generate now."[45] While I agree with Atkin theoretically on this point, his statement suggests that there is a unified "we" with a single, or at least coherent and consistent understanding of the political and social present, and a similarly coherent and consistent set of aspirations for the future. This book will show that neither exists within the Fantasy genre-culture.

The "process of creating meaning" to which Haslanger alludes is a struggle of multiple possible concepts and meanings of race we *will* see in the future. Haslanger terms the process a collaboration, and while many groups and individuals are involved, their interactions resemble an ongoing war, with a series of remarkably similar oft-repeated battles, more than a set of negotiations. Online debates about race, representation, and prejudice invoke the language of conflict: "social justice warriors" and "allies" are used variously to denote White authors and audience members who advocate racial diversity. Challenges to genre habits rarely, if ever, pass without resistance, as will be discussed in detail throughout this work, particular in the final chapter, which examines the online phenomenon known as "RaceFail 09" or the "Great Cultural Appropriation Debate of Doom."

Human bodies may no longer constitute race scientifically, but they serve as markers of difference in ways which cannot be disentangled from its history. Thus, although science and medicine have declared that race is social and not scientific, accounts of race-as-biology retain a great deal of currency.[46] Fields as diverse as censuses, the law and biomedical science invoke biologies of race in processes and practices of social governance.[47] The denunciation of race as a science-based fact has collapsed the foundations on which centuries' worth of race-based systemic discrimination stood.

The legacies of that discrimination, however, remain and are the subject of contestation in almost every facet of twenty-first-century western societies, from politics, to the law, medicine, and the arts. Society, as Tony Bennett has recently argued, can and should not be separated from culture;[48] this book recognises the connections between social and cultural productions of race in the modern world.

Race is written both *through* the body's phenotypical features and *on* it by the social assignation of associations – meanings – to its outward, visible, phenotypical features. It is thus both written and read, a discursive construct. Race that it written on the body in socio-cultural context is also a matter of lived experience and of identity for individuals. Members of minority groups tend to be more aware that their bodies are read as "raced" by majority society because they are understood as "different" where White is normative; that normativity leads Whites to be largely unconscious of the fact that they too are "raced."

A key question, then, is "what is Whiteness?" Race, as noted above, is not *solely* defined through scientific discourses, but is also linked to culture through the construct of ethnicity. Bodies are assumed to possess or have a claim to particularly stories and histories, and those stories and histories can be used to justify the presence, actions, and power of the bodies to which they belong. This has been particularly true since the nineteenth century when philologists – most famously the Brothers Grimm – collected the orally transmitted stories of the *volk* – folktales – in the belief that they could provide access to and recuperation of the essence of the racial group. Since approximately the same time – and that is no coincidence – the Middle Ages have been constructed and associated with Whiteness, a point which I return to throughout this book, particularly in chapter three.[49] Whiteness, thus, is not just the state of bodily being dependent on phenotypical features, but also encompasses culture. I have preferred to use "race" rather than "ethnicity" – which is often used as a euphemism for race in contemporary culture – for the most part throughout this book, despite its interest in stories and imagined worlds, to highlight the point that they are never *just* stories but are always connect to people – bodies – through writing, and reading.

HABITS OF WHITENESS

The central argument of this book is that Fantasy formed habits of Whiteness early in the life of the genre-culture, and is, in the early decades of the twenty-first century, struggling to break them. Those habits take multiple forms: some are to do with the bodies which have traditionally dominated its spaces – in both the real and imagined worlds; some with the voices that are most audible; and some with the kinds of sources which inspire imagined worlds, and the ways that they are used. I do not mean simply that Fantasy has an ongoing history of being dominated by White bodies, voices, and stories that are widely considered White cultural heritage, but that that history of domination shapes what can be done, and how easily, by any actor in the genre-culture network.

My account of habits of Whiteness draws on Sara Ahmed's concept of "habit worlds" in which she argues that "if habits are about what bodies do, in ways that are repeated, then they might also shape what bodies *can do*," and that "spaces acquire the shape of the bodies that "inhabit" them."[50] The spaces of genre-culture – whether physical, digital, or imagined – have acquired the shape of the White bodies that have habitually occupied them for decades. I drew also on Bourdieu's concept of habitus is my account of habits. Habitus is:

> a system of dispositions, that is of permanent manners of being, seeing, acting and thinking, or a system of *long-lasting* (rather than permanent) schemes or schemata or structures of perception, conception, and action.[51]

The second part is the most applicable here: habits of Whiteness are sustained but not unbreakable, they are, however, often *seen* as permanent, that is, as innate to the genre-culture. Habits of Whiteness in Fantasy, thus, simultaneously influence who can be present, and what is seen, thought, and done, by creating patterns of bodies and spaces alike.

Contemporary popular Fantasy inherits its habits from the twentieth century society in which it was founded. Key authors such as H. P. Lovecraft, Robert E. Howard, Tolkien, and C. S. Lewis were all themselves British or American White men who drew heavily on European myths, literature, and history for inspiration, and who populated their worlds largely with White protagonists. Whether they themselves, or their texts, were racist remains a topic of at times bitter argument among scholars, critics, and audiences. The patterns laid in the early-to-mid-twentieth century formed into habits in its last two decades as Fantasy became a major publishing category and genre in popular culture, although even as this happened there were counter-voices, such as that of African American author Samuel R. Delany. The explosion of digital technologies and the rise of multi-media adaptations and franchises has significantly shaped the Fantasy landscape in the twenty-first century, not just enabling but fostering the repetition of old habits and adding new dimensions to them. The first two chapters explore the processes by which nineteenth-century theories of race and difference have been drawn into the twenty-first through the imagined worlds of Fantasy and the social and cultural milieus in which they were created and recreated, considering the nature of media industries and audience responses as well as texts.

Fantasy habitually constructs the Self through Whiteness and Otherness through an array of racist stereotypes, particularly but not exclusively those associated with Blackness. The Middle Ages are, anachronistically, considered White space in the popular imagination, and the realms of Gritty

Fantasy – such as Martin's *A Song of Ice and Fire* and Bioware's Dragon Age franchise – which claim to represent the medieval period as it really was, reflect this. The imagined worlds are dominated by Whiteness, imagined as a (never-extant) pre-race utopia, a state which authorizes the constructed Whiteness of some fan communities, as the third chapter argues. The fourth chapter explores the representation of orcs, the most racialized of all Fantasy's monsters, principally in novels and games including: *Dungeons & Dragons*, Mary Gentle's *Grunts!*, the Warcraft and The Lord of the Rings franchises, and Terry Pratchett's *Unseen Academicals*. The racial logics which structure genre worlds mean that shifting representations do not necessarily change Fantasy's habits of Whiteness, but can rather re-inscribe them in new forms.

Fantasy creates worlds structured by imperialist nostalgia. For much of its history, the Fantasy genre has avoided engaging with imperialism and colonialism in any critical way, as has most Western popular culture. Twenty-first century Fantasy has begun to critique colonialism, imperialism, and their legacies, although indigenous voices are still significantly marginalized within the genre. Chapter five offers three case studies postcolonialism in popular culture: Daniel Heath Justice's The Way of Thorn and Thunder trilogy; Naomi Novik's Temeraire series; and N. K. Jemisin's Inheritance trilogy. In Urban Fantasy, explored in chapter six, not only imperial histories but those of migrancy, slavery, and national myth-making re-emerge in corporeal form as the magic, gods, and monster of folklore in modern cities, suburbs, and small towns. From American television programs such as *Grimm* and *Sleepy Hollow*, to the novels of Nalo Hopkinson and Ben Aaronovitch, the substrata of the past intrude into the present. As authors seek new stories and to represent the diversity of modern society cultural appropriation and representation are increasingly topics of discussion – and controversy – in Fantasy communities.

Digital communication technologies have impacted significantly on the genre-cultures of Science Fiction and Fantasy – which are so intertwined as to be functionally inseparable on any significant scale outside the imagined worlds of texts – and their affordances and challenges are the focus of the final chapter. Two different kinds of influence – affect and money – circulate within Fantasy genre-culture as it is outlined above, and influence how its multiple communities form and re-form genre identity. Online struggles over identity – of individuals, groups, and genre-culture broadly – and efforts to challenge and change Fantasy's habits of Whiteness are explored at length in the final chapter, which includes an analyses of the blogosphere phenomenon known as "Racefail 09" which draws on Eduardo Bonilla-Silva's frameworks of racist discourse. The presence of people of colour in both imagined worlds and the real one is key to changing the habits of genre, digital communication technologies, and online spaces enable that presence to be both claimed and supported.

Finally a note regarding terminology. As a general rule I follow the definitions provided by *The Encyclopedia of Fantasy*,[52] unless otherwise stated.

I use author in its traditional sense, and creator in preference when the text is not a literary one. I use audience in preference to readers, viewers, gamers etc, unless a particular distinction is necessary. Fans are considered a sub-set of audience members, that is, those who have an affective relationship with a given text or texts. I have used people of colour – and its derivatives such as fans of colour – in a very broad way throughout, and recognize that is a term which developed in in a particular national context and is not used universally even in the U.S.A. Individuals in speculative fiction communities identify in myriad ways,[53] the specificities of which I cannot hope to include here. Exploring Fantasy's habit of binary identity construction – White and non-White – necessarily risks repeating it, so I have actively sought to identify individuals using terms they have previously used for themselves – for example in biographical sketches or interviews – and to use a collective term only when necessary.

NOTES

1. Dyer, *White: Essays on Race and Culture*, 3.
2. Douglas, *Astrofuturism: Science, Race, and Visions of Utopia in Space*; Lavender, *Race in American Science Fiction*; Lavender, *Black and Brown Planets: the Politics of Race in Science Fiction*; Nama, *Black Space: Imagining Race in Science Fiction Film*.
3. Leonard, *"Into Darkness Peering": Race and Color in the Fantastic*.
4. Bearick, "Why Is the Only Good Orc a Dead Orc? the Dark Face of Racism Examined in Tolkien's World"; individual chapters in Leonard, *"Into Darkness Peering."*
5. Higgin, "Blackless Fantasy"; Langer, "The Familiar and the Foreign: Playing (Post) Colonialism in *World of Warcraft*"; Poor, "Digital Elves as a Racial Other in Video Games: Acknowledgment and Avoidance."
6. Kim, "Beyond Black and White: Race and Postmodernism in *The Lord of the Rings* Films."
7. Gatson and Reid, "Race and Ethnicity in Fandom"; Reid, "The Wild Unicorn Herd Check-in: the Politics of Race in Science Fiction Fandom"; Stanfill, "Doing Fandom, (Mis)doing Whiteness: Heteronormativity, Racialization, and the Discursive Construction of Fandom"; Young, "Race in Online Fantasy Fandom: Whiteness on Westeros.org."
8. Attebery, *Strategies of Fantasy*, 2.
9. Attebery, *Strategies of Fantasy*, 2.
10. Attebery, *Strategies of Fantasy*, 9.
11. Attebery, *Strategies of Fantasy*, 12.
12. Mendlesohn and James, "Introduction," 1.
13. Jackson, *Fantasy: The Literature of Subversion*; Swinfen, *In Defence of Fantasy: a Study of the Genre in English and American Literature since 1945*.
14. Bourdieu, *The Field of Cultural Production*, 38.
15. Bourdieu, *The Field of Cultural Production*, 39.
16. Bourdieu, *The Field of Cultural Production*, 38.
17. Mendlesohn and James, "Introduction," 2.

18. Mendlesohn, *Rhetorics of Fantasy.*
19. Erikson, "Not Your Grandmother's Epic Fantasy: a Fantasy Author's Thoughts upon Reading *The Cambridge Companion to Fantasy Literature*," 5.
20. Gelder, *Popular Fiction*, 13. Gelder draws significantly on Bourdieu.
21. Bould and Vint, "There Is No Such Thing as Science Fiction," 48.
22. Atton, "Genre and the Cultural Politics of Territory: the Live Experience of Free Improvisation," 427.
23. My thinking here is also influenced by Pierre Bourdieu's account of the relational nature of social fields. Bourdieu, *The Field of Cultural Production.*
24. Latour, *Reassembling the Social*, 131.
25. Bennett et al., "Habit and Habituation: Governance and the Social," 7.
26. Attebery does not accept this reading of fantasy-as-formula.
27. For example, Suvin, *Metamorphoses of Science Fiction.*
28. Toynbee, *Making Popular Music: Musicians, Creativity and Institutions*, 106.
29. Deleuze, *Difference and Repetition.*
30. Bennett et al., "Habit and Habituation," 8.
31. Sussman, *The Myth of Race: the Troubling Persistence of an Unscientific Idea*, 2.
32. AAA, "American Anthropological Association Statement on 'Race.'"
33. Smith, "'Curious Kinks of the Human Mind': Cognition, Natural History, and the Concept of Race," 520.
34. An earlier edition (1781) of that work had increased Linnaeus' four races to five by including 'Malays.' Painter, *The History of White People*, 79.
35. Beasley, *The Victorian Reinvention of Race: New Racisms and the Problem of Grouping in the Human Sciences*, 1.
36. Augstein, "Introduction," x.
37. de Gobineau, *The Inequality of Human Races*, 204.
38. Jacobson, *Whiteness of a Different Color: European Immigrants and the Alchemy of Race*, 1.
39. AAA, "American Anthropological Association Statement on 'Race,'" 712.
40. Jacobson, *Whiteness of a Different Color*, 4.
41. Haslanger, "Language, Politics, and 'The Folk': Looking for 'The Meaning' of 'Race,'" 176.
42. Haslanger, "Language, Politics, and 'The Folk,'" 176.
43. 'race', n.6. *Oxford English Dictionary Online.*
44. Atkin, *The Philosophy of Race*, 74.
45. Atkin, *The Philosophy of Race*, 74.
46. Sussman, *The Myth of Race.*
47. For example. Whitmarsh and Jones, *What's the Use of Race?: Modern Governance and the Biology of Difference.*
48. Bennett, *Making Culture, Changing Society: the Perspective of "Culture" Studies.*
49. Finke and Shichtman, "Inner-City Chivalry in Gil Junger's *Black Knight*: A South Central Yankee in King Leo's Court"; Young, "Whiteness and Time: the Once, Present, and Future Race."
50. Ahmed, "A Phenomenology of Whiteness," 154. Ahmed also theorizes Whiteness itself as a habit.
51. Bourdieu, "Habitus," 27.
52. Clute and Grant, *The Encyclopedia of Fantasy.*
53. Reid, "The Wild Unicorn Herd Check-in," 231–239.

1 Founding Fantasy

J. R. R. Tolkien and Robert E. Howard

The history of fantastic literature can be traced back to *The Epic of Gilgamesh* (c.1150 B.C.E.), but Fantasy as a popular fiction genre is a product of the twentieth century with its roots firmly in the US and UK. The social and cultural mores of those places and time established the habits of Whiteness which still remain influential. Given that the foundations of the genre were laid in the first half of the twentieth century, it is perhaps not surprising that the authors who were most visibly influential were White men; the patriarchal White hegemony over Western culture at that time was firmly entrenched and relatively unchallenged compared to today. Ken Gelder argues that industry and entertainment are two of the defining features of popular fiction;[1] the economic power behind industry production and the consumption of entertainment – via disposable income – was skewed in favour of White men even more than it is today.

The names which are most commonly linked to the foundation of the genre in the early-to-mid twentieth century are those of White men: Robert E. Howard, J. R. R. Tolkien, H. P. Lovecraft, and C. S. Lewis. Authors of colour, however, may equally have been involved, at least in pulp publishing, as Samuel R. Delany argues:

> We know of dozens upon dozens upon dozens of early pulp writers only as names. They conducted their careers entirely by mail – in a field and during an era when pen names were the rule rather than the exception ... we simply have no way of knowing if one, or three, or seven of them – or even many more – were blacks, Hispanics, women, Native American, Asians or whatever.[2]

Delany writes particularly of Science Fiction, but the same observations apply to pulp Fantasy. Early audiences evinced unanswered interest in the lives of authors – *Weird Tales* readers wrote to the magazine requesting that biographies be printed, for example a letter published in the January 1934 volume – but even at the time, editors and audiences alike often knew little of many. The visible authors, whose work is most commonly cited and of whom we know most, are not necessarily representative of the whole.

The structural racisms and sexisms – as well as other social inequalities – which shaped Western society when the foundations of Fantasy were laid undoubtedly contributed to both the capacity of White men to write and publish, and also to later assumptions that those who were visible were, in fact, broadly representative of writers. Privilege breeds its own success, and whatever the structural inequalities which supported some authors and disadvantaged others – and which still have significant impact today – white men and their writing contributed very significantly to the habits of Fantasy genre-culture. Tolkien's and Howard's works, more than any others, shaped High Fantasy and Sword and Sorcery, the two most commercially successful Fantasy sub-genres in the twentieth century and into the twenty-first. As Ian Nichols points out, their respective "imagined worlds of Middle-earth and Hyboria have served as the models for countless other fantasies."[3] This chapter argues that race-based ideologies behind the social systems which privileged them as White men very strongly influenced the shape of the worlds they imagined, worlds which were decidedly eurocentric and reproduced White race-thinking that had justified both British imperialism and slavery in the US since at least the eighteenth century.

Tolkien was born in South Africa in 1892, and moved to England with his mother and brother after the death of his father in 1896. He was educated at the King Edward's School, and then Oxford, where he studied Classics and English, before fighting in the trenches on the Western Front during World War One. After the Armistice he worked on the Oxford English Dictionary, then at the University of Leeds, before returning to Oxford as the Rawlinson and Bosworth Professor of Anglo-Saxon in 1925. He took up the Merton Professorship of English Language and Literature in 1959. Howard's background and life were different. Born in 1906, he moved from small Texas town to small Texas town during his childhood before his family settled in Cross Plains, Texas. In 1924, he went to Howard Payne College in nearby Brownwood to study stenography, but dropped out of the course when *Weird Tales* began publishing his stories, moving back to Cross Plains. He committed suicide in June 1936 after being told that his mother – who suffered from tuberculosis – had fallen into a terminal coma. Both Howard and Tolkien, Nichols observes, "lived in societies where they were part of a dominant race, and where racial distinctions were important."[4] Their Whiteness, and the privilege which resulted from it, is an important similarity in their seemingly very different lives.

Thousands of words have been devoted to the influence of the societies and cultures in which the two men lived on their works, by scholars and general audience members alike. The argument that the works of either author reflect the racial mores of their respective historical and cultural moments are almost invariably defensive, made against charges of racism directed at the authors, their works, or both, a point to which I will return later in this chapter. The personal writings of both men have been variously mined for evidence for or against their individual racism on multiple occasions, but such questions are secondary to the evidence of their creative production when it comes to their influence on the formation of the Fantasy genre. The author's beliefs and ideologies necessarily shape their works, as do the societies in which they lived, but it is how those attitudes were expressed in the stories they wrote which had the most profound effects on Fantasy throughout its development and into the present. This chapter seeks to reorient the discussion of the racialized worlds of Tolkien and Howard first by demonstrating the significant connections of their work with key aspects of race theory, and then by exploring the responses of twenty-first-century readers to those worlds. It is concerned with neither attacking nor defending the authors personally, but with exploring the ways their writings serve to channel centuries-old constructs into contemporary popular culture.

CREATING SUB-GENRES

Tolkien's first novel, *The Hobbit,* appeared in September 1937, with *The Lord of the Rings* published in the UK in 1954–1955. It was with the second that his influence solidified, although the process took some time. David G. Hartwell argues that "genrefication of fantasy as it exists today was motivated in earnest by the 1965 mass-market editions of *The Lord of the Rings*," first by Ace Publishing in unlicensed editions, and then by Ballantine under license later in the same year; the Ballantine editions were on bestseller lists for over a decade.[5] Following the success of *The Lord of the Rings* paperbacks, Ballantine published the "Ballantine Adult Fantasy" series, producing 65 books between 1969 and 1974, 63 of which were reprints of earlier works. The series: "helped to claim serious critical attention for fantasy, and in addition helped create a collective history for the genre,"[6] as well as laying the groundwork for its success in the later 1970s. According to Hartwell: "Fantasy ... had to be made predictable, had to be able to be sold as a product to achieve large-scale success."[7] Given the popularity of *The Lord of the Rings* it is not surprising that this commercially necessary predictability derived from it. Publishers do not have the only influence, but nonetheless are a critical link between authors and audiences in any commercially successful genre, particularly in the decades before digital media made self-published titles widely accessible. Terry Brooks' *The Sword of Shannara* (1977) is widely considered the first Tolkienian imitation.[8] It is characterized by Hartwell as "slavish imitation" of Tolkien,[9] and by Brian Attebery as "especially blatant in its point-for-point correspondence";[10] but it is in this very derivation that Hartwell locates its success. Audiences, he argues, wanted "not more *fantasy* but more *Tolkien*."[11]

The works which were published and became successful in this period confirm the accuracy of Hartwell's statement. Author Kij Johnson remarks of her experience as a reader in the later 1970s and 1980s:

> Tolkien just swept everything away and so all we had was medieval fantasy ... Then *The Sword of Shannara* came out and the idea of the

medieval fantasy as the default setting kicked in [in the late 1970s and 1980s] ... the medieval quest fantasy became the lockstep ... No matter how much the women [like Patricia McKillip and Elizabeth Scarbourough] were trying to subvert it, it still had those beats.[12]

High Fantasy series by authors like Brooks, David Eddings, Raymond E. Feist, and Robert Jordan dominated the Fantasy shelves of bookshops; their continued presence decades later attest to their popularity. Celtic worlds like Katherine Kerr's Deverry, offered variations to the medievalist theme, but were nonetheless strongly eurocentric. The influence of Tolkien's writing, particularly *The Lord of the Rings*, on Fantasy role-playing games is likewise immense.[13] Gary Gygax and Dave Arneson's 1974 *Dungeons & Dragons* imitated Tolkien's work so closely that it infringed copyright and elements had to be changed for later editions under threat of legal action.

All of the Conan tales published by Howard during his life appeared in the pulp magazine *Weird Tales* between December 1932 and October 1936. Appraisals of his influence are extremely varied, generally along lines of how focused any given history is on Fantasy or fantastic literature. In Attebery's major *The Fantasy Tradition in American Literature*, for example, he is mentioned only once, as an imitator of Edgar Rice Burroughs.[14] Farah Mendlesohn and Edward James also link his name with Burroughs' as a major writer in the pulp magazine era, and acknowledge his influence on later work: "Robert E. Howard's Conan set the model for a new kind of hero, but also for a new kind of tale, one frequently episodic and set beyond the kind of fey civilization that the late-nineteenth-century British fantasy had constructed."[15] Author David Drake wrote recently that: "Conan created S&S [Sword and Sorcery] as a publishing category as surely as Stephen King created horror."[16] Patrice Louinet comments on the genre more broadly, calling Howard: "a founding father of the Fantasy genre, rivaled only by J. R. R. Tolkien in terms of importance and influence."[17] Through Conan, and other characters like Kull the Conqueror, Howard rejected nineteenth-century sensibilities to create heroes who fought in their own interests, were not chivalrous, and were often dirty and bloody. His work "popularized the subgenre [of Sword and Sorcery], helped define its characteristic traits, and influenced several generations of later fantasy authors."[18] The Gritty Fantasy of George R. R. Martin and others, which has become prominent in the mainstream of popular culture during the first decade of the twenty-first century and is discussed at length in the third chapter of this book, owes much to this vision. Conan himself was the prototype for barbarian figures in Fantasy from Fritz Leiber's Fafhrd and Michael Moorhouse's Elric, to Martin's Khal Drogo and the "barbarian" class in role-playing and video games from *Dungeons & Dragons* to *Diablo III*, and is parodied by Terry Pratchett's Cohen the Barbarian.

A considerable number of Howard's stories – including some of his Conan tales – were reprinted in hardcover collection during the 1940s;

the late 1940s and early 1950s were a high point for reprints from *Weird Tales*.[19] In 1953, Lyon Sprague de Camp, a Science Fiction and Fantasy writer, editor, and enthusiast, began republishing Conan stories in hardback collections, but they were not widely available or outstandingly popular.[20] The very different publishing markets of hardbacks as compared to cheap pulp magazines may have been a factor. De Camp re-wrote both Howard's published originals and unpublished drafts himself until the 1960s when the Conan stories began to appear in paperbacks published by Lancer in 1965, the same year as paperback editions of *The Lord of the Rings*. The combination "created nothing short of a phenomenon" in publishing and popular culture.[21] The early books from Lancer were based on Howard originals and fragments, but after Lin Carter began working with de Camp they also produced entirely new pastiches, as well as re-casting Howard's historical tales to feature Conan.[22] After 1965, a number of well-known authors in speculative genres also wrote Conan tales – Poul Anderson, Harry Turtledove, and Robert Jordan – as did lesser known names. A 1957 list of members of the "Hyborian Legion," a Howard fan-club, meanwhile, includes other authors who had been Howard's contemporaries in the pulps – Robert Bloch, Clark Ashton Smith, and Fritz Leiber – as well as the then agent for Howard's estate, Glenn Lord. Other names central to the formation of Fantasy as a major genre in later decades appear alongside them: Marion Zimmer Bradley and Lester Del Rey.[23]

De Camp's efforts, and those of his later collaborators and followers, are often considered inferior to Howard's originals.[24] De Camp acknowledged that Howard would be termed racist by the standards of the time in which he wrote, but also said that he was "a lot less ethnocentric than many of his contemporaries," exemplifying the defensive discourse often applied to Howard by his readers.[25] He removed some of the worst and most obvious racial slurs, but did not fundamentally alter the structure of the stories or the imagined world in his editing.[26] De Camp, writing with Carter, created the character of Juma of Kush, "a black equal to Conan."[27] If the myriad adaptations and imitations in the form of movies, short stories and novels, comics, television series, and games were more often based on the work of de Camp and his collaborators than on Howard's, the problematic constructs of race and overall eurocentricity associated with the Howard and his work are nonetheless unquestionably present in the original tales.

Scholarship and lay commentary on the imagined worlds of Tolkien and Howard remarks on the social embeddedness of their works as explanation for problematic racial constructs found therein. In recent years, this has turned – particularly in scholarship – from being a primarily defensive tactic to fend off attacks on the individual authors to more in-depth discussions of the possible sources of the ideas which permeate their works. Dimitra Fimi, for example, focuses on "the evolution of views about 'race' during Tolkien's lifetime" as well as tenets of Victorian anthropology, and observes that: "When Tolkien started composing his mythology, it was still entirely legitimate and scientifically acceptable to divide humankind into race with fixed physical characteristics and mental abilities."[28] Tolkien's medieval and classical sources have also been discussed as sources for his racialized world.[29] Mark Hall writes that the "racial schema" of Howard's Hyboria "echoes some of the ideas and attitudes prevalent in the United States" at the time he was writing and points to the influence of both anthropology and history-writing.[30] To date there has been, however, no in-depth discussion of the two worlds side-by-side, nor of the common elements which, shaped by race-thinking, became Fantasy conventions, a project which this chapter now takes up.

It is not my purpose to offer a complete summary of all the permutations of race-thinking over several centuries, but rather to highlight those features of race theory which resonate particularly with the habits of the Fantasy genre. Racial logics, as discussed in the Introduction to this book, distinguishes between human groups by assigning non-necessary meanings to phenotypical features – most notably skin colour – and conceives of those features as both biologically determined and extending to "physical, intellectual and moral differences."[31] That the supposedly empirical basis for race has been disproved comprehensively, and that race is a social construct not a natural one, bears repeating. Whiteness as a racial construct, moreover, has historically mutable borders which include and exclude according to social and cultural shifts.

RACE IN MIDDLE-EARTH

Howard's Hyboria and Tolkien's Arda between them resonate with multiple major elements of race theory, from the superiority of characters coded as White and Germanic (particularly Anglo-Saxon), to polygenesis, to biological essentialism in the delineation of races, and evolution. The idea of first Germanic and then Anglo-Saxon – now White – supremacy in racial hierarchies stems principally from the nineteenth century. It relies, however, on the much older works of a Roman writer, Publius Cornelius Tacitus (56–177 C.E.), which were absolutely central to race-thinking about Whiteness from the sixteenth century on.[32] Tacitus's *Annals* and *Germania* describe the Germani, who lived to the north of the Roman Empire, did not intermingle with other peoples, were endogamous, virile, martial, and lovers of liberty. His northern barbarians, while lazy and dirty, were in other ways greatly superior to the southern Romans who had become decadent and corrupt because of the comforts of civilization. English and then American descent from the Saxons – who Tacitus does not mention but who were grafted onto his idealized Germanic barbarian stock in later centuries – was central to intertwined notions of race, language, culture, and nation from the seventeenth into the twentieth century.

Language-use and race were thought to be directly connected in the nineteenth century; in an 1851 edition of the *Germania*, R. G. Latham, an English ethnologist and philologist, asserted that:

> The present distribution of the families and nations descended from, to allied to, the Germans of Tacitus extends as far eastward as Australia, and as far westward as North America; as far north as Finmark and as far south as New Zealand.[33]

Robert J. C. Young argues that philology revolutionised race theory because "it established connections between people who might never before have considered themselves part of a group."[34] Anglo-Saxonism, particularly in its philological form, allowed Whites on both sides of the Atlantic, and indeed anywhere the British Empire had spread, to claim racial superiority over all other peoples of the world.[35] Philologists constructed the English nation, language and Anglo-Saxon race as intertwined, and the Middle Ages were considered – and still are – a key historical period of origin for all of them. Anglo-Saxonism was a key myth for ethno-national identity in the US and Australia, as well as Britain, in the nineteenth and early twentieth centuries, and the Middle Ages provided fertile ground for fictionalising that myth.[36]

James Obertino finds in Tacitus inspiration for Tolkien's Elves, Dwarves, Woses, and Orcs, and a source for the dwarven attempt to re-take Moria in the account of Varus' doomed expedition across the Rhine in the *Annals*. Sandra Ballif Straubhaar likewise argues for Tacitus's influence on Tolkien in an article on Gondorian attitudes to intermarriage with the Rohirrim.[37] It is through the dependence of modern discourses of Whiteness that Tacitus had the greatest impact on Middle-earth however. Given the tremendously important role philology and language played in the creation of Middle-earth and its inhabitants, Tolkien's academic work, and the long history linking philology with race-thinking, it is not surprising that the latter entered his work in profound ways. In his examination of connections between fascism and Tolkien's work, Paul Firchow argues that Tolkien "unconsciously absorbed ... several underlying fascist ideas," and suggests that "a medievalist specializing in Germanic languages and literatures – a field much touted by Nazi propaganda – would have been more exposed and perhaps also susceptible" than others.[38] Tolkien's ideas were, as his personal writings attest, originally formulated during his early university studies, before the rise of Nazism in Germany, so its direct influence, which Firchow argues for, is unlikely. Niels Werber also finds the influence of Germanic thinking arguing that: "an analysis of deep structure, narrative logic, rhetoric, and topology in Tolkien's works reveals in terms of geo- and biopolitics an almost frightening coherence" with "German discourses of race and space."[39] Fimi makes the crucial point that Tolkien spoke explicitly *against* equating race and language in his scholarly work, but that "the identification of 'racial' characteristics ... with ... languages was maintained in his fiction."[40] It is precisely that fiction which has been mostly widely read, imitated, and adapted. Tolkien was not a fascist, but the "noble northern spirit"[41] in which he believed was created in modern culture in the service of race theory which, in the eighteenth and nineteenth centuries in particular, imagined the White race into being and placed it at the top of a hierarchy of humanity.

The influence of philological Anglo-Saxonism on Tolkien is clearly visible in his depiction of the Riders of Rohan who "resemble the ancient English down to minute detail."[42] Tolkien had access to the culture of the Anglo-Saxons through his professional work, and drew on their literature extensively. Yet that access was not direct, a jump from the twentieth century to the first millennium, rather, his medievalism was coloured by that of earlier philologists who conceived of them in racial terms, marked out from the rest of humanity by their physical, cultural, and linguistic character. The Rohirrim, as Faramir tells Frodo, are one of the "proud peoples of the North," once the enemies of Gondor, but now their allies; they are "tall men and fair women, valiant both alike, golden-haired, bright-eyed, and strong," said to be descended from "the same Three Houses of Men as were the Númenoreans in their beginning." The key role language plays in differentiating peoples in Tolkien's world is also displayed in his description of them: "their lords speak our speech at need; yet for the most part they hold by the ways of their own fathers and to their own memories, and they speak among themselves their own North tongue."[43] Race in Middle-earth is defined by interlinked moral, physical, and linguistic factors, demonstrating clear links to philological constructs of race which had arisen during the late eighteenth and nineteenth centuries.

Tolkien's human protagonists – including Hobbits – are unmistakably influenced by historical and literary constructs of European culture. Where the Rohirrim resemble the pre-Conquest English, Hobbit life and the Shire are redolent of nineteenth-century England. If the Rohirrim as a people most closely resemble the Anglo-Saxons,[44] the Gondorrians also have some Germanic values, many of which are best illustrated in the life of Aragorn. His right to the throne of Gondor and Arnor is not solely conferred by his descent from the legendary kings of former ages, rather, he must prove himself worthy by strength of will, through battle, and through leadership. He does not enter the city of Minas Tirith as king until he has been acclaimed by its people those of the surrounding lands. This model is strongly reminiscent of Tacitus's Germani who chose their leaders by battle prowess and consent, not descent. Aragorn, moreover, is from the North – as compared to Gondor's South; his character has been shaped by that land and by his pure descent. The Gondorrians, like Tacitus's southern Romans, have fallen from the peak of their power, as Pippin sees when he first enters Minas Tirith with Gandalf: [The city] "was in truth falling year by year into decay; and already it lacked half the men that could have dwelt at ease there."[45] Judy Ford convincingly reads the renewal of Gondor and its empire under

Aragorn's kingship as "an expression of a late-ancient, early-medieval, northern European hope that the Roman Empire could be reborn, and that its reincarnated form would embrace the Germanic peoples and provide them with glory and peace."[46] The fulfilment of that wish is arguably found in the nineteenth-century Anglo-Saxonism of the British Empire as much as it is in *The Lord of the Rings*.

Some of Tolkien's peoples are inherently and essentially superior to others; both his hierarchy and the underlying construction of human difference invoke race-thinking which created racial categories based on supposed biological differences, and assigned character traits to those races. As Fimi observes, "the 'race' of the Númenóreans [from whom Aragorn and the people of Godnor descend] differed from common Men in biological and mental characteristics."[47] Faramir explains to Frodo:

> For so we reckon them in our lore, calling them the High, or Men of the West, which were Númenoreans; and the Middle Peoples, Men of the Twilight, such as are the Rohirrim ... and the Wild, the Men of Darkness ... the wild Easterlings [and ...] cruel Haradrim.[48]

Although Tolkien's characters are rarely, if ever, entirely circumscribed by their race, essentializing logics of racial difference nonetheless underpin the structure of the peoples of his world. Racialized taxonomies shape the cultures of Middle Earth, and although these leave space for multicultural and cosmopolitan readings,[49] they are also very problematic. Not only are the Good peoples of Middle-earth marked as White, Faramir's "Men of Darkness" are distinctly not. Many peoples comprise Sauron's armies in addition to the non-human trolls and orcs: "Easterlings with axes, and Variags of Kharad, Southrons in scarlet, and out of Far Harad black men like half-trolls with white eyes and red tongues" all come to the Battle of the Pelennor Fields.[50] They are effectively undifferentiated under the one – tellingly black – banner of evil, servants of Sauron, collected together within the single Othering category of non-European, non-White.

Tolkien's explanations of the differences between Good and Evil humanity – that the former descended from those who had greatest contact and affinity with the Elves in ancient times – does not obviously relate to pseudo-scientific explanations of racial difference; it smacks more of religious constructs of a "chosen people." Turning from Tolkien's delineation of human groups to his other species, however, reveals the influence of theories of polygenesis, according to which different races were the result of multiple acts of divine creation.[51] It developed in the late 1700s, and gained considerable currency, particularly in the US, in the mid-nineteenth century.[52] At its basis, this theory allowed non-Europeans – or non-Whites as the connection of skin colour and race was by then entrenched – to be considered non-human, and therefore sub-human. The creation story of Arda, published in *The Silmarillion*, recounts the making of the Children of Ilúvatar: "Elves and Men, Firstborn and Followers,"[53] names which strongly suggest that they have different moments of creation. There is no question that this is the case when it comes to dwarves, who "were made by Aulë in the darkness of Middle-earth."[54] Rebecca Brackman argues that their creation story – they are awakened before the Elves – "steeps itself in the sort of supersessionist dynamic that early Christian writers used to separate Christianity from its origin within Judaism."[55] Their creation story, however, resonates much more strongly with racial than religious thinking; dwarves are other beings entirely than the Children of Ilúvatar and have a completely different origin, unequivocally demonstrating that Middle-earth is a location of polygenesis.

Charles Darwin's theory of evolution did much to dispel the notion of polygenesis, but nonetheless was also used to dehumanize non-Europeans, particularly Africans, through the suggestion that different racial groups were more or less evolved than others. The "Negro-ape" metaphor, for example, invoked evolutionary theory to suggest that Africans were closer to apes, that is, less evolved, than Whites, and were therefore inferior.[56] It was used – and still is – as Phillip Atiba Goff et al. argue, "to bolster growing stereotypes that peoples of African descent were innately lazy, aggressive, dim, hypersexual, and in need of benevolent control."[57] According to polygenesists, Whites were the only real humans, but evolution theory was used to construct Whites as the most human. Evolution creeps into *The Lord of the Rings*. Gandalf's comment that Gollum's people "were of hobbit-kind: akin to the fathers of the fathers of the Stoors," and Frodo's response: "'I can't believe that Gollum was connected with hobbits, however distantly,' said Frodo with some heat. 'What an abominable notion.'" Gandalf assures him that it is true, remarking "I know more than hobbits do themselves."[58] It is not hard to read the exchange as one of a country squire hearing the humanity is related to apes for the first time.

Hybridity in Middle-earth is treated negatively, to the extent that it can be most accurately termed miscegenation. According to nineteenth century race theory, racial mixing or impurity – which came to be known as miscegenation in the mid-nineteenth century – led to the corruption and loss of the good qualities of both. Mixing races is problematic in Tolkien's world. The inhabitants of Lebennin, one of the lands near Minas Tirith have "mingled" blood, "there were short and swarthy folk among them whose sires came more from the forgotten men who housed in the shadow of the hills in the Dark Years ere the coming of the kings."[59] This decay of the Númenóreans into the people of Gondor, partly through intermarriage with "lesser men" is a clear case of imagined miscegenation.[60] Moreover, Tolkien describes Saruman's "interbreeding of Orcs and Men" as "his wickedest deed."[61] The complexity of Middle-earth is such that this is not the only perspective offered on intermarriage: the Appendices of *The Return of the King* include the tale of the Gondorrian King Valacar who rejuvenated his line by marrying Vidumavi, the daughter of the king of the Northmen (forebears of the Rohirrim). Straubhaar reads this as a multicultural move,[62] and while it does offer a counterpoint to miscegenation, this is merely a reversed interpretation of the same underlying structure. The point remains that whether intermarriage weakens or strengthens a people – or their ruling dynasty – the concept itself depends upon the existence of fundamental and meaningful racial difference in the first place.

Dieter Petzold remarks: "for those who accuse Tolkien of racism, the orcs are key witnesses."[63] There are few physical descriptions of them in the *The Lord of the Rings*, the most detailed is at the Fellowship's first encounter with them in Moria: "a huge orc-chieftain, almost man-high, clad in black mail from head to foot, leaped into the chamber … his broad face was swart, his eyes were like coals, and his tongue was red."[64] There is no denying that this is a racialized description, and nothing in *The Lord of the Rings* undercuts or contradicts it. *The Lord of the Rings* establishes orcs as a monstrous Other through racial discourses. They are somatically different to the White Self of Good, and embody degradation and the threat of miscegenation. The literary antecedents of orcs, moreover, are located within a millennium-old cultural tradition that constructs a dichotomy between West and East as Self and Other. There are significant similarities between them and conventional Saracen enemies in European romances of the mid-to-late Middle Ages: they are marked as somatically different to the Good characters; often have giant-like leaders; and have vastly superior numbers.[65] Locating Saracens as a source of Tolkien's orcs does not excuse or justify their racialization, but rather confirms the enduring racism which has been present in Western culture for centuries.

Two scenes in *The Lord of the Rings* demonstrate that there are multiple tribes of orcs just as there are multiple groups of humans. The first is a confrontation among Merry and Pippin's captors in *The Two Towers*:

> In the twilight he [Pippin] saw a large black orc, probably Uglúk, standing facing Grishnákh, a short, crook-legged creature, very broad and with long arms that hung almost to the ground. Round them were many smaller goblins. Pippin supposed that these were the ones from the North.[66]

In the tower of Cirith Ungol Sam notices "two liveries … one marked by Red Eye, the other by a Moon disfigured with a ghastly face of death,"[67] and the different languages spoken by Orcs are mentioned in both episodes. Orc squabbles amongst themselves, and "different cultures, languages, and philosophies" are offered as evidence of "simple humanity" by Robert T. Talley.[68] These glimpses, however, emphasize how little is known of orcs and their lives when they are not the immediate enemies of the Fellowship; this lack of knowledge both creates and maintains their racial Otherness.

RACE IN HYBORIA

Anglo-Saxonism in the US declined during the 1930s and 1940s, but was an extremely popular race theory during Howard's formative years in the 1910s and 1920s; while he did not have the professional exposure to philological constructs that Tolkien did, there is no question that it shaped Howard's thoughts. The decadent evils of civilization and the virile masculinity of northern barbarians which can be ultimately traced by to Tacitus's writings was an important belief for Howard personally and are clearly visible in the Conan stories.[69] At his first print appearance, Conan is: "a man whose broad shoulders and sun-browned skin seemed out of place among those luxuriant surroundings. He seemed more a part of the sun and winds and high places of the outlands."[70] The motif is regularly repeated. Howard himself was of Irish descent, a complicating factor in his thinking, but "Conan's popularity spoke to a public fixated on the idea of an Anglo-Saxon-centred racial hierarchy."[71]

Conan is a White American hero: self-sufficient and independent, strong, honest, and moral, abiding by his own code of honour. His "dual identity of being a savage, but being white,"[72] makes him naturally suited to lead the softer, more decadent and corrupted peoples of the south; he becomes, among other things, king of the southern, medievalist realm of Aquilonia. Pulp adventure stories, a genre in which Howard wrote and of which his Conan stories can be considered a fantasy sub-set, were steeped in the concept of the 'white man's burden' according to which "primitive" races benefit from White leadership.[73] Conan is depicted as a natural leader of peoples of other races on multiple occasions. In "The Hour of the Dragon" he instigates a mutiny on a ship crewed by black slaves who, as Benjamin Garstad observes, "were apparently docile until they found a white leader."[74] In this tale, as in others, Conan is strong, decisive, rational, and freedom-loving in contrast with: "the blacks [who] were frothing crazy now, shaking and tearing at their chains and shrieking."[75] Conan is the Germanic barbarian tribesman of Tacitus, filtered through nineteenth-century American Anglo-Saxonism and re-modeled for twentieth-century consumption.

Garstad shows that in Howard's stories – whether they feature Conan or not – slavery is "on the classic American model. It is a slavery of race in which the slaves are of another, supposedly lower, race than the masters."[76] "Shadows in Zamboula," one such story of slavery, offers a damning portrayal of racial mixing: "this accursed city which Stygians built and which Hyrkanians rule – where white, brown and black folk mingle together to produce hybrids of all unholy hues and breeds."[77] Its population is described as both "mongrel" and "hybrid" in the space of a page that also includes several paragraphs describing the racially mixed history and inhabitants of the city, a place terrorized by its own cannibal "giant black slaves."[78] There is a hierarchy of evil within the degenerate city: the black slaves are its lowest layer, and the least threat to Conan, serving partly as a plot device to drive him to meetings with Totrasmek, the sorcerous high priest of its temple who has attempted to poison its legitimate ruler, and his servant Baal-pter. Conan first encounters and kills Baal-pter, who is "brown-skinned,"[79] then dispatches Totrasmek, "a broad, fleshy man, with fat white hands."[80] Not all White people in Howard's stories are good any more than, as has been variously pointed out,[81] all black people are cannibals in them. Nonetheless, Whites are always leaders among mixed racial company, and racial difference fundamentally structures the world.

Howard gives evolution a much greater role in his world than Tolkien did in Middle-earth. In "Queen of the Black Coast," Conan's main enemy is a winged humanoid, the last survivor of a "race" of "winged and of heroic proportions; not a branch of the mysterious stalk of evolution that culminated in man, but the ripe blossom on an alien tree."[82] The same story deploys a series of negative racial stereotypes focused on the warrior servants of the title character which likewise invoke evolution. When Conan first sees the pirate band led by Bêlit, her "white skin glistened in dazzling contrast to the glossy ebony hides" of her followers; from this introduction, "the blacks," as they are consistently referred to throughout the tale, are represented as closer to animals than humans.[83] The "Negro-ape" construct,[84] is explicitly deployed when Conan comes upon one of his crew-members in the jungle: "At first [he …] thought it to be a great black gorilla. Then he saw that it was a giant black man that crouched ape-like, long arms dangling, froth dripping from the loose lips."[85] Conan is the only one of the pirate band to survive their journey up the river Zarkheba, which he does because of his racial superiority. The crew members are so "maddened by terror" by an assailant Conan later defeats that they are helpless: "already unmanned by their superstitious fears, the blacks might well have died without striking a blow in their own defense."[86] Conan, in contrast, spends considerable time in thought during the tale, and is able to survive as a result; his superior rationality enables him to manage his emotions and defeat their foe.

Bêlit, like her crew, does not survive. Although her skin is white, she is a Shemite not a Cimmerian, and because of her race is unable to resist focusing on treasure rather than survival; Howard writes: "the Shemite soul finds a bright drunkenness in riches and material splendor."[87] Conan, having defeated the winged-ape and its attendant pack of savage dogs, finds her dead, hanging from the yard-arm of her galley, strangled by a necklace of rubies, her greed having literally killed her. Shemites, according to Howard and as their name suggests, are the ancestors of "Arabs, Israelites, and other straighter-featured Semites."[88] The manner of Bêlit's death displays a distinct current of anti-Semitism that tapes into negative stereotypes about the supposed greed of Jews. The passage also illustrates the way that Howard uses racial logics, he attaches physical, moral, and intellectual attributes to biological groupings.

Howard imagined his world as an earlier, pre-historic and forgotten era of our own. Familiar names of peoples and places – Picts, Atlantis, Kush,

S(h)emites – taken from history and mythology suggest this in the Conan stories, and it is confirmed in "The Hyborian Age," an essay written to sketch out the history of Conan's world. It begins with a disclaimer – "nothing in this article is to be considered as an attempt to advance any theory in opposition to accepted history"[89] – but ends by stating that the peoples of the modern world are "far older than they realize, their history stretches back into the mists of the forgotten Hyborian age."[90] Hall reads the work as "meta-history" and argues for a possible "critique of eugenics and anti-miscegenation laws" in it,[91] based on the fact that according many of the races of Hyboria are mixed and yet are not lacking in "vitality and vigor."[92] He acknowledges that Howard's short stories may suggest differently, a possibility that is confirmed by Garstad's compelling argument that miscegenation between slave and master races consistently brings about the downfall of both in Howard's tales. Garstad argues that in the stories, "races which maintain their integrity also maintain their strength and virility."[93] It is the stories, not the pseudo-historical essay, which have had the greatest impact on Fantasy. Moreover, the different attitudes Hall and Garstad find to racial mixing, as with the different interpretations of intermarriage found in Tolkien's writing as discussed above, both depend on the belief that distinct races do exist.

EUROPE-CENTRED AND EUROCENTRIC

The worlds both Tolkien and Howard imagine as settings for their stories are Europe-like and medievalist; they create geographical and social landscapes which support the white ethnoscapes of their people.[94] Ditomasso argues that "medievalism as a literary construct does not always mean medieval in the sense of a fixed period in Western history," but nonetheless observes similarities between Hyboria and the Middle Ages:

> Kingdoms and city-states rather than democracies and nation-states, a pre-industrial and largely pre-scientific technological base, an economy based on barter or some sort of metallic standard, pre-gunpowder armies and methods of warfare, a feudal social and political structure, and parochialism, superstition, race-consciousness, and even racism on the part of the population.[95]

The article argues that Howard's racism is true to the kind of historical period in which his works were set, suggesting that for the imagined world to be believable, its people *had* to be race-conscious and racist. It is my suggestion, however, that Howard's world is not racist because it reflects medieval realities – although it is true that the medieval world was itself racist – but that modern perceptions of the Middle Ages, particularly in popular culture, are significantly shaped by modern representations rather than historical fact. Howard's own work, as well as Tolkien's, contributed considerably to the shape of those perceptions. As I have shown above, however, the medievalist works both men wrote were very strongly influenced by modern, post-medieval constructs of race and difference, and by the concept of Anglo-Saxonism.

Tolkien, as has been variously observed, drew on his professional interests in the European Middle Ages to create Arda – and Middle-earth in particular.[96] He worked with history, literature, myths, and legends of the Middle Ages deliberately and extensively, and his medievalism is evident in almost every aspect of the world he created, including but not limited to its geography, political structures, cultures, weaponry, and level of technology. As Michael D. C. Drout argues, although Tolkien "explicitly and overtly severed the connections between real European history and Middle-earth, there remains a structural substratum of story-structure, names, and parallels that links early Anglo-Saxon and Germanic culture to Tolkien's imaginative creation."[97] Howard's medievalism has been much less discussed than Tolkien's, and his library shows no evidence of particular interest in that period.[98] Nonetheless, their worlds have similar hallmarks associated with the western European Middle Ages. Both, furthermore, are deeply soaked in modern racial ideologies which found a focus in re-imaginings of the Middle Ages.[99]

The maps Tolkien included with *The Lord of the Rings* have been variously credited with making maps *de rigeur* for High Fantasy works, while the reasons Tolkien provided them, and their uses, are many: "authentication, understanding, inner consistency, or world expansion."[100] The map of Middle-earth in *The Lord of the Rings* does not resemble a map of modern Europe, but it does locate the action in the corresponding part of the globe: there is a great sea to the west, icy wastes to the north, and hotter, dryer lands to the south. The various topographical features – from the forests to mountains, caves, marshes, rivers, and grasslands, are all more or less common to Europe; the Fellowship encounter no sandy deserts or tropical rainforests. Although the remark is made in passing in the Prologue to *The Fellowship of the Rings*, Tolkien does locate the Shire historically and geographically: "Those days ... are now long past, and the shape of all the lands has changed; but the regions in which Hobbits then lived were doubtless the same as those in which they still linger: the North-West of the Old World."[101] Tolkien's stories may be set before even pre-history, but they took place in Europe nonetheless.

Howard's imagined world Hyboria was conceived of as a forgotten pre-history of our own, although he was much more explicit about describing its peoples as the ancestors of modern peoples and its lands as their pre-cataclysmic homes. Conan travels much more widely than the protagonists of either *The Hobbit* or *The Lord of the Rings* in the kinds of landscape that he passes through, even if his wanderings are not as minutely mapped as theirs. Where the action of Tolkien's novels is restricted to the north and west of Middle-earth, and his protagonists encounter climate and topographical features which are distinctly like those of Europe, Conan travels to jungles and deserts in seemingly more far-flung realms. Yet two rough maps of Hyboria drawn by Howard demonstrate how absolutely Europe-centred he imagined it to be. Both consist of rough outlines of his imagined lands laid over hand-drawn maps of Europe, including the north coast of Africa, reaching west to include the Iberian peninsula, north towards but not including all of Scandinavia, and east to the Caspian Sea.[102] His entire world is literally encompassed by Europe and its margins.

There is no particular reason that either Tolkien or Howard as individual authors should not have imagined their worlds as very early versions of Europe. There is no evidence to suggest that either intended, much less foresaw, the future impact of their work. Their works nonetheless provided the templates that made 'Europe' – with greater or lesser levels of magic – became the default location for both High Fantasy and Sword and Sorcery. European settings, taken in isolation, are not necessarily problematic in the terms of a discussion of race, and given that both authors were White men of the early twentieth century, it is perhaps not surprising that they chose those locations. When those European settings are linked, however, with the kinds of racial thinking that imbue the writings of both authors, they become much more troubling because they resonate with the political and power structures which have shaped the world historically in the past several centuries. Linking geography with race-thinking turns their works from Europe-centred, to eurocentric. Tolkien and Howard's writings, as I argue above, have become influential because of their popularity across multiple decades. If their worlds reflect the socio-cultural contexts in which they were produced, it is their reception that has made them more than just historical artifacts, and it is to this that I now turn.

EARLY RESPONSES

Discussions of the racial elements of Tolkien's and Howard's work from before the 1980s are few and far between. The letters pages of *Weird Tales* contemporary with Howard's stories say nothing of them, for example.[103] Some two decades later and across the Atlantic, *The Lord of the Rings* appears to have come in for some criticism. In his 1955 review of *The Two Towers* and *The Return of the King*, "The Dethronement of Power," Lewis wrote that readers could "imagine they have seen a rigid demarcation between black and white people" linked to an unambiguous line between good and evil, but argues that the "mixed" motives on the side of good in the books prevent readers who found racism in them from being able to "brazen it out."[104] I have not been able to locate reviews or other criticisms of the kind Lewis refers to, but his comments demonstrate that they must have been made.[105] There are multiple reasons for the contemporary silence around Conan and what seem to have been the most hushed murmurs about Middle-earth, including the social and cultural milieu in which they wrote.

What I offer here is a short discussion of the discussions that did emerge as Fantasy developed as a genre.

In 1968, Neil Isaacs suggested that "fannism," as found among devotees of Tolkien's work, "acts as a deterrent to critical activity."[106] The statement is overly sweeping, and not ultimately true. The nature of pre-digital fan communication, however, makes locating evidence difficult. Face-to-face discussions leave no trace to be recovered decades later. Many fanzines, moreover, had very limited print runs and circulation and are held only in limited numbers of archives, if at all, meaning that negative evidence – that is, of the absence of commentary – is far from definitive. Evidence in fact does exist of critical readings of, and discomfort with, representations of race in Middle-earth among fans as early as 1963, a letter written by one John Boardman and published in the tenth issue of the fanzine *Xero*.[107] Boardman begins by expressing liking for *The Lord of the Rings*, but finds "subtle racism" in it, based on its references to miscegenation and divisions of humanity into "High, Middle and Low," and what he considers "mono-chromatic" representation of elves and orcs.[108] It seems highly unlikely that his was the only concerned voice amongst the many fans of Tolkien, even if it is the only one which seems to have survived in print.

De Camp published several essays and books which at least touched on the issue of racism in the mid-to-late 1970s. His *Blond Barbarians and Noble Savages* contained essays on H. P Lovecraft's Aryanism, Howard's obsession with the Celts, and with "barbarian." They trace the cultural and intellectual histories of the racial constructs that so occupied the two men, and made a number of very clear-cut statements about the inherent falseness of the ideas they espoused. Explanations of Howard's views offered by de Camp included:

> many of Howard's views would today be called "racist." In presenting such views, Howard merely followed most popular fiction writers of the time, to whom ethnic stereotypes were stock in trade. If a racist, Howard was, by the standards of his time, a comparatively mild one.[109]

De Camp also offers social context as an explanation of Howard's views, and implies that they were more intellectual than personal:

> Howard's attitudes were compounded by a conventional Southern white outlook, with sentimental sympathy for the Confederacy and a sense of outrage at the depredations of the carpetbaggers. He vented conventional Texan views of Negroes and Mexicans but noted some Negroes and Mexicans whom he admired.[110]

These statements foreshadow many of those which have been widely espoused since and which continue to be in the present day about Howard and Tolkien alike.

Historicizing an author and his work is an extremely common strategy, one which widely used to explain away problematic statements or elements in creative work, much in the way that de Camp did for Howard's. A recent Reddit thread, from the "tolkienfans" section, includes the comment that "when you have an author that was around when serious colonialism was alive and well, it raises a few questions ... From someone that was born in 1892 ... I've seen worse."[111] Comments on the genre-forum *Chronicles: Science Fiction and Fantasy Community* make precisely the same move in defending charges of racism levelled at both Jackson's films and Tolkien's novels: "You have to read the book and take into account when it was written."[112] A thread on *Stormfront.org* takes this to an extreme in relation to Tolkien's opposition of the Nazis: "You have to remember that Tolkien was a veteran of WWI and his closest friends were killed in combat. As a patriotic Englishman he would naturally carry a grudge against Germans."[113] Another thread from the same website also speculates about Howard's ideas were he alive; contrasting Dark Horse's comics version with the casting of Jason Momoa, an actor with Native American and Hawaiian heritage, as Conan in the 2011 *Conan the Barbarian* it says: "im sure Howard would be proud of what theyve done [sic]."[114] As Gary Romeo writes, one of the three main arguments made defending Howard against charges of racism is that he "was a product of his time and racism was as natural as breathing back then."[115]Audience members use this technique to create distance from or, in the case of the avowedly White Supremacist *Stormfront* proximity to, the authors to legitimize their enjoyment of the creative works, enabling the Whiteness associated with Fantasy's foundational authors and publishing milieu to reach forward into modern times without critical examination. The discussions on forums across the political spectrum have strong similarities which demonstrate that they have more to do with readers and how they perceive themselves than with the authors around whom they nominally revolve; they represent challenges to, and defences against, genre habits of Whiteness.

Historicizing the author's life and writing is at best a purely personal defence, that is, it speaks to the (possible) character of the individual. This makes it a shallow defence because, as I argue above, it is the writing of Howard and Tolkien – not their personalities – which have so profoundly influenced the Fantasy genre.[116] Whether the racial logics and stereotypes that contributed significantly to the genre's habits of Whiteness stemmed from personal bigotry or cultural norms and influences have no impact on their ongoing legacies. Such defences imply that those norms have been discarded and that the works which they inflect do not carry them forward into new times and places; neither is true, as I argue throughout this book. As Saladin Ahmed puts it, Tolkien's "half-sublimated wranglings with race are more complex and fraught than either his shrillest detractors or his most fawning defenders would have us believe," but there is nonetheless "irreducible ugliness" in his works and Fantasy has inherited "ideological baggage ... from our shared progenitor."[117] Speaking of Lovecraft and the use of his image for the World Fantasy Award statuette, Nnedi Okorafor writes that for minorities in the arts, "many of The Elders we honor and need to learn from hate or hated us."[118] Whatever emotions were felt by Howard and Tolkien, the legacy of their writings, Ahmed's "ideological baggage," is undeniable.

Paul Shovlin rightly argues that most early responses to Howard's racism, such as de Camp's comments:

> were centred in apologetics ... [and] are mobilized by critics who are mainly concerned about what the implications of race in Howard's work are for them as a reader and fan base and him as an author they respect.[119]

The absence of criticism of Howard's racist stereotyping in 1930s fandom is at least in part due to the fact that they were not troubling to the majority of his contemporary audience; there were no implications for his readers.[120] In the post-War 1950s when *The Lord of the Rings* was first published, the racist excesses of Nazism had made the general public more attuned to White racial logics and stereotypes; Lewis's passing defence reflects this. De Camp, however, was editing and writing Conan stories in the Civil Rights era when race relations and injustices were at the forefront of politics in the United States. His decision to edit out some of the worst racist epithets, the creation of Juma of Kush, and various essays on race in Howard's thoughts and writing are not just personal but are also commercial ones, arguably designed to reduce the potential negative implications of being a fan of the stories, and their potential to cause offense to readers. Fans of colour may not have had widely audible voices in fan communities in the mid-twentieth century, but the hegemony of Whiteness in wider culture was made visible, and attacked. Being a fan of worlds structured by racial logics and stories which include racist stereotypes has potential implications in the contemporary climate – both fandom and wider society – that did not exist in earlier decades.

Digital media, moreover, enable a much greater range of voices to be heard than was previously the case in SFF fan communities.[121] Those same communities, however, at times actively work to silence criticism of racial representations and to construct normative identity within them as White, as I show elsewhere of *Westeros.org*.[122] Nonetheless, from about the start of the twenty-first century, voices concerned with the racial stereotypes and biases evinced in the founding works of the genre and held by their authors have become far more visible within Fantasy genre-culture than they were in earlier decades. Digital technology, particularly after the advent of Web 2.0, impacted tremendously on fan communities – and continues to do so – including on the ways fans communicate with each other.[123]

Blogs, discussion boards, online journals, and social media sites enable fan communities which are numerically larger than even the biggest convention or society to form. Online communication is also relatively decentralised. A physical fanzine might be produced by one or a few people, even if it cir-culated among many more, but a discussion board or even blog comments, can have hundreds or even thousands of contributors and readers and usu-ally no single central gate-keeper for content.

The current prominence of Fantasy as a genre within popular culture plays a role here by increased numbers of potential commentators to Tolkien's and Howard's works. Tolkien's in particular came into the broad public eye in the early 2000s through Jackson's film adaptations, increasing the numbers of potential readers (and viewers) at the same time as techno-logical developments made it exponentially easier to share their responses. Blog posts are more likely than not to be written as attacks on, not defences of, either Tolkien or Howard and their respective works, unless they are responses to a specific criticism from another audience member or fan.[124] Some deploy critical theory and close textual analysis,[125] while others are expressed as attacks on the authors themselves.[126] Posts of either kind rarely go unchallenged, at times in extremely heated terms. YouTube videos, mainly referring to Jackson's films, have also appeared in recent years, both asserting that they are racist and claiming that they are not;[127] as with blog posts, the latter kind is almost invariably triggered by a direct or perceived attack. Criticisms, however, are generally responses to the text themselves, whether the originals or adaptations. Digital media increase the fans' ability to communicate with each other, and one result is an increase in the visibil-ity of discussions and debates about Fantasy's habits of Whiteness.

CONCLUSION

Twenty-first-century Fantasy genre-culture developed its habits of Whiteness early in the previous century when it became a publishing category and entered significantly into popular culture. That the two most influential authors, whose works established the most commercially successful sub-genres in the five decades since, were White men is no accident, but rather a product of the wider social and cultural settings in which those men wrote, and also in which they have been read, imitated, and adapted. The medieval-ist worlds they imagined were both strongly influenced by modern discourses around race which developed throughout the eighteenth and nineteenth centuries, particularly Anglo-Saxonism. Scholars explore the sources of the ideas that formed their racialized worlds – as I have done in this chapter; and fans make similar moves to justify the more overt extrusions of rac-ism by talking about their "time and place" as they argue about the indi-vidual racism of each. Insights into the personal beliefs, their sources, and the relationship each of these factors has on imagined worlds, can provide background and nuanced understanding of Tolkien and Howard and their works, but taken within the context of the Fantasy genre as a whole, those nuances are largely insignificant. What matters, what has shaped the genre most, are the broad brushstrokes which place racial difference at its heart. Middle-earth and Hyboria, which are in many ways very similar, became the default setting for Fantasy, making race the conventional framework around which difference is built in the genre, it shapes worlds, societies, peoples, cultures, and conflicts.

NOTES

1. Gelder, *Popular Fiction: The Logics and Practices of a Literary Field*, 1.
2. Delany, "Racism and Science Fiction."
3. Nichols, "A Comparison of the Ideology of Robert E. Howard's Conan Tales and J. R. R. Tolkien's *The Lord of the Rings*," 35.
4. Nichols, "A Comparison of the Ideology of Robert E. Howard's Conan Tales and J. R. R. Tolkien's *The Lord of the Rings*," 40.
5. Hartwell, "The Making of the American Fantasy Genre," 372.
6. Mendlesohn and James, *A Short History of Fantasy*, 76.
7. Hartwell, "The Making of the American Fantasy Genre," 373.
8. Katherine Kurtz's *Deryni Rising* (1970) and *Deryni Checkmate* (1972) are medievalist fantasy published in the Ballantine series previously, but are not Tolkienian.
9. Hartwell, "The Making of the American Fantasy Genre," 375.
10. Attebery, *The Fantasy Tradition in American Literature*, 155.
11. Hartwell, "The Making of the American Fantasy Genre," 375. Italics in the original.
12. Interview conducted at the International Conference on the Fantastic in the Arts, Orlando FL, 2013. See also James, "Tolkien, Lewis and the Explosion of Genre Fantasy," 64–71.
13. Barton, *Dungeons and Desktops: The History of Computer Role-Playing Games*; Tresca, *The Evolution of Fantasy Role-Playing Games*, 23–46; Thompson, *The Frodo Franchise: The Lord of the Rings and Modern Hollywood*, 233.
14. Attebery, *The Fantasy Tradition in American Literature*, 118.
15. Mendlesohn and James, *A Short History of Fantasy*, 36.
16. Drake, "Storytellers: A Guided Ramble into Sword and Sorcery Fiction," 8.
17. Louinet, "Robert E. Howard, Founding Father of Modern Fantasy for the First Time Again," 163.
18. Shanks, "History, Horror, and Heroic Fantasy: Robert E. Howard and the Creation of the Sword and Sorcery Genre," 3.
19. Benefiel, "Shadow of a Dark Muse: Reprint History of Original Fiction from Weird Tales 1928–1939," 458.
20. Shanks, "History, Horror, and Heroic Fantasy," 11.
21. Louinet, "Robert E. Howard, Founding Father of Modern Fantasy for the First Time Again," 166.
22. Holmes, "Lin Carter: The Inept Pasticheur," 163.

23. The list is held in the Eaton Collection in the library of the University of Calironia, Riverside.
24. See, for example, Drake, "Storytellers"; Louinet, "Robert E. Howard, Founding Father of Modern Fantasy for the First Time Again," 165–166. See Burke, "De Camp vs. Howard: Rewriting Conan," for a close analysis of multiple versions by de Camp compared with Howard's original texts, and a "purist manifesto."
25. de Camp, "Howard and the Races," 129.
26. de Camp, "Editing Howard," 117.
27. Saunders, "Revisiting 'Die, Black Dog!'" Juma first appeared in "The City of Skulls," a short story in the collection *Conan* from Ace in 1967. He appears 9 issues of Marvel's *The Savage Sword of Conan* and 1 of its *Conan the Barbarian* comics, and also in Leonard Carpenter's *Conan the Hero* (1989).
28. Fimi, *Tolkien, Race, and Cultural History*, 132.
29. For example, Chism, "Middle-Earth, the Middle Ages, and the Aryan Nation: Myth and History in World War II."
30. Hall, "Crash Go the Civilizations: Some Notes on Robert E. Howard's Use of History and Anthropology," 33.
31. Beasley, *The Victorian Reinvention of Race: New Racisms and the Problem of Grouping in the Human Sciences*, 1.
32. Kupperman, "Angells in America," 38; Painter, *The History of White People*, 33.
33. Latham, *The Germania of Tacitus with Ethnological Dissertations and Notes*, i.
34. Young, *The Idea of English Ethnicity*, 57.
35. As Painter points out, in Ralph Waldo Emerson's *English Traits* (1856), "the American was the same as the Englishman, who was the same as the Saxon and the Norseman," *The History of White People*, 183. Rudyard Kipling's poem *The White Man's Burden* is one of the best known – and now infamous – illustrative examples of the discourse of superiority.
36. Horsman, *Race and Manifest Destiny: The Origins of American Racial Anglo-Saxonism*; MacDougall, *Racial Myth in English History: Trojans, Teutons, and Anglo-Saxons*. See also Young, "Whiteness and Time: the Once, Present, and Future Race."
37. Straubhaar, "Myth, Late Roman History, and Multiculturalism in Tolkien's Middle-Earth."
38. Firchow, "The Politics of Fantasy: *The Hobbit* and Fascism," 23.
39. Werber, "Geo- and Biopolitics of Middle-Earth: a German Reading of Tolkien's *The Lord of the Rings*," 229.
40. Fimi, *Tolkien, Race, and Cultural History*, 145.
41. Tolkien, *The Letters of J. R. R. Tolkien*, pt. 1183.
42. Shippey, *The Road to Middle Earth*, 152.
43. Tolkien, *The Two Towers*, 887.
44. Fimi, *Tolkien, Race, and Cultural History*, 150.
45. Tolkien, *The Return of the King*, 984.
46. Ford, "The White City," 71.
47. Fimi, *Tolkien, Race, and Cultural History*, 147.
48. Tolkien, *The Two Towers*, 887. Moreover, as Fimi observes, Treebeard "presents an evaluative classification of different Middle-earth beings from highest to lowest' when he first meets the hobbits Merry and Pippin. Fimi, *Tolkien, Race, and Cultural History*, 142.

49. Straubhaar, "Myth, Late Roman History, and Multiculturalism in Tolkien's Middle-Earth"; Young, "Diversity and Difference: Cosmopolitanism and *The Lord of the Rings*."
50. Tolkien, *The Return of the King*, 107.
51. Polygenesis was not only attributed to divine creation in real world discourses, and took on a scientific bent in the nineteenth century in particular.
52. Painter, *The History of White People*, 70.
53. Tolkien, *The Silmarillion*, 18.
54. Tolkien, *The Silmarillion*, 42.
55. Brackman, "'Dwarves Are Not Heroes': Antisemitism and the Dwarves in J. R. R. Tolkien's Writings," 87.
56. Lott, *The Invention of Race*.
57. Goff et al., "Not Yet Human: Implicit Knowledge, Historical Dehumanization, and Contemporary Consequences," 293.
58. Tolkien, *The Fellowship of the Ring*, 71.
59. Tolkien, *The Return of the King*, 982.
60. Fimi, *Tolkien, Race, and Cultural History*, 148. According to Appendix B, during the Third Age, "the wisdom and life-span of the Númenóreans ... waned as they became mingled with lesser men," Tolkien, *The Return of the King*, 1423.
61. Tolkien, "Orcs," 418.
62. Straubhaar, "Myth, Late Roman History, and Multiculturalism in Tolkien's Middle-Earth." His mixed heritage leads directly to civil war.
63. Petzold, "'Oo, Those Awful Orcs!': Tolkien's Villains as Protagonists in Recent Fantasy Novels," 77.
64. Tolkien, *The Fellowship of the Ring*, 423.
65. Young, "Diversity and Difference," 360–361.
66. Tolkien, *The Two Towers*, 582.
67. Tolkien, *The Return of the King*, 1181.
68. Talley, "Let Us Now Praise Famous Orcs: Simple Humanity in Tolkien's Inhuman Creatures," 24.
69. Hinckley, "Conan the Oxymoron: The Civilized Savage of Robert E. Howard and Frank Frazetta"; Joshi, "Barbarism vs. Civilization: Robert E. Howard and H. P. Lovecraft in Their Correspondence."
70. Howard, *The Coming of Conan the Cimmerian*, 11.
71. Chambliss and Svitavsky, "From Pulp Hero to Superhero: Culture, Race, and Identity in American Popular Culture, 1900–1940," 13.
72. Shovlin, "Canaan Lies Beyond the Black River: Howard's Dark Rhetoric of the Contact Zone," 100.
73. Chambliss and Svitavsky, "From Pulp Hero to Superhero," 6–7.
74. Garstad, "'Death to the Masters!': The Role of Slave Revolt in the Fiction of Robert E. Howard," 244.
75. Howard, *The Hour of the Dragon*, 140.
76. Garstad, "'Death to the Masters!'," 245.
77. Howard, "Shadows in Zamboula," 530–531.
78. Howard, "Shadows in Zamboula," 532. De Camp's editing of what he considered Howard's worst racial slurs did not extend to this story, which is reprinted word for word in *Conan the Wanderer*, and Ace paperback, in 1968.
79. Howard, "Shadows in Zamboula," 542.
80. Howard, "Shadows in Zamboula," 545.

81. For example, Finn, "'I Had No Idea He Was a Racist Douchebag.'"
82. Howard, *The Coming of Conan the Cimmerian*, 138.
83. Howard, *The Coming of Conan the Cimmerian*, 126.
84. Described in chapter one of Lott, *The Invention of Race*.
85. Howard, *The Coming of Conan the Cimmerian*, 141. Direct similes of this kind are used in other of his stories, including "Shadows in Zamboula."
86. Howard, *The Coming of Conan the Cimmerian*, 143.
87. Howard, *The Coming of Conan the Cimmerian*, 136.
88. Howard, *The Coming of Conan the Cimmerian*, 398.
89. Howard, *The Coming of Conan the Cimmerian*, 381.
90. Howard, *The Coming of Conan the Cimmerian*, 398. Connections between Hyboria and the modern world were reinforced by de Camp long after Howard's death. de Camp, "Kush."
91. Hall, "Crash Go the Civilizations," 32–35.
92. Hall, "Crash Go the Civilizations, 35.
93. Garstad, "'Death to the Masters!'," 248.
94. I use the term in the light of Isiah Lavender's *Race in American Science Fiction*.
95. Ditomasso, "Robert E. Howard's Hyborian Tales and the Question of Race in Fantastic Literature," 151–152.
96. Chance, *Tolkien the Medievalist*; Chance and Siewers, *Tolkien's Modern Middle Ages*; Drout, "A Mythology for Anglo-Saxon England"; Shippey, *The Road to Middle Earth*; Shippey, *J. R. R. Tolkien: Author of the Century*.
97. Drout, "A Mythology for Anglo-Saxon England," 230.
98. After Howard's suicide, his books were donated to Howard Payne College – now Howard Payne University – by his father. They are now in the Robert E. Howard Museum in Cross Plains, Texas. A brief catalogue was printed in 1984 (Herron, "Robert E. Howard's Library"), while a more complete, online version is also available. See Burke, "The Robert E. Howard Bookshelf."
99. Young, "Whiteness and Time."
100. Ekman, *Here Be Dragons: Exploring Fantasy Maps and Settings*, 15.
101. Tolkien, *The Fellowship of the Ring*, 3.
102. Howard, *The Coming of Conan the Cimmerian*, 423, 425.
103. The representation of women in stories and on the covers are, in contrast, extensively discussed.
104. Lewis, "The Dethronement of Power," 12. The essay first appeared in *Time and Tide* and was reprinted in *Tolkien and the Critics* in 1968.
105. Bearick, "Why Is the Only Good Orc a Dead Orc? The Dark Face of Racism Examined in Tolkien's World," 862.
106. Isaacs, "On the Possibilities of Writing Tolkien Criticism," 1.
107. The letter was reprinted in 2004 as Boardman, "Letter." See also Hunnewell, *Tolkien Fandom Review from Its Beginnings to 1964*, 9–10.
108. Boardman, "Letter," 238.
109. de Camp, *Literary Swordsmen and Sorcerers: The Makers of Heroic Fantasy*, 149.
110. de Camp, *Literary Swordsmen and Sorcerers*, 149.
111. Various, "Racism in Middle Earth."
112. "*LOTR*: Racist?"
113. "*LOTR* Southern Humans."
114. "Conan Comics from Dark Horse."

115. Romeo, "Southern Discomfort: Was Howard A Racist?" Mark Finn, writing a rebuttal of Romeo's essay a decade later suggests that Texas society and culture were changing rapidly during Howard's lifetime and that an individual's beliefs and statements cannot be simply explained by context. "Southwestern Discomfit: An Analysis of Gary Romeo's Controversial Article on Robert E. Howard and Racism."
116. Also because, as Okorafor put it of Howard's friend Lovecraft: "the fact that a lot of people back then were racists does not change the fact that Lovecraft was a racist." Okorafor, "Lovecraft's Racism The World Fantasy Award Statuette, with Comments from China Miéville."
117. Ahmed, "Is *Game of Thrones* Too White?"
118. Okorafor, "Lovecraft's Racism The World Fantasy Award Statuette, with Comments from China Miéville." In 2014 a petition calling for the award to be changed to an image of Octavia Butler was circulated by author and editor David Jose Older, partly sparked by Okorafor's response to the statuette. At the time of writing the Awards committee have commented that they are "in discussion" about changing the statuette. Flood, "World Fantasy Awards Pressed to Drop HP Lovecraft Trophy in Racism Row."
119. Shovlin, "Canaan Lies Beyond the Black River," 91–92.
120. The lurid covers of the magazine, often featuring nude women, did however draw comment, not because they represented women badly but because they might mislead the uninformed into thinking the magazine was pornographic.
121. Reid, "The Wild Unicorn Herd Check-in: the Politics of Race in Science Fiction Fandom."
122. Young, "Race in Online Fantasy Fandom: Whiteness on Westeros.org."
123. See, for example Pearson, "Fandom in the Digital Era."
124. For the former see, for example, Acrackedmoon, "The Tolkien Fanboy Fallacies." For the latter see, for example, Finn, "'I Had No Idea He Was a Racist Douchebag.'"
125. Anaesthetized, "The Othering of Orcs: A Post-Colonial Reading of Peter Jackson's Lord of the Rings Trilogy."
126. Sanford, "Robert E. Howard Was a Racist. Deal with It."
127. Billingr, "The Hobbit Race Is Based on the European Race. Please Stop PC in the Media"; Jon, "World According To Jon: Are Hobbits Racist?"

2 Forming Habits
Derivation, Imitation, and Adaptation

Ursula K. le Guin's *A Wizard of Earthsea*, first published in 1968 by the small press Parnassus, is one of the most critically lauded Fantasy books ever written. Published towards the beginning of the Fantasy boom sparked by paperback versions of Conan and *The Lord of the Rings*, it has recently been called a "wellspring" of Fantasy by Margaret Atwood,[1] and introduced what have become lasting tropes of the genre: the "school of magic," and that the Word – a speech act – and true names are powerful.[2] The political elements of Earthsea, however, did not elicit imitation to the same degree, notably its brown-skinned protagonist Ged and the peripheral role planned by white-skinned people in most of the series. Le Guin commented in a recent edition that "a great many white readers … were not ready to accept a brown-skinned hero;"[3] to this day, she says, "some readers notice this [his skin-colour], many don't."[4] Audience expectations enable individuals to read over the fairly subtle indications of the skin-colour of Ged and many of the peoples he encounters. This chapter illuminates the processes by which the genrefication of Fantasy from the late 1970s to the present ingrained those same expectations, considering particularly the sub-genres High Fantasy and Sword and Sorcery, and demonstrating that Fantasy's habits of Whiteness were challenged even as they were being formed.

A not inconsiderable number of successful Fantasy authors from the 1960s onwards did not write principally in either the High Fantasy or Sword and Sorcery sub-genres, Anne McCaffrey and Andre Norton among them, while Marion Zimmer Bradley's best-known work, *The Mists of Avalon* (1983), also does not sit comfortably here; all three authors also have significant Science Fiction elements in many of their works.[5] A single chapter cannot hope to discuss in any detail all the permutations of the genre, much less the vast numbers of works – both literary and audio-visual – that were produced in the last two decades of the twentieth century. Rather than attempting this, I focus on the two most commercially successful sub-genres, which are unquestionably at the centre of Fantasy as a genre. During the 1970s and early 1980s, "there was a glut of sword-and-sorcery books, movies, comics, and cartoons, though many of these works were derivative and of poor quality."[6] These foreshadowed and then were over-taken by quest narratives in the 1980s,[7] most of which were in the Tolkienian mode of High Fantasy.

Neither Tolkien's nor Howard's work created a complete sub-genre, much less a complete genre. The Whiteness so central to both their worlds only became habit – convention – through repetition; this chapter traces that repetition as it occurs first through imitation and then adaptation.

Farah Mendlesohn and Edward James argue that "superficially, the two types can look similar" because of "medievalist to other kinds of pre-industrial settings, purple prose and a sense of moral order."[8] Many of the elements that are side-lines to their discussion of Fantasy structures, including settings, are of central concern to my exploration here because content as much if not more than narrative form shapes the Whiteness of the genre. In this chapter I argue that there are four interconnected elements of Fantasy convention found in both Sword and Sorcery and High Fantasy of the 1980s and 1990s which contribute significantly its habit of Whiteness: cultural and physical geography; medievalism; the somatic markers of protagonists; and race logics which connect physical and non-physical traits to biological descent.

This chapter begins with an exploration of the shape of prominent Fantasy worlds of David Eddings, Robert Jordan, Fritz Leiber, Michael Moorcock, and *Dungeons & Dragons* (*D&D*), showing that racial logics and eurocentrism are consistently present.[9] It then offers a counter-point, examining the Sword and Sorcery writing of Samuel R. Delany and Charles R. Saunders, both African American authors whose voices were prominent in challenging the Whiteness of Fantasy in both creative and critical writing.[10] Both men wrote heroic Fantasy which had protagonists of colour, people who inhabited worlds which were neither eurocentric nor structured by racial logics; the contrast highlights how constructed the Whiteness of the genre is. Delany's work is better known and has been more widely explored by scholars, although this due in large part to the fact that he also writes Science Fiction, which tends to attract far more scholarly attention than Fantasy. Saunders' work, like the vast majority of Sword and Sorcery, has been left largely undiscussed.

The chapter then moves to the twenty-first century with an exploration of transmedia franchising – a major feature of the contemporary genre – using three works featuring the character of Conan. The section considers the ways in which adaptations can bring much earlier, out-dated, and disproven concepts of race and difference into the popular imagination as products iterate and reiterate their stories and the structures of their imagined worlds. It considers the role of three important media forms – comics, film, and games – and the ways they influence constructions of race and racialized worlds through examinations of: Dark Horse's *Conan the Barbarian* comic series which adapts Howard's original stories; the 2011 movie of the same name; and Funcom's massively multi-player online role-playing game (MMORPG) *Age of Conan*.

Imitation, derivation, and adaptation are all significant factors in driving the repetition of tropes, structures, and form that creates a genre; by linking them, this chapter illuminates the ways in which Fantasy's habits of White-ness form and re-form. Real world essentialized racial hierarchies based on descent derived largely from race theory developed in conjunction with the pseudo-science of the Enlightenment era. Optimistic claims of a vast reduction in the influence of such notions in Western culture, assert that, for example: "the images of race reflected in the dual mirrors of science and popular culture at the beginning of the [twentieth] century were fundamen-tally different from those reflected at the end."[11] Racial hierarchies, however, remain integral to not only material which is overtly White supremacist, but to the power relations which structure western society. Fantasy is one area of popular culture in which such concepts remain strong, and is a micro-cosm of popular culture.

REPETITIONS OF RACE

Racial logics which link physical and non-physical traits to biological descent are present in both Tolkien's and Howard's worlds, and are also written into the sub-genres that derived from them. David Eddings' *Pawn of Prophecy* (1983), the first book of his Belgariad and Mallorean series, quickly establishes that the personal attributes of individuals are closely linked to their racial descent. Multiple "racial stocks" live in the kingdom of Sendaria where the hero Belgarion grows up, but racial descent is still telling:

> Rundorig would have been their leader, but because he was an Arend, his sense was a bit limited ... Arends, of course, were very brave, but were also notoriously thick-witted.[12]

The idea that non-physical traits can be passed down from one generation to the next across thousands of years is far from unique to Eddings' worlds.[13] Mat, one of the protagonists of Jordan's *The Eye of the Wheel* (1990), the first book in his long Wheel of Time series, instinctively uses the war-cry of his ancestors. One of his companions remarks: "the blood of Arad's line is still strong in the Two Rivers. The old blood still sings."[14]

The impact of *Dungeons and Dragons* (*D&D*) and its many transme-dia products, while fairly infrequently discussed by historians of fiction in Fantasy, ought not to go unremarked. Even if the trickle-down influence of the game is not considered, its most popular realms were shared worlds in which large numbers of novels, written by multiple authors, were set. Hundreds of novels have been written for each of the Forgotten Realms and Dragonlance settings, for example.[15] In the early editions of *D&D* "humans are the normative race, and given the Anglo-centric depiction of human culture in the game, humans can be interpreted as representing 'white peo-ple.'"[16] The manuals for the first two editions of the game contained only illustrations of White characters in their hundreds of pages, and the third edition (2000), had very few.[17] This structure was maintained in *D&D* – despite the myriad other playable races – until the fourth edition, released in 2008, which Tresca argues: "set out to remove the humanocentric bias of the racial descriptions."[18] As Matthew Sernett writes in the *Races and Classes* guide to that edition:

> Dwarves are described as suspicious, greedy, and vengeful. Elves are known to be aloof, disdainful, and slow to make friends. Gnomes are reckless pranksters. Half-orcs have short tempers. Each race in the 3rd Edition *Players Handbook* brings with it classic flaws – except humans … maybe humans were described in such glowing terms as a means of explain why we presented them as the dominant race in all of D&D's published settings.[19]

The fourth edition added corruptibility as an inherent weakness of humans. This passage highlights the racial logic of the game world – non-physical traits are linked to biology – and adding a flaw to humanity does not undercut this. Game rules that favour specifically White humanity and privilege human player-characters over non-human characters which are often marked as non-White, combined with the dominance of humans in "all of D&D's published settings" as Sernett puts it,[20] established Whiteness as both normative and desirable.

The tendency to link non-physical with physical traits according to biological descent and thus reproduce racial logics even when there are no overt references to a particular real-world culture is common in Sword and Sorcery worlds, as it is in those of High Fantasy. The Melnibonéans of Michael Moorcock's Elric stories are a case in point; a humanoid race resembling conventional elves, their difference from the humans of that world is emphasised in various ways throughout the stories – particularly through their different aesthetics – as is their callous and selfish nature which is both cultural and inherent; their culture, based heavily on tradition, helps keep their amoral impulses in check.[21] Zimmer Bradley's world of Darkover is another example, one from a series which crosses back and forward between Fantasy and Science Fiction. The Comyn Families, which hold power on the planet of Darkover, are the result of a dedicated eugenics program between human settlers and indigenous Chieri which fostered *laran*, a telepathic power, which is linked to red hair. Whether the non-physical attributes are supernatural as on Darkover, or (a)moral tendencies as with the Melnibonéans, race thinking structures these worlds.

The tendency to use somatic markers associated with race to indicate character in Fantasy in the 1980s and 1990s was so strong Diana Wynne-Jones satirised it in her *A Tough Guide to Fantasyland* (1996):

> Black hair is Evil, particularly if combined with a corpse-white complexion. Red hair *always* entails magical Powers … Brown hair has

to be viewed in combination with eyes, whose colours are the real giveaway ... Fair hair, especially if it is silver-blonde, *always* means goodness.[22]

Protagonists are often marked to the reader as racially White by their physical features: Belgarion from Eddings' Belgariad and Mallorean series, for example, is one of a long line of sandy-haired boys,[23] while the child Errand, who later becomes the god of all humanity Eriond in these series, has "pale blond hair" and blue eyes.[24] Rand al'Thor saviour of the in Jordan's Wheel of Time series, meanwhile, has light blue-grey eyes, white skin, dark-red hair. Feist's Pug, one of the heroes of *Magician* is an exception, with black hair and eyes, and "dark" skin, "like unclouded chocha or coffee."[25] The vast majority of Fantasy protagonists, whatever the sub-genre in which they appear, are described or shown to have physical characteristics associated with Whiteness.

Myles Balfe argues that conventional Fantasy representation of lands and peoples marked as foreign and Other draw heavily on "pre-existing cultural discourses to construct their 'incredible geographies.'"[26] Characters marked as "us" and "good" in the genre, he observes, are also marked "Western;"[27] geography, culture, and race are linked in profound ways. Balfe identifies Jordan's lengthy Wheel of Time series and *D&D* as examples of this trend, and the many others include Guy Gavriel Kay's *Fionovar Tapestry*, Eddings' Belgariad and Mallorean books, Feist's Midkemia books – particularly the first four, and Terry Goodkind's Sword of Truth series. Terry Brooks' Shannara series takes place in a land that was revealed to be a future post-apocalyptic version of the Pacific Northwest of the US in the Genesis of Shannara books (2006–2008); its human inhabitants are marked as White. Even in worlds where west does not equate to Western, Whiteness is dominant.

As Laurie Finke and Martin Schihtman argue, "the fantasy of the Middle Ages has always been the exclusive province of European colonialism, representing the historical legitimation of white, Christian, European domination;"[28] this is as true for the conventions of Fantasy as it is in the vast majority of modern culture. The medieval elements common to High Fantasy and Sword and Sorcery are invariably associated with the White Self, for example in the construction of humans as a playable-race in *D&D* discussed above. Eddings, for example, clearly references Viking culture for his Chereks with their berserkers, worship of the Bear God, axes, and icy-homeland but does not use any identifiable source. Even less specific gestures towards the Middle Ages are used to identify many other cultures as medieval-European. Thus, Feist's Kingdom of the Isles is a feudal monarchy, albeit one with an active merchant class in later books. Its nobles live in castles, have hunt-masters, and fight with European style weaponry.

Ahistorical references to medieval European cultures are also common in Sword and Sorcery worlds, it is very rare for one to exist that does not have at least some. They are, however, often less central to the action of the various episodic stories as the wanderings of protagonists are commonly much geographically wider. Fritz Leiber's Fafhrd and the Grey Mouser stories, the first of which was published in 1939, were second only in success to Howard's tales.[29] Leiber described his world in the gaming magazine *The Dragon* in 1976, using the conceit that "wargamers wanted to know about the geography and terrains of the World of Nehwon and which earth solders most resembled in weapons and tactics the warriors of the chief lands of Lankhmar [the city around which most of the tales are set]." The people of that city, he writes are like "southern medieval," their neighbours are like "northern medieval," while those of the "Eastern Lands" are like "Saracens, Arabs, Parthians, Assyrian ... they ride the camel and the elephant."[30] The physical, cultural, and racial geography of his world is not only similar to that of the real world, but is directly linked to it. Where Howard imagined Hyboria as an early precursor to history, Leiber's stories are those of a parallel world; the landscapes and ethnoscapes of both are similar, and both contribute to the habits of both the sub-genre of Sword and Sorcery, and the Fantasy genre more broadly.

Medievalist feudal monarchies, made palatable to modern readers by a strong sense of *noblesse oblige* among high-born protagonists, is conventionally contrasted with an exoticized and often "Oriental" empire; the Mallorean and Tamul empires in Eddings' books, and Feist's Tsurani and Kesh are examples, all of which are marked as pan-Asian by their cultural and physical geographies and are subject to Orientalist discourse. The reader experiences them only through the filter of the White protagonists, even when characters from those realms – often the emperor himself – take a significant role in the story.[31] Each is saved from collapse by the presence and action of Whitecharacters, including the Mallorean which is a realm of "enemy" Angaraks in the *Belgariad* until their evil god Torak is killed at the end of that series.[32] These "White saviour" narratives construct the Othered empires as static, incapable of change without external intervention, moreover, the change that does come is extremely limited and result in no political or social development, merely a shoring up of the existing power structure.[33]

COUNTER-VOICES

The dominance of White protagonists and European medievalist cultural references in the burgeoning Fantasy genre was perhaps nowhere more vehemently criticised than in a 1975 essay by Saunders. Saunders penned a stinging attack on representation of Black characters in the pulps, linking Howard's name with those of H. P. Lovecraft and Clark Ashton Smith. Saunders begins the essay, titled "Die Black Dog! A Look at Racism in Fantasy Literature," by talking about his own experience: "the ethnic epithets that spew form the mouth of Conan are all-too-well represented in the grim world of reality. When blatant racism does occur in a Fantasy tale, the black reader is rudely jerked from its escapist world."[34] He compares "Shadows in Zamboula" to "having a front row seat at a Ku Klux Klan rally," and argues that Howard had "a latent fear of blacks." He does allow that there may be some elements of white guilt in Howard's tales too, and praises de Camp and Carter for their addition of Juma the Kushite, "a black equal to Conan."

Saunders had published a short story featuring the black warrior Imaro, who has been characterised as "an alternative to the big, white, muscled lunk" of convention,[35] in the small-press zine *Dark Fantasy* in July of 1974. His short stories and novellas about Imaro were collected into the novels *Imaro* (1981), *Imaro II: The Quest for Cush* (1984) and *The Trail of Bohu* (1985) by DAW; the first two were re-issued by Night Shade in 2006 and 2007. Saunders conceived of Imaro partly as an "anti-Tarzan,"[36] and of Nyumbani, the Africa-inspired continent he inhabits as part of "a world in which Africa was never toppled from its ancient glories as it was in ours."[37] DAW attempted to market the first novel as "The Epic Novel of a Black Tarzan" and were only prevented from doing so by the threat of legal action from the estate of Edgar Rice Burroughs.[38] Burroughs and H. Rider Haggard, along with Howard, were significant influences on Saunders as he wrote stories intended to provide alternative representations of Africa and its peoples to theirs.[39] Imaro was widely received as a "Black Conan" in the 1980s and still is today,[40] perhaps as much because of the relative popularity and visibility of Conan compared to Tarzan in late-twentieth and early-twenty-first-century culture.

Delany is one of if not the best-known African American authors of Fantasy, although like many authors, he writes across genres. His Science Fiction has garnered a great deal more attention than his Sword-and-Sorcery *Return to Nevèrÿon* series (1979–1987), particularly when it comes to explorations of race.[41] The tales – eleven short stories and novellas published in four books – take place from the city of Nevèrÿona to the margins of its empire. The empire – located variously in the region of the Mediterranean, Africa, or Asia according to the pseudo-archaeological framework Delany constructs for the stories – is one of brown- and black-skinned people at its centre, and pale-skinned, blue-eyed, blond-haired "barbarians," who are often enslaved, living at its periphery.[42]

Saunders and Delany challenged Fantasy's habits of Whiteness by their very presence as African American authors; as Nnedi Okorafor points out, "there were very few writers of colour specifically working in the field" in the 1970s and 1980s.[43] The stories they wrote and the worlds they created also do so because they do not use the conventions discussed in the previous section of this chapter. Nyumbani and the empire of Nevèrÿona are not Europe-like settings; their protagonists are black and brown skinned; and the major cultures of their worlds are not based on those of medieval Western Europe. Saunders world, as noted above, was inspired by the desire to "wrote back" to Western stereotypes of Africa and its people that were – and still are – expressed in the form of Fantasy convention. Neither he nor Delany, however, merely "flip" the somatic markers of their protagonists, but rather create worlds in which the racial logics that structure so many Fantasy worlds do not exist.

Both create worlds inhabited by diverse peoples with diverse cultures and homelands; Saunders' are predominantly inspired by those of the real-world,[44] while Delany's are less clearly so, even though he presents his world as a pre-historic version of our own. The fair-skinned yellow-haired barbarians of the world do not inhabit icy northern and western lands or live in medievalist cultures; they are not White in the way that Howard's Cimmerians or Eddings' Alorns are White. The somatic markers of individuals – yellow hair, brown skin and so on – demonstrate the diversity of the people who inhabit his world, but they are not attached to non-physical attributes, that is, they are not constructed using racial logics. The many different peoples Imaro encounters in his travels in Nyumbani and beyond are differentiated by physical and cultural characteristics, but the physical and non-physical are, as in Delany's world, not connected; much of the first novel is concerned with demonstrating that Imaro's character, and those of the Ilyassai people, are a product of culture and individual tendency, not of racial descent.

The presence of Delany and Saunders, and the natures of their works and worlds, demonstrate that Fantasy's habits of Whiteness are patterns developed through time and repetition, patterns which can be deviated from and perhaps ultimately changed. They collectively and individually inspire participation in genre-culture by authors and audiences from minority backgrounds – this is particularly the case for Delany, whose work is intersectional and engages strongly with gender and sexuality as well as race.[45] As Okorafor says, "since the 1990s a critical mass of authors who identified themselves as writers of colour has emerged,"[46] some of whose work is explored in depth in later chapters, partly because of the pioneering works of Saunders and Delany. Nonetheless, a great deal of twenty-first-century Fantasy has not broken – and does not seek to break – its habits of Whiteness.

MULTI-MEDIA STORYTELLING

Fantasy, like much of twenty-first-century popular culture, is littered with multi-media franchises, the multiple attempts – more and less successful – to adapt *The Lord of the Rings* to radio, animated film, movies, and videogames are a case in point. Martin's A Song of Ice and Fire series, HBO's *Game of Thrones* based on it, and the plethora of games, graphic novels, and other forms deriving from one or both is another example, one which combines adaptation of original narratives and transmedia storytelling, which creates new narratives for new media forms.[47] The following section of this chapter explores the ways that adaptation from text to visual and audio-visual media can affect constructions of race. Focusing on twenty-first-century works featuring Conan, it also considers the way that adapting older texts can be particularly problematic because of audience demands for fidelity to an original and the role played by licensing agreements.

Dark Horse's Conan the Barbarian Comics

Conan first appeared in a comic, titled "Conan the Barbarian," in 1970. It was published by Marvel, which continued to produce Conan comics, sometimes although generally not based on Howard's original stories, until 2000. Dark Horse took over the license for comics in 2003, it is held from Conan Properties Inc., a subsidiary of Paradox Entertainment Inc., a Norwegian company which owns some of the rights to Conan and Hyboria; a significant number of Howard's original stories are now in the public domain, so they do not control a complete franchise.[48] Many of the comics Dark Horse has published across five series and a range of mini-series and one-offs are new stories, not adaptations of Howard's originals. The series *Conan the Barbarian* (2012–2014), however, is an adaptation of Howard's "Queen of the Black Coast," written by Brian Wood,[49] and it is this series I focus on here. There is a growing body of scholarship on race in comics, it does not, by and large, engage with Fantasy, or with comics as adaptations,[50] and is mostly concerned with superheroes and representation of African Americans in "real world" comics.[51] Licensed comics, as Nicolas Pillai observes, are often treated with "active disdain" by scholars working in comic studies, but are also an integral part of most major transmedia franchises in contemporary popular culture.[52]

Howard's story has three parts: the first tells of the meeting of Conan and Bêlit – the Queen of the title – and the other two of the adventure that leads to her death. Dark Horse's series inserts a series of adventures between the first two chapters of Howard's work, significantly extending the length of this episode of Conan's life. The first three issues correspond with the first section of Howard's tale – up to Conan and Bêlit's meeting – and the final four with its end. Between the two parts of this framing narrative they have adventures in each other's homelands – Cimmeria and Shem – and in other parts of the world as well. Each finds the others' homeland and people unwelcoming, and feels alien in them. As with any similar adaptation, certain elements are emphasized by the nature of the visual medium. The comic series also expands on a number of cues Howard includes in his work, increasing the impact of problematic racial constructs.

From her first appearance Bêlit is depicted with skin so white as to be almost colour-less; she is far whiter than Conan, whose skin is tan to beige throughout. The skin colour of the crew, "the blacks" of Howard's tale, varies markedly throughout the series, and indeed in the space for a single issue at time. They are savage, almost bestial at their first appearance: hairless, shirtless – unlike Conan – and hyper-muscled, their mouths are open in shouts showing pointed teeth, their eyes have no coloured iris, and their fingers are curled into claws while their skin is black, very dark browns, and charcoal greys. The effect is heightened by the fact that for the first four pages of battle scene they are shown without weapons, a contrast to Conan who has first a bow and then a sword in his hands, which are often drawn in close up. The hero fights with relatively technologically advanced weapons but his enemies are depicted as being so close to animals that they appear to have no need of them. In the third issue, once Conan has joined Bêlit's band and is conversing freely with rather than fighting them, their features become normalized, and their skin at times has very similar shades to his own. The overall effect strongly associates savagery with darker skin tones in a way which builds on the cues in the original story; in the comics series, the crews' skin darkens as they become beasts in battle, but it is only they who have changing colour, only they who seemingly devolve in pressured situations.

Howard gives no details of how Bêlit came to be the pirate leader. Wood, however, provides a back-story for Bêlit and her crew. As N'Gora, the first mate, explains:

> Half the men here once crewed the *Obsidian*, a timber barge out of Abombi ... The ancient forests of the black kingdoms are home to many valuable woods, valued by rich men of Argos and Shem. Bêlit came to us then.[53]

When Conan asks what help she could give he is told:

> Perspective. We were blinded and bound by the value of our cargo. We were placing that above the lives of the crew. We dumped the cargo and fled, Bêlit aboard the *Obsidian* with us. She knew the raiders, knew where they lived.[54]

Under her command, the former timber-barge crew became successful pirates: "Bêlit has led us to victory after victory after victory. We are all of us as rich as nobles, yet we will never leave her. She *liberated* us. She *delivered* us."[55] The tale he tells is a "White saviour" narrative, and is strongly couched in the language of slavery and emancipation. N'Gora's account of how Bêlit turned merchant seamen into pirates is an example. Bêlit displays superior knowledge and has the ability to see the world rationally and form a much broader perspective than do the men who become her crew. Bêlit "liberated" them, but in return became their "mistress," ruling them with her success born of rationality and control: "she is cautious when it is tactically sound to be so, and fierce when required."[56]

N'gora does not use the words "slave" or "slavery," but the language he chooses and the situation he describes invokes the history of European slave-trading in Africa under a veneer of capitalism. He and his crew considered themselves to be commodities, and not very valuable ones at that, "blinded and bound," enslaved to the value of the goods aboard their ship. The desire in rich, civilized lands for the natural resources of "the ancient forests of the black kingdoms" invokes the European desire for resources which drove imperialism not only in Africa but around the world, and paved the way for slavery. Bêlit thus becomes an emancipator from the evils of history and commerce simultaneously, her physical and symbolic Whiteness is literally a beacon of liberation which emblematizes her superiority over her followers. They then enter a state of voluntary slavery to her, electing not to enjoy the rewards of their successful entry into the plundering capitalist system which had previously dominated them, but rather to bind themselves perpetually in a new form of service. Bêlit saves the men from one form of slavery, but they remain subject to the power of her Whiteness.

The final episode of Conan's adventures with Bêlit parallels Howard's story very closely and draws much of the narrative and dialogue from it, including references to racist stereotypes. When Conan encounters N'Gora, who has been driven mad by fear: "At first he thought it was a common gorilla;"[57] the phrase in Howard's story is "great black gorilla."[58] The comic takes out the word "black," but the colours used for N'Gora's skin in the panels that follow are very dark browns and, in several just black; they are much darker than in many other of his appearances. The comic, moreover, expands on his transition. Where Howard writes briefly of his "inhuman mask," the comic contrasts: "the animal that was now N'Gora ... [with] the human side that had so clearly fled him."[59] The implication is that N'Gora, unlike Conan who is not overcome by fear and never loses his humanity, has always been part animal.[60] The influence of the nineteenth-century idea that people of colour were less evolved than Whites is clear: it is found in Howard's original as discussed in the previous chapter, and, far from being removed or challenged in the twenty-first-century adaptation, is reiterated and reinforced through the visual element of the comic.

The most overtly racialized elements of Bêlit's death are largely although not entirely removed. In Howard's story Conan finds her hanged by a ruby necklace from the yardarm of the *Tigress* – literally killed by her greed – but in the comic she hangs from a rope, shown only through the drawing. The comic also removes Howard's remark that "the Shemite soul finds a bright drunkenness in riches."[61] The underlying suggestion that it was Bêlit's lust for treasure that doomed her and her crew, however, remains. The most overt signs of anti-Semitism of Howard's story are adapted out of the comic, but the anti-Blackness is not. Given that Conan, still the White barbarian hero of nineteenth-century Anglo-Saxonist fantasies, is the sole survivor of the crew of the *Tigress* because he is not overcome by either greed or fear, the entire episode can be read as an assertion of racially superior rationality in the same manner as Howard's story.

In the last volume of the series Conan has travelled to Kush after burning the *Tigress* at sea with Bêlit's body and all their loot aboard. The people he encounters there are marked as "African" by their dark-brown skin,

dreadlocked hair, and tribal-style jewellery and tattoos. Conan has suc-
cumbed to despair and sits in a tavern drinking and fighting any one he
can, although none defeat him. The tavern-keeper Thessy, a Kushite woman,
explains to him that she and other locals call him "ghost man" not because
of his white skin as Conan thinks, but because "you're dead inside." She
forces him to confront his despair and to move on with his life; when she
beats him in a fight and threatens to kill him he must admit to himself that
he wants to live despite having lost Bêlit. The character of Thessy is unique
to the comic, and her role in it is that of a "magical negro:" she exists only
as part of Conan's story, having none of her own, and has insight into his life
others – including himself – do not and uses it to assist him.

Creating a comic book, Will Brooker argues, "especially with a long-
established character, is inherently a form of editing and creative collage."[62]
Brooker is writing specifically about Batman here, but the same can also be
said of Conan. The process is one of adaptation, but also one of original
creation; in the Conan the Barbarian series discussed here, only about
one-third of the material is drawn directly from Howard's story, the rest is
entirely new. Taking parts of the old, re-working, and inserting new material
in the twenty-first century at times removes some of the most overtly racist
aspects of Howard's work but this is not always the case and the process can
also reiterate them in new and more extended ways, including through the
addition of the visual elements of the comics medium.

CONAN ON FILM

The 1981 movie *Conan the Barbarian*, which included Arnold Schwarzeneg-
ger in the lead role, it perhaps the best remembered of a wave of B-grade
Sword and Sorcery films which appeared that decade. It made more than
$100 million at the box-office, more than twice that of the eponymous 2011
film which was a box-office bomb. I focus on the later film, subsequently
Conan, for several reasons: the relationship of the 2011 film to both Howard's writing and the game *Age of Conan*; and that the release date makes it
a better vehicle for considering some of the issues arising from twenty-first-
century Fantasy film. 1980s and 1990s B-grade films in speculative genres
were distinguished in part by the low-grade special effects – the monsters
Conan fights, for example, are obviously models. Improvements in special
effects resulting from technological developments in computer-generated
images are arguably a significant factor in the improved performance of
Fantasy and Science Fiction film in the first decade of the twenty-first century,[63] *Conan* places its heroic-Fantasy protagonist in an epic Fantasy storyline: what begins as a personal quest to avenge the death of his father and
the destruction of his home takes on epic proportions when Conan saves
all of Hyboria from an evil wizard, Khalar Zym. His adventures along the
way – he becomes a pirate, and frees a group of slaves – echo elements of

some of Howard's stories, but the film's overarching narrative is not based on any single one of them.

The prologue of the movie establishes a pseudo-historical backstory, telling of the time of "the dark empire of Acheron – whose power Khalar Zym hopes to regain – where cruel necromancers sought secrets of resurrection" and "enslaved to civilized world" so that "only the barbarian tribes were left to rise up against them."[64] Prologues of this kind are a common technique in films where the world of the narrative is far-removed from that of the modern world, and serve as a "bridge" between them.[65] In *Conan* the prologue invokes multiple conventional Fantasy elements to establish the genre setting, from the purple over-blown prose, to the "ancient" map with line-drawn castles, the mention of an evil, Othered empire, and the real-world cultural references assigned to the peoples it mentions. The footage accompanying the voice-over shows the soldiers of Acheron on horseback, dressed in robes and turbans, wielding curved swords while the barbarians are white-skinned, wear heavy furs, and their swords are straight. The iconography constructs evils of Acheron as Oriental – although they are light-skinned – and the barbarians, Conan's ancestors, as White.

The first scenes of his childhood reinforce this: the sequence opens with footage of a pre-industrial village, indistinguishable from any other medievalist village of historical or Fantasy film, set against the backdrop of a snow-covered hillside. Alec Worley argues that in the 1980s movie, "the mythical realm of Hyboria resonates by visually echoing earthbound history. Conan's wintry homeland of Cimmeria resembles the Scandinavia of Viking saga, while the barren plains of the south exude a certain Middle Eastern exoticism."[66] The look of the 2011 *Conan* is markedly similar, although its referents are historical only as filtered through the conventions of genre films and comics. The overall effect of the geographical visual cues is to mark the character of Conan as White before he appears on the screen. The world Conan inhabits as an adult when he leaves Cimmeria is littered with non-specific cultural and geographic exoticism, from slave colonies to ruins, mysterious monasteries, and deserted fortifications. Its people are equally non-specific, but are always marked as different to Cimmerians by their clothing, and at time by their skin-colour. In the first scenes where Conan appears as an adult, he is accompanied by Ukafa, a dreadlocked dark-skinned warrior. They are about to attack the "Ziguran Slave Colony," when Ukafa says "these are common slavers Conan, not the man you seek. Why attack?" Conan responds: "no man should live in chains."[67] The scene establishes him as a leader who values freedom while simultaneously emphasising his Whiteness through the visual contrast with his Black companion who plays at best a supporting role.

The casting of the film differs from the common pattern of Hollywood Fantasy. Momoa, who played the adult Conan and is now better known for his role as Khal Drogo in HBO's *Game of Thrones*, is an actor of Native Hawaiian and Native American descent. Casting an actor who is not White to play such a role is extremely unusual in a film industry better known for "whitewashing" – casting White actors to play characters who are not White in original texts – in adaptations.[68] The Sci-Fi Channel's *Legend of Earthsea* (2004) miniseries is a notorious example; the changed race of the protagonist and people led le Guin to publically condemn it.[69] Conan's two sidekicks in the film – Ukafa and Ela-Shan – were respectively played by: Bob Sapp, an African American wrestler and martial arts expert, and Saïd Taghmaoui, a French actor of Moroccan descent. Having both the hero and his sidekicks played by actors who are not White is extremely unusual for a Fantasy film; the nine members of the Fellowship in Jackson's *The Lord of the Rings* films were all played by White actors while, as Sue Kim points out, the evil Uruk-hai were played by Maori and Pacific Islander actors.[70] The relative diversity of the *Conan* supporting-role actors, however, is significantly undercut by the roles that they play, merely enabling Conan's story without having their own genuine agency or narrative.

The marketing material for the film makes explicit claims about its relationship with Howard's work, for example on the iTunes store: "deftly adapted from the original works of Robert E. Howard and faithful to the mythology and psychology of his iconic character."[71] Publicity for it also worked hard to differentiate the film from its earlier namesake. In a 2011 interview Momoa said that neither he nor most of his co-stars had seen the earlier film and that their version owed much more to other media:

> I'm a fan of Frank Frazetta … With the books, there's eight decades of Conan material, so it's just so much greater than that. We tried to stick really clear to the Robert E. Howard fans and the comic book fans.[72]

Although audiences and critics alike panned the film its attempts to invoke the feel of Howard's Hyboria was widely considered to have succeeded, mainly because of its extreme level of violence.[73]

Positioning the film in this way allows its creators to abrogate some responsibility for problematic elements, including the representation of race and gender. As I have argued elsewhere of Jackson's *The Lord of the Rings* film and game franchise, licensing agreements and pressure to create a consistent world in which the different elements of a franchise can be set, can iterate and reiterate racial logics and representations at the same time as they actively work against challenging troubling aspects of any given world.[74] The legacy and history of Conan and Hyboria, as trademarked objects within the popular culture landscape, is much more fragmented than that of Middle-earth because of the myriad pastiches, entirely original stories, and comic-book, television, and film versions that have been produced since the mid-1960s. The race logics which structured Howard's world, however, have been an integral part of most if not all of them, while the twenty-first-century emphasis on authenticity and accuracy to the original works adds pressure to reproduce concepts of race that have long been proven false.

CODING CONAN

A significant amount of scholarly attention has been paid to issues surrounding race in Fantasy gaming in recent years, but it has, almost without exception, focused on *World of Warcraft*.[75] *Age of Conan* was developed by the Norwegian studio Funcom, and first released as the subscription-based *Age of Conan: Hyborian Adventures* in 2008; it was re-released as *Age of Conan: Unchained* in 2011 when a free-to-play option was introduced. Players can still choose to subscribe for "premium" content and access. Although, as with any game, precise details of player numbers are hard if not impossible to obtain according to Funcom after a luke-warm reception and significant loss of players in its first six months,[76] *Age of Conan* surpassed 2 million in mid-2011, boosted by around 300 000 gamers who took up the free-to-play option.[77] Like Dark Horse's comics and *Conan*, the game is produced under licence from Conan Properties International LLC.

Age of Conan is shaped not only by the nature of the world Howard created but also by the video-game industry itself, which like Fantasy is marked by Whiteness: from stereotypical and under-representation of minorities,[78] to racism in player communities,[79] the unavailability of avatars of colour with realistic appearances,[80] and the lack of minorities working in the industry.[81] Fantasy worlds – in any medium – tend to consider race "an immutable and deterministic quality of being;"[82] video-games add new dimensions to this because of their dual rule-based nature: they rely ultimately on binary coding as a medium, and also do not allow the kind of negotiation between players that pen-and-paper games can engage in. The medium lends itself to perpetuating racial logics. That the rules-based nature of games relies on the codification of difference means that ludic elements must be considered in any evaluation of the construction of race. Although some critics have claimed that the immersive qualities of games render analysis of representational elements unimportant, many players do not share Espen Aarseth's oft-cited ability to see through and past the digital body of the player character.[83] Representation of race, particularly of people of colour and minority groups, is of considerable interest to players and critics alike.[84]

DIGITAL HYBORIA

There are four playable-races in *Age of Conan*, all human: Aquilonian, Cimmerian, Stygian, and Khitani. The racial and cultural geographies of the game world reflect those of Howard's Hyboria which were directly linked to those of the real world in his conception. Players not only recognise but make explicit the connections between the game and real-world historical peoples. A fan-created Wiki states that:

> Cimmerians are proto-Celts ... Stygians are evocative of a dark, twisted,
> Egypto-Babylonian people ... the Aquilonians have a culture similar

to that of the Carolingian Franks as well as the Greco-Romans ... the Khitani are similar to the Chinese/Korean of ancient history.[85]

Khitai is heavily exoticized in an Orientalist mode; it is described by the game website as "the most mysterious land in the Dreaming East."[86] In the visuals of the game, skin-colour, clothing, and weaponry all contribute to these constructions for individual characters, while political structures – kingdom vs empire for example – and architecture do the same for races.

The character creation tool is embedded in the opening scenes of the game and, unlike *World of Warcraft* where the player begins in the homeland of her character, in *Age of* Conan each begins as a slave on a galley about to be shipwrecked. The first choice is gender, which must be selected before either race or class, the other two major choices in the creation process. Making a character male or female has no direct impact on the options that are subsequently available, although as Esther MacCallum-Stewarr points out, the narrative of the game and player attitudes suggests that women and men are not equal.[87] Once gender is selected the avatar appears and the player may choose her race and class.

When the player selects one of the four "Culture" options, an explanatory text box pops up to provide information about it. That information links directly to race, for example: "the Khitani are slender with sharp features and parchment-yellow skin," and "Cimmerians are a northern race of barbarians, fair skinned and dark haired." Somatic markers are specified in the text and reinforced by the image of the character displayed in the centre of the screen. The text boxes also detail the class that is not available to any given race: "Aquilonians can never become sorcerers," while "Stygians can never become soldiers." The full range of classes available in the game is displayed down the right of the screen. They are grouped into four categories, based on archetypes of gaming – Soldier, Priest, Rogue, and Mage – with three sub-categories in each. The options which are not open to any given race are greyed out, reinforcing the fact that some races are, in this digital world, unable to learn particular skill-sets and act in a particular ways. When a class is selected, a pop-up text box again appears, briefly describing the nature and style of fighting of that type of character, and the armour and weapon types she has access to.

It is not possible *not* to have a race selected at any point during character creation: once gender has been selected Cimmerian is highlighted by default. The same is true for class: Guardian, a sub-category of Soldier, is the default setting for Cimmerians. As a result, at no stage can the player have a digital body that is not explicitly racialized both physically and in terms of the skills and styles of play that are open to her. A fan-created wiki asserts that "there are only cosmetic differences between players of the same class, *Age of Conan* has no racial bonuses,"[88] yet when it comes to creating the player's character and to her style of game-play, the choice of race is significant because it restricts what class can be played. Culture, physical appearance, and the skills a character may learn are all inextricably bound together in the coding of the game and this is communicated to the player from the opening screen, before she has properly entered the world, an extremely common feature of MMORPGS, and indeed many RPGs. The construction is that of race logic as it makes connections between physical and non-physical attributes explicit. In the game world they are 'real' and inescapable, although this is emphatically not the case in the real world.

As with the vast majority of MMORPGS, the appearance of the player character can be customized, but only within the restrictions of the game coding which often do not allow a genuinely diverse range of options. David R. Dietrich argues, based on a survey of both online and offline RPGs, that: "the patterns of restrictions on character creation seem to constitute omissions based upon the unquestioned standards of normative whiteness."[89] Players of colour, particularly those of African descent, often find themselves unable to create avatars that resemble them; Dietrich shows that skin-colour, hair, and facial features – the somatic markers most associated with race – are habitually restricted to White. In *Age of Conan*, only Stygian characters can have dark skin-shades – up to a medium brown – although they can also have skin-shade that is indistinguishable from those available to Cimmerians and Aquilonians. Facial expression can be altered, and some features varied in the advanced customization screen, but as with the vast majority of MMORPGs that offer this kind of customization the ability to create an avatar that does not have White features is lacking. The same is true for hair-style, often a point of discontent for players of colour.[90] A female Stygian character may have "beaded" hair and a range of "straight" hair options, but no curly style is available, while male Stygians have two "curly" options, but they are not the tight curls common to people of African descent. The playable characters of Hyboria are shaped, as is almost invariably the case, by exclusionary norms of Whiteness.

The four playable races are not the sole inhabitants of digital Hyboria any more than they were of Howard's imagined world. After character creation, there is a short cut scene of the slave galley being shipwrecked before the player-character wakes on a beach on the pirate Island of Tortage which is "teeming with all cultures."[91] In the first few minutes, the player meets two non-player-characters (NPCs): Kalanthes of Ibis, a black-skinned, white-haired Nemedian man who offers advice, and Casilda, a white-skinned blond woman who needs rescuing. Both are "quest-givers," that is, they offer the player-character advice or information, or make requests of her, that lead to certain actions. They are thus involved in the action of game, but in peripheral ways. While having racially diverse NPCs in the game – most regions, it should be said, are not as diverse as Tortage – is positive in comparison to games such as *Dragon Age 2* which is dominated by White NPCs, the limited range of choices available to players remains problematic. NPCs are part of the digital world but do not affect it directly; their actions are programmed, that is, they can only react to player-characters and have no agency of their own. The cumulative effect is that three of the four playable – that is, potentially agential – races are marked as White, while the vast majority of passive, non-agential races are not. The digital world – like Howard's literary one – by and large exists as a backdrop for the actions of White heroes. Representation – and lack of it – combines with ludic elements to reinforce Fantasy's habits of Whiteness.

When it was first released, the game-world attracted criticism from some players for not being true to the world of Hyboria as Howard had created it. It "was not in keeping with the author's vision," they argued, because it did not have built-in racial prejudice: "the interracial mingling in the game between Aquilonian, Cimmerian and Stygian races was the most unrealistic element."[92] Others, however, commented strongly against Howard's racism, evincing no desire to see it replicated in the game. One, cited on a gaming journalism website, says: "Conan is a misogynist and a racist, a fantasy reflection of his creator's worldview." The author who cites the comment argues against this reading, asserting that "Howard's supposed racism was actually a very clever literary device," designed to "quickly put a read in a world with a minimum of exposition or confusion."[93] I have no wish to repeat my arguments of the previous chapter here to assert the underlying – and at times overlying – racist world-view of Howard's work; stereotyping is not a clever literary device.

The different attitudes evinced above illuminate some of the hazards that game-developers – and indeed anyone involved in adaptation of most if not all early Fantasy material – face. Players not only expect but demand fidelity to the imagined world of a given author – Tolkien is another case in point – even if they are willing to accept the creation of new narratives and other elements of the process. Scholars may suggest that accuracy is not a useful concept when considering adaptations, but audiences often do not agree and this can influence game-makers, particularly in franchises whether they are aiming to engage an already knowledgeable fan-base.

A related issued deriving from the commercial nature of popular culture is the impact of licensing agreements. The convoluted history of the rights to Conan and Hyboria, and the fact that in many countries the original stories are now out of copyright because of the length of time since Howard's death, mean that *Age of Conan* is less tightly connected to other works with which it shares a license than, for example, games set in Middle-earth.[94] Nonetheless, the first adventure pack, *The Savage Coast of Turan* (2011), was explicitly related to the 2011 *Conan the Barbarian*, and was designed to allow players to experience the setting and characters, and use weapons based on those in it. The Orientalist imagery of the the film was transposed directly into the game, reaching a much wider audience as a result.

CONCLUSION

The sprawling worlds of role-playing games and almost infinite number of narratives that can be set in them – either in the course of game-play or through novels, comics, and other media forms – have significant scope for diversity nonetheless. A "favourite" theme of Margaret Weis and Tracy Hickman, who collaborated on the original Dragonlance novels which achieved bestseller status, is "that of the need for different peoples to lean tolerance regarding each other's ways."[95] Krynn, the world of Dragonlance, suffers a vast volcanic eruption that changes its geography and destroys many cultures when the Kingpriest of Istar embarks on a fascistic genocidal campaign to wipe-out races that are considered "impure."[96] Although role-playing game-worlds like the many realms of *D&D* are structured by race, as noted above and explored in-depth in chapter four, players and authors alike are able to subvert the expectations these rules might create and tell stories that make anti-racist statements. Gamers and writers have the capacity to resist the ideologies built into the worlds in which they play.

Nonetheless, Whiteness is the default setting for Fantasy worlds, even when they do not conform closely to the conventions of either Sword and Sorcery or High Fantasy. A genre by definition depends on repetition of elements to exist; by the 1980s, Gary K. Wolfe argues, Fantasy was "radically unstable" in form but not appearance,[97] not least because of the fundamentally commercial nature of its creation. Publishers – Ballantine, Ace, and DAW – were instrumental in the making of the adult market, which, as Wolfe observes, "tended to define itself in terms of works that bore at least a surface resemblance to Tolkien."[98] Academic engagements with Fantasy tend to shy away from its centre to focus on those works which can be considered new or different to the "white noise" of conventional background, and to seek ways of valorising the genre as an object of literary study. As a result, "surface" elements are often at best secondary in scholarly discussions, despite their key role in the making of genre as a significant popular culture market. De Camp's oft-quoted remark in the introduction to the *Swords and Sorcery* (1963) anthology illustrates the point: "the tales collected under this name are adventure fantasies, laid in imaginary prehistoric or medieval worlds, when (it's fun to imagine) all men were mighty, all women were beautiful, all problems were simple, and all life was adventurous."[99] Setting and character-type were – and are – significant factors binding the genre and its sub-genres together. When *The Lord of the Rings* was printed in paperback in 1965, it emerged against a backdrop of imagined worlds that were united by the Whiteness, and it resonated with them. The influence of the combined weight of worlds is, as I argue further in the next chapter, still extremely strong.

NOTES

1. Russell, "Margaret Atwood Chooses *A Wizard of Earthsea*."
2. Mendlesohn and James, *A Short History of Fantasy*, p. 2 of chapter 7.
3. Le Guin, *A Wizard of Earthsea*, 222.
4. Le Guin, *Cheek by Jowl*, pt. 1189.

5. See the chapter "The 1970s" in Mendlesohn and James, *A Short History of Fantasy*.

6. Shanks, "History, Horror, and Heroic Fantasy: Robert E. Howard and the Creation of the Sword and Sorcery Genre," 12.

7. See the chapter on "The 1980s" in Mendlesohn and James, *A Short History of Fantasy*.

8. Mendlesohn and James, *A Short History of Fantasy*, 119. They are more concerned with the structure of the respective modes, pointing out that the former tend to involve closure but the latter do not.

9. I provide representative examples of trends and conventions, taken from some of the most widely read works, as comprehensive lists would run to hundreds if not thousands of genre titles.

10. Octavia Butler is another African American author who made significant contributions to challenging the overarching Whiteness of speculative genres. As all but one of her novels is Science Fiction rather than Fantasy, I do not discuss them in this chapter. *Kindred*, the exception to this rule, is a time-travel novel, usually read as Science Fiction despite there being no scientific explanation for the time-travel offered in it.

11. Riper, *Science in Popular Culture*, 223.

12. Eddings, *Pawn of Prophecy*, 26–27.

13. Racial traits are also a feature of his Elenium and Tamuli series.

14. Jordan, *The Eye of the World*, pt. 5080.

15. Catalogues of the products produced for these and other realms tend to be produced by fans, and the publishers only list those which are available at any given time. One fan website lists 209 *Dragonlance* novels at the time of writing, as well as numerous gaming products, and comics. See "Complete Product List."

16. van Dyke, "Race in *Dungeons & Dragons*."

17. Tresca, *The Evolution of Fantasy Role-Playing Games*, 80. See also van Dyke, "Race in *Dungeons & Dragons*."

18. Tresca, *The Evolution of Fantasy Role-Playing Games*, 80. Tresca quotes Gary Gygax, one of the original designers of the game, as saying that only humans could be properly role-played.

19. Sernett, "Human Frailty," 20.

20. Sernett, "Human Frailty."

21. Moorcock's work elsewhere pushes against deliberately against eurocentric conventions: in his Hawkmoon stories it is the Western peoples who are barbarians threatening to conquer and destroy the rest of the world.

22. Wynne-Jones, *A Tough Guide to Fantasyland*, 48.

23. Eddings, *Pawn of Prophecy*, 28. Multiple references to Garion's descent, linked to hair-colour, are made throughout the various novels in which he and they appear, his father, for example, "like most members of his family" was "born with that sandy-colored hair." Eddings and Eddings, *Belgarath the Sorcerer*, 761.

24. Eddings, *Magician's Gambit*, 295.

25. Feist, *Magician*, 507.

26. Balfe, "Incredible Geographies? Orientalism and Genre Fantasy," 87.

27. Balfe, "Incredible Geographies?" 76.

28. Finke and Shichtman, "Inner-City Chivalry in Gil Junger's *Black Knight*: A South Central Yankee in King Leo's Court," 107.

29. Shanks, "History, Horror, and Heroic Fantasy," 11.

30. Leiber, "Fafhrd and the Grey Mouser Have Their Say."

31. Sarabian of the Tamul empire is one example, and Zakath of the Mallorean is another.

32. Feist's *Prince of the Blood* is another example.

33. White saviour narratives are not exclusive to Fantasy. They are common in multiple areas of popular culture, notably Hollywood films such as *Dances with Wolves* (1990), *Dangerous Minds* (1995), and *Avatar* (2009). See Hughey, "The White Savior Film and Reviewers ' Reception."

34. Saunders re-published the essay on his blog in 2011. All quotes are taken from the later version. Saunders, "Revisiting 'Die, Black Dog!'" "Black dog" is a common epithet in Conan stories, including *The Hour of the Dragon* and *Shadows in Zamboula*.

35. Mendlesohn and James, *A Short History of Fantasy*, 129.

36. Saunders, "Revisiting Imaro," 6.

37. Saunders, "What Is Africa to Me?," 2.

38. Saunders, "Revisiting Imaro," 6.

39. Bell, "A Charles R. Saunders Interview," 90; Saunders, "Revisiting Imaro," 6.

40. See, for example, Amazon reviews of the 2006 edition and Holmes, "Imaro and Me."

41. A major monograph on the subject, Jeffrey Allen Tucker's *A Sense of Wonder: Samuel R. Delany, Race, Identity, and Difference*, does not include a chapter on the series.

42. Delany, *Neveryóna*, pt. 629. The institution of slavery is not, however, a racial one in the historical American model, and is eroded and destroyed throughout the stories. See Keizer, "'Obsidian Mine': The Psychic Aftermath of Slavery."

43. Okorafor, "Writers of Color," 180.

44. Imaro is a member of the Ilyassai, a warrior tribe based on the Masai who live in a grassland like the Serengeti, "the vast yellow reaches of the Tamburure plain." Saunders, *Imaro*, 14.

45. His "A Tale of Plagues and Carnivals" (1985) is about the AIDS crisis, for example.

46. Okorafor, "Writers of Color," 180.

47. The multi-volume graphic novel, *A Game of Thrones*, adapted by Daniel Abraham with art by Tommy Patterson is an example of the former; the 2012 video-game *Game of Thrones*, developed by Cyanide is an example of the latter.

48. For a discussion of the status of Howard's various works see Herman, "The Copyright and Ownership Status of the Works and Words of Robert E. Howard."

49. Illustrators change throughout the series: the entire series is coloured by Dave Stewart; Becky Cloonan penciled issues 1–3 and 7; James Harran issue 4–6; Vasilis Lolos issues 8 and 9; Declan Shavely 10–12; Mirko Colak 13 and 14; Andrea Mutti issue 15; Davide Gianfello 16–18; Paul Azaceta 19–21; and Riccardo Burchielle 22–25.

50. An exception is Craig Smith's work on motion comics "Motion Comics: Modes of Adaptation and the Issue of Authenticity." Nicolas Pillai's recent article is another "'What Am I Looking At, Mulder?': Licensed Comics and the Freedoms and Transmedia Storytelling." Pillai does not regard licensed comics as adaptations, and indeed many are not.

51. Nama, *Super Black: American Pop Culture and Black Superheroes*; Nelson, "Studying Black Comic Strips: Popular Art and Discourses of Race"; Singer, "'Black Skins' and White Masks: Comic Books and the Secret of Race."

52. Pillai, "'What Am I Looking At, Mulder?'," 103.
53. Wood, *Conan: Queen of the Black Coast.* The comics cited throughout this chapter are un-paginated in both hard copy and digital form, so no page numbers are given for them.
54. Wood, *Conan: Queen of the Black Coast.*
55. The italicized words are also italicized, as well as bolded, in the original. Wood, *Conan: Queen of the Black Coast.*
56. Wood, *Conan: Queen of the Black Coast.*
57. Wood, *Conan the Barbarian: The Song of Bêlit Part 2.*
58. Howard, *The Coming of Conan the Cimmerian*, 141.
59. Howard, *The Coming of Conan the Cimmerian*, 141; Wood, *Conan the Barbarian: The Song of Bêlit Part 2.*
60. See chapter one of Lott, *The Invention of Race.*
61. Howard, *The Coming of Conan the Cimmerian*, 136.
62. Brooker, *Hunting the Dark Knight: Twenty-First Century Batman*, 66.
63. Redfern, "Genre Trends at the US Box Office, 1991 to 2010," 148.
64. Nispel, *Conan the Barbarian.*
65. The technique is frequently used in "historical" medievalist films, Elliott, *Remaking the Middle Ages: the Methods of Cinema and History in Portraying the Medieval World*, 201–202.
66. Worley, *Empires of the Imagination: a Critical Survey of Fantasy Cinema from Georges Melies to The Lord of the Rings*, 197.
67. Nispel, *Conan the Barbarian.*
68. The practice has been the target of significant fan-activism in recent years. This was sparked particularly by M. Night Shyamalan's *The Last Airbender* film, which did this in such egregious ways that "race-bending" is now a widely recognized term, and the title of an ongoing movement. Racebending, "Racebending.com." See also Lopez, "Fan-Activists and the Politics of Race in *The Last Airbender.*"
69. Le Guin, "A Whitewashed Earthsea."
70. Kim, "Beyond Black and White: Race and Postmodernism in *The Lord of the Rings* Films," 877.
71. "Plot Summary, *Conan the Barbarian* (2011)."
72. "New 'Conan' Star Never Saw Arnold's 'Conan.'" Frazetta's images were also highly influential on the 1982 film, and its producers had sought to have him work as a visual consultant on it.
73. The "Critics Consensus" on the review website *Rotten Tomatoes* is that: "While its relentless gory violence is more faithful to the Robert E. Howard books, Conan the Barbarian forsakes three-dimensional characters, dialogue, and acting in favour of unnecessary 3D effects." "*Conan the Barbarian* (2011)."
74. Young, "Racial Logics, Franchising, and Video Game Genres: *The Lord of the Rings.*"
75. For example, Higgin, "Blackless Fantasy"; Nakamura, "Don't Hate the Player, Hate the Game: The Racialization of Labor in *World of Warcraft*"; Langer, "The Familiar and the Foreign: Playing (Post) Colonialism in *World of Warcraft*"; Monson, "Race-Based Fantasy Realm: Essentialism in the *World of Warcraft.*"
76. MacCallum-Stewart, "'The Street Smarts of a Cartoon Princess.' New Roles for Women in Games," 229.
77. "Over 300,000 Players Join *Age of Conan: Unchained* in First Month."

78. Leonard, "'Live in Your World, Play in Ours': Race, Video Games, and Consuming the Other"; Phi, "Game Over: Asian Americans and Video Game Representation"; Burgess et al., "Playing With Prejudice: The Prevalence and Consequences of Racial Stereotypes in Video Games."
79. Gray, "Intersecting Oppressions and Online Communities: Examining the Experiences of Women of Color in Xbox Live"; Thomas, "KPK, Inc: Race, Nation, and Emergent Culture in Online Games"; Rowland and Barton, "Outside Oneself in *World of Warcraft*: Gamers' Perception of the Racial Self-Other."
80. Dietrich, "Avatars of Whiteness: Racial Expression in Video Game Characters."
81. Packwood, "Hispanics and Blacks Missing in Gaming Industry."
82. Higgin, "Blackless Fantasy," 21.
83. Aarseth, "Genre Trouble."
84. See, for example, Jemisin, "Identity Should Always Be Part of the Gameplay"; Monson, "Race-Based Fantasy Realm." I return to the issue of representation and fandom in gaming in a discussion of the *Dragon Age* franchise in the following chapter.
85. "Race." Connecting Fantasy races and places explicitly with those of the real-world is an extremely common practice, so much so that it has its own "TV Tropes" page, "Fantasy Counterpart Culture."
86. Funcom, "Locations."
87. The text-box that appears gives the same information: Wo/men "in the harsh and brutal world of Hyboria grow to be strong and quick-witted." MacCallum-Stewart explores, however, the ways that the game's opening sequences position male and female characters very differently and the impact this has on players. MacCallum-Stewart, "'The Street Smarts of a Cartoon Princess'," 228–230.
88. "Race."
89. Dietrich, "Avatars of Whiteness," 99.
90. See, for example, Jemisin, "Identity Should Always Be Part of the Gameplay."
91. "Tortage."
92. MacCallum-Stewart, "'The Street Smarts of a Cartoon Princess'," 229.
93. Eckhrdt, "Racism in *Age of Conan*'s Hyborian Age."
94. I have discussed the impact of licensing on games in franchise based on Peter Jackson's film adaptations of *The Lord of the Rings* and *The Hobbit* elsewhere, Young, "Racial Logics, Franchising, and Video Game Genres," esp. 1–5, 8.
95. Stout, "The Novels of Margaret Weis and Tracy Hickman," 7.
96. King, "Characters, Places and Things in the *Dragonlance* Novels," 101–103, 129. The Kingpriest of Istar appears in Weis and Hickman, *Legends I: Time of the Twins.*
97. Wolfe, *Evaporating Genres: Essays on Fantastic Literature*, 31.
98. Wolfe, *Evaporating Genres*, 31.
99. de Camp, *Swords and Sorcery*, 4.

3 The Real Middle Ages
Gritty Fantasy

Gritty Fantasy,[1] a sub-genre created in the late twentieth and early twenty-first centuries, is marked by low-levels of magic, high-levels of violence, in-depth character development, and medievalist worlds that are "if not realistic, at least have pretensions to realism" in their depictions of rain, blood, and mud.[2] The most well-known example is George R. R. Martin's A Song of Ice and Fire series, the spin-off HBO television show *Game of Thrones*, and attendant franchise. Joe Abercrombie is another prominent author, as are R. Scott Bakker, and Steven Erikson, while games such as Bethesda's *The Elder Scrolls V: Skyrim* and Bioware's *Dragon Age* franchise are further examples. Gritty Fantasy is constructed in opposition to Tolkien-derived High Fantasy by creators and consumers alike: Martin famously derides the "Disneyland Middle Ages" of conventional High Fantasy for its unrealistic worlds and inauthentic invocations of history.[3] Gritty Fantasy, despite its apparent break with some of the more sanitized and unrealistic elements of genre convention, has retained High Fantasy's medievalist euro-centricity and problematic constructions of race and racial difference.

A wide range of reasons for the popularity of the sub-genre have been suggested, including: the industry copying successful works, reactions against the kinds of High Fantasy many current authors grew up reading, increased audience exposure to violence in culture more generally, and audience desire for in-depth connection with characters.[4] Readers identify a number of often similar factors, including "looking for something that is more grounded in a sense of reality," than apparently escapist High Fantasy.[5] One commented that the realism of the worlds "make a medieval world that feels lived in, rather than ideologically constructed."[6] The sub-genre is not, however, universally admired. In one now infamous article, the conservative website *Breitbart.com* vehemently condemned it as: "mockery and defilement of the mythopoeic splendour that true artists like Tolkien and Howard willed into being with their life's blood."[7] Others take issue with sexism, violence, and racism within the genre, critiquing the notion that these are "historically authentic."[8] This chapter takes up the question of historical authenticity as it pertains to representations of the Middle Ages, not to examine whether or not any such claim is true, but to interrogate why they are so significant to authors and readers of a genre which by definition creates imagined worlds.

Fantasy, like any genre, is more diverse than generalisations can admit; nonetheless, it works with pseudo-medieval settings and a largely White cast of characters featured in a very large proportion of Fantasy marketed to mainstream audiences for decades, as outlined in the previous chapters. Gritty Fantasy appears to make over the first of these assumptions with its claims to represent, as Martin has called it, "the real Middle Ages" by including mud, blood, sex, and violence – at times all at once.[9] This claim is closely connected to its rejection of clear delineations of good and evil; physical mud inevitably accompanies murky moral waters. Gritty Fantasy does not, however, generally challenge the assumption that Fantasy is by, for, and about White people. Rather, as I argue here, texts, authors, and audiences draw directly on the habits of Whiteness established largely through the kind of Fantasy it claims to have rejected. Not only does Gritty Fantasy invoke eurocentric Fantasy conventions, it also reflects and reproduces race theory of the eighteenth and nineteenth centuries in its medievalist constructions of Whiteness.

MEDIEVALISM AND FANTASY

Fantasy and the Middle Ages are intimately, inextricably connected in the current popular imagination. The fact that the *Sims Medieval* computer game, for example, includes "wizard" as a career choice while making much of its realistic depiction of the Middle Ages passes without comment in reviews of the game.[10] A more telling indication of modern audiences' concepts of the Middle Ages is the blurb accompanying the YouTube trailer for the movie *Orcs* (2010): "They are savage, bestial and barbaric. They are mythical, medieval and warmongering. They are monstrous, sadistic creatures devoid of human emotion." "Medieval" sits comfortably amidst this list; the only question raised by viewers of the clip in the comments section was: "what are medieval orcs doing in the USA?"[11] All the adjectives applied to orcs here could also be applied to "the real Middle Ages" of Gritty Fantasy.

The supposed historical realism of *A Song of Ice and Fire* and *Game of Thrones* was so widely credited for their appeal that in 2012 medieval historian Kelly de Vries wrote an article in *Foreign Affairs* asserting that the real medieval period was not interesting enough to sustain a television drama.[12] De Vries was far from the first academic to caution against, or be wary of, associating Fantasy with medievalism. Reneé Trilling remarks:

> the kitsch and self-conscious irony of a Medieval Times or a Jorvik Viking Centre threaten to devalue the objects of our study as serious intellectual enterprises ... Such an approach pushes toward an absolute separation of the Middle Ages as not only past, but also the realm of fantasy, where those [Monty Python] self-flagellating monks exist comfortably alongside wizards and dragons.[13]

Given that Fantasy has a reputation for being escapist and trivial, it is not surprising that academics whose lives and intellect are devoted to study of the Middle Ages are wary of too close an association, as Trilling suggests. A growing number of scholars, however, are interested in the very nexus Trilling finds problematic and recognise the cultural power of a period that is considered simultaneously past and ahistorical.[14]

Works which engage with the Middle Ages as both past and imagined are often termed neomedievalist. David Marshall has recently offered a useful summation of the many different manifestations of neomedievalism as:

> a self-conscious, ahistorical, non-nostalgic imagining or reuse of the historical Middle Ages that selectively appropriates iconic images … to construct a presentist space that disrupts traditional depictions of the medieval.[15]

He contrasts it with what he terms romantic medievalism which is both pastist and nostalgic. Thus, a presentist neomedieval text "looks into the mirror of the Middle Ages and asks it to reflect back histories of modernist or postmodernist identities," while a romantic medievalist pastist work regards the Middle Ages as Other and sees "the past and present as bounded temporal objects that cannot come into contact."[16] For Marshall, the "mode of identification" is a key difference between neo- and romantic medievalisms. Romantic medievalisms, he suggests, identify with the medieval "in an imaginary form, an imitative relation to that past," while neomedievalism "relates to the medieval through something more like symbolic identification, finding a structuring principle that nevertheless stresses the irreparable gap between medieval and (post)modern."[17] Gritty Fantasy works, with their overt imaginative elements bounded by claims to represent the "real Middle Ages" in historically authentic ways, challenge such delineations.

Even scholars of neomedievalism have generally not engaged in depth with the desire to connect Fantasy with "the real Middle Ages" and tend to focus on the abandonment of historical veracity. Richard Utz, for example, comments:

> Neomedieval texts no longer need to strive for the authenticity of original manuscripts, castles, or cathedrals, but create pseudo-medieval worlds that playfully obliterate history and historical accuracy and replace history-based narratives with simulacra of the medieval.[18]

The tension between real and imagined worlds, and how it is managed by authors and audiences is a key focus of this chapter, which explores the connections between medievalism and Whiteness in Gritty Fantasy, with a particular focus on the discourses surrounding "the real Middle Ages" in texts and their reception.

The idea of the "real Middle Ages," how it is defined, and how it is attached to discourses around race and Whiteness is central here. This chapter is not, as noted above, concerned with establishing historical fact, although it is indebted to over a decade of work by scholars of the Middle Ages who have problematized the meaning of "race" in the Middle Ages,[19] and have connected race, the medieval and medievalism in meaningful ways. What matters here is not what the Middle Ages *were* like, but what they are *thought and said* to have been in the popular imagination of the twentieth century. According to many authors and readers of Gritty Fantasy, medieval times were violent, misogynist, and White; mud, blood, and rape can be added to the Fantasy mix, but racial and cultural diversity cannot.

NORMATIVE WHITENESS IN THE *DRAGON AGE* AND *A SONG OF ICE AND FIRE* FRANCHISES

For all that both authors and audiences of Gritty Fantasy emphasise about its differences from High Fantasy epics, claiming it represents the Middle Ages as they really were with all the blood and mud kept in not sanitized out, it has the same conventions surrounding race and medievalism I have identified in previous chapters. In its exploration of the sub-genre, this chapter focuses on two case studies: Martin's *A Song of Ice and Fire* and the franchise derived from it, including *Game of Thrones*; and Bioware's *Dragon Age* video-games and their attendant franchise. The two worlds – which centre on the continents of Westeros and Thedas respectively – were built for different media and now have both developed into still growing transmedia entities. Both imagined worlds are heavily influenced by eurocentric Fantasy conventions.

In Martin's novels and HBO's *Game of Thrones*, a significant proportion of the action takes place in the North and West of the imagined globe. Although the storyline which follows Daenerys Targaryen sees her travel through the East and South, this journey is with the sole purpose of returning to and conquering Westeros, a much identified analogue of medieval England. Bioware's *Dragon Age* franchise, which makes genuine and at times successful attempts to engage with issues of race in complex, challenging, and unconventional ways, nonetheless locates the action of its games in imagined places analogous to Europe. David Gaider, the lead writer for all three games – *Dragon Age: Origins* (DAO), *Dragon Age II* (DA2), and *Dragon Age: Inquisition* (DAI)[20] – remarked in an online discussion of diversity in the game-worlds that Ferelden, where the first game takes place, is "a fictionalized version" of medieval England.[21] The action of all the games and paratextual material – novels, comics and so on – takes place on Thedas, a continent based on Europe. DAI takes the player to Orlais, a previously unexplored country which is recognisably "French" compared to Ferelden's Englishness. Both franchises – like others in the Gritty Fantasy sub-genre including Abercrombie's *First Law* trilogy and its sequels – reinforce eurocentric world-views by centring the narrative action in places marked as Western.

Racial Whiteness linked to geographical Western-ness is the norm in Gritty Fantasy. Martin's northern Starks may be dark haired, but this is comparative and serves to mark them as different to the Southern Lannisters and the Targaryens, who are yellow and white blond respectively; all are clearly white-skinned. Visual media works, such as *Game of Thrones*, make such markers of race particularly prominent, as discussed in the second chapter; Daenerys Targaryen, as played by the actress Emilia Clarke with platinum blond hair, is sardonically referred to as "the blondest girl in the world" by some critics of the show.[22] Although the story lines of some characters, Daenerys included, see them travel far beyond the borders of the kingdom of Westeros to places loosely modelled on other parts of the real world, Westeros itself is still locus of the various narrative threads. Daenerys, for example, is constantly seeking a way to gain power and an army to lead back there to reclaim the throne of her dynasty.[23]

The *Dragon Age* world perhaps best indicates the strength of normative Whiteness in Gritty Fantasy. *DAO* made significant attempts to problematize Fantasy's habits of Whiteness by, for example, allowing players to change the skin-colour of their avatar – whether as a human, elf, or dwarf. The possible skin tones and hair types were unable to represent genuinely non-White – particularly Afro-American – skin and features.[24] Moreover, the opening sequences of the game include the character's immediate families whose skin, hair, and features remained noticeably Caucasoid whatever changes the player made. This was identified as a major flaw by players,[25] and attempts were made to rectify this in the sequel, although the general population in *DA2* and *DAI* are still predominantly White.

Bioware's attempts to engage critically with both historical racism and Fantasy's conventional Whiteness were not without problems, but were nonetheless often welcomed, and contrast positively with the gaming industry and community's ongoing failures to address their own habits of Whiteness. Fantasy author and gamer, N. K. Jemisin, for example, remarked: "Bioware tried, which is more than most game companies have done, and they did it on more than a superficial level."[26] At the character-creation stage before the start of game-play in *DAO*, the first game in the franchise, the description of elves outlines their history:

> Once enslaved by humans, most elves have all but lost their culture, scrounging an impoverished living in the slums of human cities. Only the nomadic Dalish tribes still cling to their traditions, living by the bow and the rule of their old gods as they roam the ancient forests, welcome nowhere else.[27]

Players encounter casual racism as elves that they do not as humans or dwarves – the other two options in *DAO*, for example, non-player characters accosting them with comments like "you there, elf." That the player's experience in *DAO* changes if their character is an elf is significant, particularly as "in-game 'racism' usually is bigotry in name only, not in action";[28] *Skyrim*, for example, has been critiqued for its inconsistent representation of racial prejudice.[29]

One of the defences against charges of racism levelled at Gritty Fantasy works is that they tend to show *all* cultures as savage and brutal. Good and evil is not demarcated as Western and Eastern because, the argument goes, such works refuse to construct moral binaries. If a work like Martin's does not allow simple goodness to any character and demonstrates the failings of all societies, it nonetheless taps into Western literature's long history of Orientalism. The Dothraki, for example, are slavers who engage, in the novels and the TV series, in public acts of sex and violence at weddings; this construct invokes orientalist imaginings of Otherness as sexually depraved. The medievalist, White Self may not be perfect, but the Eastern Other is invariably marked as comparatively worse because of particular cultural practices which are repellent according to contemporary mores. If Gritty Fantasy challenges dichotomies of good and evil, its worlds and stories still revolve around White characters who live in medievalist worlds.

USING THE PAST

Both Martin and Gaider have remarked on specifics of real-world history which inspired aspects of their respective worlds. Martin has remarked that The Wall in *ASOIF*, for example, is "inspired by Hadrian's Wall" in the United Kingdom;[30] although resemblances to the Great Wall of China are often raised by others,[31] he insists on its single, European, source. Like many other Fantasy authors whose worlds draw explicitly on history, Martin often emphasises his research and the information it provides about what the past was really like: "If you read about the real Middle Ages, as I do all the time, it was a brutal time for everybody."[32] His emphasis on research and the impact of medieval European history on his work is strong enough that not only is a bibliography offered on his own website, but journalists have also offered possible sources for interested readers.[33]

In his rejection of the patterns of the Fantasy genre, Martin cites not only history but historical fiction as a strong influence:

> The contrast between that [historical fiction] and a lot of the fantasy at the time was dramatic because a lot of the fantasy of Tolkien imitators has a quasi-medieval setting ... they don't really seem to grasp what it was like in the Middle Ages. And then you'd read the historical fiction which was much grittier and more realistic ... I said what I want to do is combine some of the realism of historical fiction with some of the appeal of fantasy.[34]

These remarks are about establishing the fact that his own work is not like several decades of conventional Fantasy as much as they are about the Middle Ages, historical fiction, or their influences. The history which inspires specific features of Westeros and the wider world is not the sole focus of Martin's comments; he invokes a much more generalised historicity with his assertions that his work represents "what it was like in the Middle Ages." These broader claims are authorised by the specifics – like Hadrian's Wall – to which he attaches his world and stories, and are often made in defensive ways against, for example, criticisms of gender relations or the treatment of women.

The kinds of statements Martin makes about the Middle Ages and how they inspire his work problematize Marshall's categories of romantic medievalism and neomedievalism. They suggest a relationship which is "self-conscious" and which "selectively appropriate[s] iconic images to construct a presentist space that disrupts traditional depictions of the medieval";[35] substitute "conventional" for "traditional" and this apparently describes Martin's medievalism. Martin's insistence that his world is inspired by specific events or artefacts – Hadrian's Wall may be classical rather than medieval but this is rarely acknowledged – emphasises their historicity, placing the source of inspiration in a past *within* time rather than ahistorically out of it.

Gaider's statements about the medievalism of the *Dragon Age* franchise do not have the same rhetorical emphasis on the realism of the imagined world as Martin's, although like Martin he cites real-world medieval history as inspiration. Specific geo-political locations are, for example, often given as the inspiration for a particular setting: "Ferelden is analogous to medieval England,"[36] and "Antiva has the same kind of sense ... as the Italian city-states in the Middle Ages,"[37] while "you could maybe say they [the Free Marches] are the Holy Roman Empire."[38] The world of *Dragon Age* to date is marked as both medieval and European, however, it also references the real world outside these temporal and geographic boundaries.

In a discussion thread on Bioware's official website, a player asked if "elven alienages," segregated parts of cities where only despised elves live, were based on historical realities: "you could make the comparison betwee the Elves and the Jewish Ghetto, NA [North American] native reservations, the Palestinians in Israel, the indigenous South Africans under aparthied, the Helots in Sparta, [and] Anglo-Saxon serfs under the Normans."[39] Gaider responded to the question, commenting: "the medieval Jewish ghettos were the original inspiration behind the alienages, yes. It grew to encompass other things, of course, but all of Thedas started as a fictionalized version of European history, so that is indeed where it began."[40] By acknowledging the relevance of non-European and non-medieval situations, Gaider recognises that the *Dragon Age* world is temporally, geographically and culturally multiple – or at least suggests that it might be – in ways that Martin specifically rejects; the European Middle Ages are important inspiration but are not constructed as *the* point of origin.

The type of engagement with the Middle Ages suggested by Gaider's statements aligns closely with Marshall's summation of neomedievalism as "self-conscious, ahistorical, [and] non-nostalgic."[41] The *Dragon Age* games, moreover, take up what Carolyn Dinshaw has described as the "ethical potential" of ahistorical, multi-temporal medievalist worlds to render "justice that might have been absent in the past" by challenging conventional approaches to gender, sexuality, and race.[42] Elves in the *Dragon Age* world were historically enslaved by humans, are the targets of significant prejudice, and serve as a racial Other.[43] When *DAO* was released, Gaider remarked that if players chose to make their avatar an elf: "they're going to be treated very differently by NPCs [non-player characters] they encounter, a lot of humans they encounter are going to be prejudiced against them, and there's an element of racism in the game when it comes to that."[44] Although the association of species with race in Fantasy is problematic, this situation is a significant challenge to Fantasy convention, not least because it takes up an issue which is often ignored.

READING RACE

If the *Dragon Age* franchise has been praised for its engagement with racism, its use of the default settings of Fantasy have come under fire, for example on *The Border House* blog which supports diversity of all kinds in gaming.[45] Author Chuck Wendig, who has written extensively for video-games, cited *DAO* in an article which critiqued the tendency for medievalist Fantasy settings to be exclusively White. Wendig finds that in *DAO*, and *World of Warcraft*, Whiteness is the default setting for humanity as well as elves and dwarves: "I can go ahead and change the skin colour of these humans, but somehow the characters still look distinctly white – but painted some other color."[46] The problem is, as David Dietrich shows, extremely wide-spread in video games which allow players to modify the appearance of their characters; skin tones, facial feature, and hair are particularly at issue.[47] The *Dragon Age* franchise has seen gradual improvements, but some players found that even the most recent game, *DAI*, did not offer skin tones and hair styles to construct a Black avatar,[48] although the level of diversity among non-player characters was much higher than the norm for similar works.[49]

The *Dragon Age* franchise has garnered mixed reception for its engagements with race, but responses to race representation in both *ASOIF* and *Game of Thrones* from mainstream media outlets have been largely negative. In an article on *Slate* which itself sparked a storm of criticism, Nina Rastogi asked "is *Game of Thrones* racist?" While she allowed that "*Game of Thrones* doesn't fall into the kind of essentializing that books like its forebear, *Lord of the Rings*, have been accused of," she also laments that "even in a fantasy world with the freedom to untether itself completely from our own, the "exotic other" has to look so boringly familiar."[50] The problematic casting of the Dothraki in *Game of Thrones* was a common topic in otherwise positive reviews in, for example, *Time* and *The Atlantic*.[51] Saladin Ahmed, a Fantasy author himself, suggested on *Salon.com* that many of the problematic racial tropes of medievalist Fantasy like *ASOIF* can be traced back to Tolkien's work. He argues that in Martin's novels, "an entire non-white culture [the Summer Isles] is presented as holding skewed values," adding of the Dothraki that "HBO has nudged Martin's creation fully into racial caricature by casting a seemingly random variety of colored people." Ahmed thereby explores the minor roles allowed to minority characters in the novels. Ahmed's article offers a more detailed reading of race in both novel and television than the reviews cited above, and he concludes that "if Westeros has its race problems, they are simply a powerful reflection of America's."[52]

THE WHITENESS OF THE MIDDLE AGES

Turning from the works and their reception in the media – both genre and mainstream – to audience, particularly fan discussions of race, illuminates the strong connections between Whiteness and medievalism in the Western popular imagination.[53] It is impossible to know how many or what proportion of audience members – including game-players – take part in online discussions of race, or any other topic, or how representative the opinions of those who post may be of the general audience. Clear patterns of rhetoric and content can, however, be discerned in debates about race on fan-forums and other websites relating to the *Dragon Age* and *ASOIF* franchises. The final chapter in this book will explore the dynamics of debates about race and Fantasy – particularly the lengthy blogosphere phenomenon known as RaceFail 09 – in more detail, here I focus particularly on those discussions which invoke the perceived Whiteness of the European Middle Ages. The different kinds of medievalism and approaches to race displayed in the works and invoked by their creators do not necessarily have an effect on the ways particular audience members receive the works and do not erase the strong expectation of Whiteness attached to medievalist Fantasy.[54]

Online debates about mainstream Fantasy's habit of Whiteness in literature, television, games and other media, without exception see participants deploy the "monochrome Middle Ages" argument: that only White people lived in Europe during the Middle Ages, and that since the Fantasy world is inspired by medieval Europe, it should be largely if not exclusively populated by Whites.[55] It has been used so frequently that multiple bloggers writing about racism in Fantasy critique it extensively.[56] While authors, including Martin as noted above, are willing to deploy similar arguments about the need for historical authenticity in relation to gender representation, and accusations of misogyny, I have found very few examples of an author using the argument explicitly to defend against charges of racism.

The shape of the argument demonstrates that there is a very strong desire amongst Fantasy audiences for the imagined worlds they encounter to resonate with their existing assumptions about the Middle Ages. Those assumptions are a product of both the habits of the genre, but also of a much deeper and longer entanglement between medievalism and Whiteness which has been present in Anglophone culture since at least the nineteenth century.[57]

Inconsistencies in any fictional world can be jarring to audiences and detract from the narrative; "lacking consistency, a world may begin to appear sloppily constructed, or even random and disconnected."[58] Since Secondary Worlds are increasingly likely to be inconsistent as they grow in size and scope, analogies to the real world are particularly useful to Fantasy authors because they provide a template in which not every detail needs to be either imagined or explained to the audience. Genre conventions operate in very similar ways. Mark J. P. Wolf points out that inconsistencies can exist at more or less intrusive levels of the world and narrative, and also observes that avid fans are more likely to notice them than casual readers.[59] Most if not all of the audience members who participate in the debates discussed below appear to fall into the first category because of the level of importance they place on what are perceived to be inconsistencies between the imagined world and the historical real world.

Casting actors of colour to play roles which are considered authentically White by some audience members is a common catalyst for use of the monochrome Middle Ages argument. Examples are not limited to Gritty Fantasy and include: Idris Elba playing the Norse God Heimdahl in the 2010 film *Thor*;[60] and the casting of Angel Coulby as Guinevere in the BBC's series *Merlin*.[61] Casting actors of colour as characters who are White in the source text of an adaptation is another trigger; Nonso Anozie, a black British actor, playing the "pale as milk" Xaro Xhaon Daxos of Qarth in *Game of Thrones* is one example.[62] Fantasy which draws on European myth and legend faces similar challenges around casting to adaptations of specific works because audience members are likely to have pre-conceived ideas about the appearance of characters.[63]

The monochrome Middle Ages argument is also used to defend against criticism of, or challenges to, the Whiteness of an imagined world; both the *Dragon Age* and *ASOIF* franchises have seen this occur in the blogosphere and on discussion boards. One example comes from *Westeros.org*, one of the major fan sites for both Martin's novels and *Game of Thrones*. In a thread titled "Why no Asian Race?" the original poster wrote:

> I know what it sounds like but there are no Asian characters or race ... I know these lands are based on our own world and each isn't exactly like our but come on where/what are they ... Come to think about it no Australian influenced race too ... I'm not trying to be racist but help me by pointing me in the right direction ... I know its fiction but everything is influenced from whats around us. I'm not taking it to serious but whats up with leaving them behind?[64]

The multiple apologies for asking the question, and the caveats included demonstrate how fraught an issue race is on forums of this kind.

The first two responses represent common attitudes as they dismiss the issue as unimportant: "ASOIAF needs Mexicans goddamit" and "This is fiction. You are taking it too seriously." The third, however, engages in more detail: "Even though some elements in ASOIAF are inspired from real world, it is not a matter of giving each race/region a representation. GRRM[65] has absorbed many aspects from medieval European history into this series because he was deeply influenced by them on some levels. We can't expect him to just include a race of people in this universe just for the sake of it." Later comments in the same thread use the same kind of logic, for example: "in real history contact between China and Medieval Europe was very limited and mostly compromised [sic] trade of luxury goods along the Silk Road."[66] Although the choices of Martin as the author are considered important, they are circumscribed by history.

Players commenting on the Bioware Social Network *Dragon Age* discussion boards take up the issue of race critically in multiple threads with titles including "Diversity in Thedas," "more Asian people in DA," "DA3: Colorblind casting," "Ethnicity," and "Bioware should break a barrier and put a African American character in DA2" which went for some 18 pages with around 400 posts and attracted external discussion.[67] In all of these threads, the supposed exclusive Whiteness of medieval Europe is invoked on both sides of the at-times lengthy and bitter debates. For example: "there's no reason for Thedas to be monoracial, it'd be unlikely for a medieval northern European to have met someone of a different skin colour, but for a mediterranean it'd be quite possible," and "Thedas is obviously a land steeped in the culture, legends, and socio-historical realities of Northern Europe. Mixing in more non-white humans would ruin their careful reconstruction of the Dark Ages."[68] For these players, as for the *Game of Thrones* audience members, accurate, representation of the racial composition of northern Europe in the Middle Ages – or at least what they believe to be accurate – is of prime importance.

Consistency in the imagined world is a significant theme in many iterations of the monochrome Middle Ages argument. Gaider, posting on the thread "Diversity in Thedas," wrote: "You'll find dark-skinned people in the nation of Rivain, which is quite a ways off to the north. This far south those of Rivaini descent ... are fairly rare ... Our intent was to create an internally coherent setting, not to reflect ethnic diversity as it's found in our world in modern times."[69] This is one of the very few places in which an author directly invokes this type of argument in a discussion of race in their created world. Martin has done on only one occasion, although he uses the same argument frequently in discussions of violence and misogyny. When a fan raised the issue of lack of representations Asian characters in 2014, replied: "Westeros is the fantasy analogue of the British Idles in its world, so it is a long long way form the Asia analogue. There weren't a lot of Asians in Yorkish England either."[70] The need for coherence and consistency in a

Secondary World is well recognised; the success of such a world depends on its believability to the audience. A world which draws on history must, according to this argument, reflect the past as it is *thought to have been* by its prospective audience. Fantasy works like *ASOIF* and *Dragon Age* engage not only with history but also with genre convention and are thus under an added layer of pressure to conform to audience expectations.

The logical fallacy in arguing that a Fantasy world – which is not real by definition – should be historically accurate is regularly pointed out by critics of the argument. Wendig, for example, comments "England in the Middle Ages didn't really have werewolves, blood-forged swords, or ancient black spires that channel magic ... If we can have werewolves, why can't we have black people?"[71] While the need for internal coherence is real, as *The Border House* blog comments, "when you create a fantasy world you are not bound to create a world with regressed social relations."[72] Recent work, such as Jemisin's Killing Moon and Inheritance series and David Anthony Durham's Acacia trilogy, are set in pre-modern worlds which are not aligned with the European Middle Ages, an increasingly common trend in Fantasy which is explored in detail in later chapters.

The assumption that the racial composition of the European continent was uniform across its entire geographical spread and unchanging for centuries underpins the argument and reveals its lack of genuine engagement with historical accuracy. The power of the monochrome Middle Ages argument, or at least of the drive for historical authenticity, is demonstrated not by those who use it to argue against increased racial diversity in medievalist Fantasy, but by those who argue for it. In his critique of the Whiteness of *DAO* and other works, Wendig argues that there was, in fact, demonstrable racial diversity in medieval England, specifically arguing for the presence of people of African origin:

> Certainly the England of old was not home to any other races ... Except, we have evidence there of Moors, who were clearly black-skinned. The influence of Romans, many of whom were dark-skinned or who brought slaves of different races, persevered as well. No, the country wasn't exactly a paragon of ethnic diversity, but it also wasn't nearly as white-washed as [this game suggests].[73]

The implication of this kind of statement, which is just one example of a very common trend, is that historical authenticity is paramount to a neomedievalist world of the kind the *Dragon Age* franchise creates. It suggests that a monochromatic world would be not just acceptable, but desirable and even necessary, if medieval Europe had been populated only by Whites. The use of the same conceptual framework for argument about race, and Whiteness in particular, is not unique to the Fantasy genre. Recent research has demonstrated that both White supremacist organizations and anti-racist organizations reproduce essentialist ideologies.[74] The debates which are, on the surface, about medievalism and consistency in the imagined world reflect arguments around race and racism in wider society.

In the many claims and counter-claims about the racial composition of Europe in the Middle Ages, little, if any, evidence is offered or requested. In the above quote from Wendig the word "Moors" was hyperlinked. At the time of writing the link no longer functions, however it originally took readers to a short online encyclopaedia entry about the Moors which indicated that they were an Islamic people who lived in North Africa and Spain, but made no mention of skin-colour, or of any presence in England. Even this information, which is tangential at best to the immediate point of Wendig's article, is significant evidence compared to many claims, such as those quoted above from the "Why no Asian race?" thread on *Westeros.org*. One participant in the "Diversity in Thedas" thread wrote: "actually, there were dark-skinned people in medieval Europe, though many of them were slaves." Another replied:

> There were not many black slaves (if any in most countries) during the medieval period, it is only at the very end of this period that Portuguese and Spanish nations began to explore the to [sic] any extent the African coastline. It is only in the early modern period (the renaissance) that European nations became seriously interacting [sic] with the slave trade.[75]

Both comments make with significant factual claims, none of which were supported by links to evidence, any indication of the source of poster's knowledge, or any claim to expertise on their parts. This is the general pattern followed in these types of debate, and is also exemplified in the comments from *ASOIF* and *Game of Thrones* fans quoted above. I make this point not to argue that only academics should comment on history, or to deride the argument or knowledge of the people who make such comments, but to demonstrate that the call for historical accuracy in Fantasy worlds is based on a *feeling* about what the Middle Ages were like and that debates rest on claim and counter-claim, not on any evidence-based account of the past.

The nostalgic tendencies of modern medievalism are well established, and have been discussed in recent years, for example in a specially-themed 2011 volume of the journal *post-medieval*.[76] Fantasy as a genre is often dismissed or derided as nostalgic by Marxist thinkers such as Darko Suvin, Frederic Jameson, and China Miéville,[77] and scholarly medievalists alike.[78] In the light of these approaches the desire to construct medieval Europe as exclusively White is easily read as nostalgic longing for a never-extant time when the world was not just eurocentric, but simply *was* White Europe. Such a reading is, however, complicated by the willingness of audience members who *are* calling for greater diversity to accept the primacy of historically accurate renderings of race even when they contest the shape of that accuracy. Exploration of the way modernity is constructed in opposition to the Middle Ages sheds further light on the issue.

Participants on both sides of debates such as those outlined above, have a marked tendency to use the term *politically correct* in a negative way. The original post in a thread titled "Dark Fantasy and Political Correctness" discusses gender and race relations in the *Dragon Age* world and states: "now I do understand the reasoning behind this, Bioware wants to avoid offending people and loosing sales, and they want to allow you to play the character as you see fit. To be frank I agree with them ... [but] I think Bioware went a bit too far."[79] The statement suggests that gestures towards, or attempts at, inclusiveness are motivated by the desire for profit and are imposed on players and game-makers by corporate interests.

The "more Asian people in DA" thread includes examples of negative references to political correctness from both sides of the diversity debate. One post reads: "I'm Black and I like to have diversity in my games, not for any "politically correct" reasons but because it helps emmerse [sic] me in the game."[80] The next post argues the opposite view but which likewise insists on the undesirability of political correctness:

> Diversity is fine as long as answers are provided as to the "how" and "why" different cultures are all mingling in places where people likely wouldn't wander twenty miles from where they were born ... Though there is no need to be rude, overly [sic] political correctness will be the death of everything, especially stories that are worth a damn.[81]

Posts such as this emphasise the need for an internally consistent world and suggest that such consistency can only be achieved if the game accurately represents the past. Political correctness is aligned not just with modernity, but also with corporatisation and its supposed impositions on games and gamers.

The idea that, for example, greater diversity in an imagined world would destroy the value of the work is also found in audience commentary on Martin's work: "Imagine how bad Game of Thrones would have been if Martin had political correctness in mind when he wrote the series. I shudder to think."[82] Casting of the character Xaro in *Game of Thrones* attracted controversy, as noted above, and saw similar language used. The choice of actor heads a *Rolling Stone* list of the ten biggest changes between the books and series in an article which remarks: "in the book, Xaro Xhoan Daxos is lily-white and gay rather than black and straight;"[83] the article makes much less of the change in sexuality than the change in race. The casting was described by one *Westeros.org* user as "folly" and dismissed as an "unhappy concession to PC [politically correct] fashionistas" with the added comment "PC stories are boring and stupid – it's honest stories which PC police will (furiously) watch, seeking stuff to get outraged about."[84] The term "political correctness" itself suggests an inherently inauthentic action or statement, so it is a powerful rhetorical device when deployed to counter a call for greater diversity in racial representation.

AUTHENTICITY AND IDENTITY

Given the significant number of texts which have grown up around both *A Song of Ice and Fire* (*ASOIF*) and *Dragon Age*, there is no question that either world can genuinely be entirely the creation of an individual author. Nonetheless, Martin is by far the most visible public figure associated with the *ASOIF* franchise and there is a strong narrative of individual genius – directly opposed to corporate creation – attached to him. A profile piece in *The New Yorker*, timed to coincide with the debut of *Game of Thrones* in 2011, paints him in this way: "[he] left Hollywood in 1994, determined to do what he wanted for a change ... He wanted castles and vistas and armies, and producers always made him cut that stuff."[85] Similar accounts are common throughout mainstream media.[86] Bioware's writing team, particularly David Gaider the lead writer quoted above, is similarly strongly constructed as the creative force behind and public mouthpiece of *Dragon Age*. Thus, although Gaider talked about the collaborative nature of both game and comic writing in a 2012 interview, his was the sole voice.[87] The following discussion focuses on their public statements because they are the respective creative figureheads of the two franchises.

The figure of the author is central to the structural separation of politically correct modern consumer culture from imagined "real" medievalist worlds. Martin-as-author has been successfully constructed in opposition to mass-culture, particularly the Hollywood film industry he left. His desire to tell a particular type of story is cast as personal, and therefore valid, even laudable. The *New Yorker* article which exemplifies this narrative connects it to his fan-base: "Although *A Game of Thrones* was not initially a hit, it won the passionate advocacy of certain independent booksellers, who recommended it to their customers, who, in turn, pressed copies on their friends. A following was born."[88] An even more mutually beneficial and dependent relationship is constructed in a 2013 article from Melbourne's *The Age* in which Martin talks about asking Elio Garcia, the "superfan" who manages *Westeros.org* about points of "lore."[89] The author and his fans are represented effectively as a subculture, independent of and separate to mass culture, they are authentic – having been self-created, as opposed to having been constructed by corporate marketing techniques.

Although the myth of the individual, inspired author cannot be as easily attached to video-games as it can be to books, the underlying dichotomy of authentic creation contrasted with corporate control has been adapted to the making of the *Dragon Age* games. Authorship, Wolf argues, "can be conceptualized as a series of concentric circles extending out from the world's originator";[90] this re-conceptualization is evident in the ways creation of the *Dragon Age* world is represented. In the passage quoted, it is Bioware the game publisher, not the creative team behind *DAO*, that is taken to have driven the creative choices considered "politically correct." The writing of *DAO* was widely praised, and was considered by many to be "a key component in the game's success," so it is perhaps not surprising that it is the focus of questions in many journalist features on the game.[91] A constant theme emerges in which the process of creation is markedly separated from corporate interference. When asked if the company influences "the writing in DA," Gaider responded: "they say what their goals are, and we implement those goals. In terms of do they come down and say don't use that word or these phrases? No, no."[92] Fellow writer Ann Lemay explained the collaborative nature of game-making – "we all need input and support from others in countless ways" – but similarly focussed on the creative elements of the process: "any writing that's done on the floor will see regular revision, tweaking, etc."[93]

There is no reason to consider any of these statements as either false or disingenuous, nonetheless, their combined weight constructs a discourse in which the value of the game world is separated from monetary considerations and corporate influence, that is, political correctness. Once, as discussed above, Gaider had posted on the "Diversity in Thedas" thread to answer the initial query about why *DAO* appeared largely White, a number of participants invoked his authority as "the communities [sic] head" in attempts to close down the debate.[94] Debates about representation in *ASOIF* and *Game of Thrones* likewise see Martin invoked as *the* authority on the imagined world: "GRRM doesn't need to derive his whole world from ours."[95] The imagined author-figure(s) offers not only a barrier between the audience and profit-driven consumer culture, but also a conceptual get-out-of-gaol-free card that can be played if pressure to genuinely reflect reality becomes too strong.

The image of the artist-as-genius has a long history in Western thought, and although theory and criticism have declared the death of the author, the myth retains significant power in modern culture. Jack Stillinger observes that "the single most important aspect of authorship is simply the vaguely apprehended presence of human creativity."[96] Colin Manlove argues that Fantasy is "markedly constant in its devotion to wonder at created things" and this tendency to place high value on the processes and products of creation is nowhere expressed more clearly by Fantasy audiences than in their devotion to author-figures.[97] While this devotion can become fraught – as has occurred for Martin when fans became frustrated with long delays between books in *ASOIF* – it is a key feature of the ways audience members, particularly fans, conceive not only of authors but of themselves.

The audience members who take part in the debates quoted above can be considered fans because of the depth of interest in and attachment to the works they discuss, and their active participation in communities which revolve around those texts. Matt Hills argues that to be a fan, as opposed to simply an audience member, is "to claim an 'improper' identity ... based on one's commitment to something as seemingly unimportant and 'trivial' as a film or TV series."[98] He also argues that "'good' fan identities are constructed against an ... imagined Other: the 'bad' consumer."[99] Both aspects of fan identity as Hills conceives of it are visibly at work in these debates, particularly on the part of those who deploy the monochrome Middle Ages argument. Authentically medieval worlds are associated with individuals who value the works more than the rules of a mainstream consumer society which is considered oppressive. The emphasis on the creativity of the author-figure, moreover, adds cultural value to the apparently "trivial" Fantasy work, placing it in dialogue with art forms such as painting and music as well as works assigned literary merit by wider society.

Political correctness in debates around race in Fantasy is strongly aligned with the constructed-ness of modern consumer culture and contrasted with the supposed honesty and authenticity of the historical medieval world and the imagined medievalist world. Audience members construct themselves as alienated from consumer culture and affectively attached to the Fantasy worlds they see as its opposites. As one person said on the thread which called casting a black actor as Xaro Xhoan Daxos in *Games of Thrones* "folly": "ASOIAF is not our world. And that's why we watch ASOIAF."[100] The Fantasy world is considered at once "fictional" and not to be taken too seriously, but also real in a way everyday life is not, not least because it claims to represent the Middle Ages as they "really" were: full of violence, rape, mud, blood, and White people. Affective attachment to that vision of the Middle Ages, which is understood as both historically and artistically authentic, valorises both individual and communal fan identities.

Fandom, particularly science-fiction and Fantasy fandom, has traditionally been the domain of young White men, who often assume their own normativity in those communities,[101] although evidence which demonstrates the inaccuracy of this perception is increasingly coming to light.[102] Mel Stanfill rightly states that "the fans depicted in mainstream media representation are unrelentingly white."[103] Genre-author Mark Newton acknowledged several decades of domination by "straight, white men," and argued in 2011 that fan communities were becoming less tolerant of works lacking gender and racial diversity;[104] the blogosphere phenomenon known widely as RaceFail 09, which is discussed at length in the final chapter of this book, is strong evidence of this. Speculative genre fandoms have long been perceived as White, even though changes to what is considered acceptable are not, however, occurring without opposition as the debates explored in this chapter demonstrate.

In his seminal *Textual Poachers* (1992), Henry Jenkins argues that fan communities have "particular interpretive conventions." Jenkins' theory is the foundation for scholarship which identifies "correct" reading practices in given fan communities.[105] Right ways of reading, however, are constructed through power struggles over what Lucy Bennet terms "intra-communal oppositional identities."[106] The debates explored here demonstrate that the convention of reading Whiteness as normative – in both the text and the community itself – are both challenged and defended, at times acrimoniously, within communities such as *Westeros.org* and the *Bioware Social Network*.

Some fans defend the normativity of Whiteness within their communities by using the medievalism of Martin's world and that of *Dragon Age* – and others like them – to claim that very identity, pushing against, for example, challenges to the lack of gender and racial diversity. Fan communities are always-already undergoing continual processes of creating collective identity, defining themselves in opposition to other fandoms, policing "bad" fan behaviours within their own community, and separating themselves from mere consumers. Fan communities, like many if not all iterations of Selfhood, coalesce around the creation of Otherness. The nature of that Otherness can vary; fan community struggles around gender, for example, have been variously documented.[107] Sara Ahmed's concept of "affective economies" is useful for exploring the dynamics of fan communities in the light of these shifting locations of Otherness.[108]

Ahmed theorises her model based on White supremacist narratives of identity which are more overtly concerned with race and hatred than most, albeit not all, narratives of SFF identity. In using it I do not mean to suggest that all SFF fan communities are White supremacist or constituted by hatred, but rather to draw attention to the ways in which constructions of normative identity as White develop structurally. In affective economies, Ahmed argues, affect "is distributed across various figures" and the "metonymic slide ... between figures constructs a relation of resemblance between the figures: what makes them alike may be their 'unlikeness' from 'us.'"[109] Affect is "economic; it circulates between signifiers in relationships of difference and displacement."[110]

A collective Other is created from distinct and potentially disparate figures in this formulation. A fan community based on a men's rights forum might explicitly and overtly express hatred for women and one on *Stormfront.org* might do the towards people of colour, but the justifications for that hatred are also likely to be filtered through discourses of fandom. Fan communities that are not explicitly or consciously aligned with extremist political movements – external communities of hatred – nonetheless display similar dynamics in constituting their own normative identities through negative affect directed towards an Other. For fan communities generally that Other can take multiple different forms, gender and race are just two of many and some are not connected to wider identity constructs; fan vs consumer identity is a common formation, as noted above.

Ahmed argues that: "the passion of ... negative attachments to others is redefined simultaneously as a positive attachment of the imagined [White] subjects."[111] The proximity of racial Otherness, in this discourse, brings a community of the Self into being, one which is delineated by hatred of the Other simultaneously explained as love of the White Self in White nationalist spaces. Fan communities are always-already structured by a narrative of affective connection – usually figured as love – for a text, corpus, or genre. In White nationalist narratives of Self, "it is the love of white, or those recognizable as white, that supposedly explains ... [the] shared 'communal' visceral response of hate."[112] In narratives fan communities tell about themselves, similar structures become intelligible with the substitution of a few words it is the love of genre [or author or text], or those recognisable as fans, that explains shared visceral responses of negative affect. Those who are not recognizable as fans – defined by love of genre – are excluded, open to and even deserving of hatred when they intrude into social spaces of fan communities. When members of a digital community like *Westeros.org* or the Bioware Social Network question the world of the text the community which coheres around positive affect towards it – love – reconstitutes itself by directing negative affect towards them, constructing that questioning as a sign of Otherness on racial grounds.

IDENTIFYING WITH THE PAST

Challenges to and defences of normative Whiteness in Fantasy works and in fan communities do not exist in a vacuum; Maureen T. Redding has argued that in the US "the current political climate is powerfully influenced by a fantasy ... of white loss of privilege," which in part at least stems from the increasing visibility of that same privilege.[113] Richard Dyer argues that Whiteness "secures its dominance by pretending not to be anything in particular," that is, by being the norm.[114] The twenty-first century has been marked by claims that Western society and culture, particularly in the US but also in Europe and Australia, is post-race. The nuances of meaning attached to "post-race" vary greatly, but one key argument is that race is no longer the most salient cause of inequality. For example, in the US, the election of Barack Obama is taken as evidence that race no longer impedes opportunity by partisans on both sides of politics.[115] The nostalgia of *Dragon Age* players' and *ASOIF* audiences' medievalism can be understood as a desire for post-race society redirected to the past so that the Middle Ages are imagined as a pre-race utopia. The different catalysts for the monochrome Middle Ages argument identified above – casting, changes from source texts in adaptations, and direct questions – all challenge the normativity of the utopian Whiteness in medievalist Fantasy texts by refusing to accept its invisibility.

The discourse of "the real Middle Ages" iterates and reiterates textual imitation of the past, constantly re-affirming its own nostalgia even as Fantasy's seemingly inherent ahistoricity appears to deny it. The same discourse simultaneously emphasises the gap between the medieval and the modern by contrasting those same texts with the constructedness of politically correct consumer culture. The medievalist Fantasy world is thus considered simultaneously real and not real. While they cannot agree on whether there was, in fact, any racial or cultural diversity in Europe – particularly England in the case of *Dragon Age* and *ASOIF* – during that era, participants in debates about racial representation in Fantasy are united in their opposition to the constructed nature of modern culture. Their beliefs about the Middle

Ages are mutually exclusive and, as they are generally expressed without recourse to evidence, demonstrate that in this context historical authenticity depends on feeling not fact. Such debates engage in what Svetlana Boym terms "restorative nostalgia" which "does not think of itself as nostalgia, but rather as truth and tradition." This is deployed in selective ways which are contingent on perspective but united by their separation of the "real" medieval from the "politically correct" modern.[116]

Marshall argues that the mode of identification between past and present is a key difference between neomedievalisms and romantic medievalisms and suggests that the former "locates parallels to the medieval in our own practice, whereas more nostalgic medievalisms attempt to create those parallels."[117] This distinction highlights the contradictions inherent in the different neomedievalisms at play in and around the *Dragon Age* and *ASOIF* franchises. When the writers of *DAO*, for example, draw inspiration from "medieval Jewish ghettos," and expand on that inspiration to encompass other historical situations in order to comment on the contemporary world, their practice is neomedievalist. Martin's insistence on a single course of inspiration for key features of his imagined world, and his repeated iterations that it represents "the real Middle Ages," over-ride the ahistoricity of the Fantasy world. In their debates about diversity in medievalist Fantasy worlds, moreover, fans compete to re-create the Middle Ages in the mould of their own idealised imaginings. The digital community they constitute in opposition to questioning, criticism, and critique of the imagined medievalist world performs Whiteness without reference to the race of its individual members.

The pre-race utopia of the White Middle Ages, which can only be seen with selective vision, is doubly problematic because it is used to both authorise and authenticate the Whiteness of not only imagined worlds, but the fan communities attached to them. The fear of exclusion attached to asking questions like "why no Asian race?" is clear. The poster understands that she or he is not abiding by the expectations of the community and is worried about being accused of racism, or being a troll, of taking things too seriously – all of which do occur in the thread, and all of which call his or her identity as a fan into question. To abide by the demands of the normative Whiteness of the community less than whole-heartedly is to be instantly cast as an outsider, a "bad" audience member seeking to impose politically correct liberal consumerism on the authentic medieval-*ish* text and its community of fans.

The Whiteness of the imagined Middle Ages is replicated in the fan community, which constructs a relationship with the past that challenges theoretical concepts of medievalism and neomedievalism. Both concepts rely on the existence of a fracture between the medieval and the modern, however, concepts of racial identity rooted in the Middle Ages depend on the opposite, on continuity. "Racial medievalisms," as I argue elsewhere, work "*against* any sense of alterity," they are nostalgic without admitting to loss.[118] The perceived political correctness of modernity threatens the purity of the imagined communities, but does not succeed in destroying it.

Wolf suggests that "an invented culture … does not come with the baggage of an existing culture," however, this does not hold true when it references real-world culture overtly and deliberately.[119] The idea that Gritty Fantasy represents "the real Middle Ages" in ways that earlier medievalist texts do not is central to its existence as a sub-genre. It further suggests that the works which fall under its umbrella, and the authors who create them, have direct access to medieval reality as part of their creative process. As I have argued elsewhere, however: "modern ideas about and engagements with the medieval past do not bridge a gap in time from now to then but rather tunnel through the many intervening strata and are influenced by that journey."[120] The Fantasy genre has not escaped the influence of intellectual and scientific projects which connect the Middle Ages with Whiteness. Gritty Fantasy works can make a rhetorical break with Fantasy convention but have not translated this to practice when it comes to its default settings.

In the nineteenth-century European, colonial, and formerly colonial countries looked to the Middle Ages as for their ethno-national origins,[121] and nationalist medievalism has not been entirely abandoned even in the twenty-first. Insisting that the authentic Middle Ages not only were White but must remain that way when they are re-imagined in Fantasy worlds mirrors those desires and moves at two levels. A real world community fulfils its own fantasy of Whiteness by insisting that its members accept the Whiteness of the imagined world as both past and present. The authentic Middle Ages, re-constructed by the author-as-artist, mitigate the alienation of modern industrialized culture by enabling fans to construct both individual and communal identities. The nature of the "not-fans" against which fan identity constructs itself is intersectional and constantly changing – only those which are overtly aligned with White supremacy constantly maintain an active and explicit program of identity work along lines of race. Nonetheless, when any fan community insists on the primacy and authenticity of the monochrome Middle Ages, it constructs a White identity for itself. The resulting imagined communities – both on and off the page and screen – bring into being, albeit incorporeally, the longed-for racial purity of nineteenth-century medievalist ethno-nationalisms.

NOTES

1. Grimdark is an alternate label. I prefer Gritty Fantasy to other options because "grit" is the single most important consideration for inclusion within this sub-genre fan, author in, and media discussions.
2. Haley, "Fantasy Family Tree," 45.
3. Poniewozik, "GRRM Interview Part 2: Fantasy and History."
4. Faircloth, "Why the Turn Towards Gritty Realism In Epic Fantasy? Authors Sound Off!"
5. Idlewilder, "Painting With Grey: The Development and Popularity of 'Gritty Fantasy.'"

6. Duke, "Gritty Fantasy: Why Do I Love It So?"
7. Grin, "The Bankrupt Nihilism of Our Fallen Fantasists."
8. Abraham, "'Concerning Historical Authenticity in Fantasy, or Truth Forgives You Nothing'"; Roberts, "Historically Authentic Sexism in Fantasy. Let's Unpack That."
9. Radish and Martin, "George R. R. Martin Interview, *Game of Thrones*."
10. Roberts, "Go Back in Time with *The Sims Medieval*"; Bernstein, "*The Sims Medieval* Updated Q&A - The Hazards of Medieval Life."
11. ArchstoneDistb, "*ORCS!* Trailer."
12. De Vries, "*Game of Thrones* as History." Multiple blog posts written by academics also take up the issue, for example, Smith-Akel, "A Historical Dissection Of *A Game Of Thrones* Part I."
13. Trilling, "Medievalism and Its Discontents," 220.
14. The 2010 and 2011 volumes of the journal *Studies in Medievalism*, numbers 19 and 20, have much of the early conversation. Another important source is Robinson and Clements, *Neomedievalism in the Media: Essays on Film, Television, and Electronic Games*.
15. Marshall, "Neomedievalism, Identification, and the Haze of Medievalism," 22.
16. Biddick, *The Shock of Medievalism*, 83.
17. Marshall, "Neomedievalism, Identification, and the Haze of Medievalism," 27–29.
18. Utz, "A Moveable Feast: Repositionings of 'The Medieval' in Medieval Studies, Medievalism, and Neomedievalism," v.
19. Hahn, "The Difference the Middle Ages Makes: Color and Race before the Modern World"; Heng, "The Invention of Race in the European Middle Ages I: Race Studies, Modernity, and the Middle Ages"; Heng, "The Invention of Race in the European Middle Ages II: Locations of Medieval Race"; Lampert, "Race, Periodicity, and the (Neo-) Middle Ages."
20. Gaider is also credited as the author of *Dragon Age* novels and comic series.
21. Various, "Diversity in Thedas. ..."
22. Doyle, "Enter Ye Myne Mystic World of Gayng-Raype: What the 'R' Stands for in 'George R.R. Martin.'"
23. A 2014 guide to the whole world of Westeros reinforces it centrality, presenting all the information contained in is as a compilation by a Maester for the king. Thus, the only way to know the world outside the action of the narrative is mediated by a White perspective. Martin, Garcia, and Antonsson, *The World of Ice and Fire*.
24. For a broader discussion of this issue in games see Dietrich, "Avatars of Whiteness: Racial Expression in Video Game Characters."
25. Various, "Diversity in Thedas. ..."
26. Jemisin, "Identity Should Always Be Part of the Gameplay."
27. *Dragon Age: Origins*.
28. Poor, "Digital Elves as a Racial Other in Video Games: Acknowledgment and Avoidance," 391.
29. Naik, "Breaking the Immersion - *Skyrim*'s Racism Lacks Authenticity."
30. Hodgman and Martin, "John Hodgman Interviews George R.R. Martin."
31. Jones, "*Game of Thrones* Season Three: How the Show Is (Re)Making History."
32. Radish and Martin, "George R. R. Martin Interview, *Game of Thrones*."
33. Miller, "The Real-Life Inspirations for *Game of Thrones*."

34. Poniewozik, "GRRM Interview Part 2."
35. Marshall, "Neomedievalism, Identification, and the Haze of Medievalism," 22.
36. Various, "Diversity in Thedas. ..."
37. Gaider, "David Gaider Speaks to Save Game on the New Comic *Dragon Age: The Silent Grove* #1."
38. Garcia and Gaider, "David Gaider Answers *Dragon Age 2* Questions at PAX."
39. Various, "Elven Alienage = Jewish Ghetto?"
40. Various, "Elven Alienage = Jewish Ghetto?"
41. Marshall, "Neomedievalism, Identification, and the Haze of Medievalism," 22.
42. Dinshaw, *How Soon Is Now? Medieval Texts, Amateur Readers, and the Queerness of Time*, 153.
43. Poor, "Digital Elves as a Racial Other in Video Games," 383–385; Young, "'It's the Middle Ages, Yo!': Race, Neo/medievalism, and the World of *Dragon Age*."
44. Pucik and Gaider, "Interview with *Dragon Age: Origins* Lead Writer, David Gaider."
45. Cuppycake, "Bioware on Racial Diversity in *Dragon:Age II*"; Quinnae, "No More Excuses: 'It's the Middle Ages, Yo!'."
46. Wendig, "The Pasty White Person Is King."
47. Dietrich, "Avatars of Whiteness: Racial Expression in Video Game Characters."
48. Jemisin, "Your Groundbreaking Is Not My Groundbreaking."
49. Wiggins, "*Dragon Age*: Inquisitioning While Black."
50. Rastogi, "Is *Games of Thrones* Racist?"
51. Poniewozik, "Review of *Game of Thrones*, 'Winter Is Coming'"; Serwer, "*Games of Thrones*: When Fantasy Looks Like Reality."
52. Ahmed, "Is *Game of Thrones* Too White?"
53. *ASOIF* and *Game of Thrones* have large audiences who do not otherwise read Fantasy, and who do not consider themselves to be fans of either the novels or the series. In this work – as discussed in the introduction – I use "fan" to denote an individual who has an affective attachment to a given work or works, and who participates in a like-minded community by, for example, posting on or reading discussion boards, writing fan-fiction, cosplay, and attending conventions.
54. For a discussion of the historical connections between medievalism and Whiteness see Young, "Whiteness and Time: the Once, Present, and Future Race."
55. See also Young, "'It's the Middle Ages, Yo!'"
56. Abraham, "'Concerning Historical Authenticity in Fantasy, or Truth Forgives You Nothing'"; Sernett, "Racism in Fantasy."
57. See, for example, Young, "Place and Time: Medievalism and Making Race"; Young."
58. Wolf, *Building Imaginary Worlds: The Theory and History of Subcreaton*, 43.
59. Wolf, *Building Imaginary Worlds*, 43.
60. Council of Conservative Citizens, "Marvel Studios Declares War on Norse Mythology."
61. Mié, Ankhesen. "So, I'm Watching 'Merlin,' Right ..." *At The Bar*, 2010. http://www.ankhesen-mie.net/2010/07/so-im-watching-merlin-right.html.
62. Unknown, "'Game' Changers: The 10 Biggest Changes Between *Game of Thrones* and the Books."
63. Casting white actors to play characters of colour in adaptations is a common phenomenon, particularly in Hollywood films. The practice is colloquially

known as "racebending" or "white-washing," and is the target of ongoing activism. Racebending, "Racebending.com."

64. Various, "Why No Asian Race?"
65. A commonly-used abbreviation for George R. R. Martin.
66. Various, "Why No Asian Race?." I have discussed the discursive construction of Whiteness in Martin's world and the fan community westeros.org in detail elsewhere, see Young, "Race in Online Fantasy Fandom: Whiteness on Westeros.org."
67. Cuppycake, "Bioware on Racial Diversity in *Dragon:Age II*."
68. Various, "*DA3*: Color-Blind Casting."
69. Various, "Diversity in Thedas. ..."
70. Comment section in Martin, "Great Times at the Jean Cocteau."
71. Wendig, "The Pasty White Person Is King."
72. Quinnae, "No More Excuses."
73. Wendig, "The Pasty White Person Is King."
74. Hughey, "The (dis)similarities of White Racial Identities: The Conceptual Framework of 'Hegemonic Whiteness.'"
75. Various, "Diversity in Thedas. ..."
76. Workman, "Editorial."
77. For example, Jameson, "Radical Fantasy."
78. Trilling, "Medievalism and Its Discontents."
79. Various, "Dark Fantasy and Political Correctness?"
80. Various, "More Asian People in *DA*."
81. Various, "More Asian People in *DA*."
82. Various, "Political Correctness and *WoW* - Where Do You Stand."
83. Unknown, "'Game' Changers: The 10 Biggest Changes Between *Game of Thrones* and the Books."
84. Various, "Race in *Game of Thrones*: A Request to Not Repeat the Folly of Xaro."
85. Miller, "Just Write It: A Fantasy Author and His Impatient Fans."
86. Salter, "The Fantasy King."
87. Gaider, "David Gaider Speaks to Save Game on the New Comic *Dragon Age: The Silent Grove* #1."
88. Miller, "JUST WRITE IT !: Onward and Upward with the Arts."
89. Salter, "The Fantasy King," 29.
90. Wolf, *Building Imaginary Worlds*, 269.
91. Kane and Gaider, "The Writing Of BioWare's *Dragon Age II*: David Gaider Speaks."
92. Garcia and Gaider, "David Gaider Answers *Dragon Age 2 Questions* at PAX."
93. Gunthera1 and Lemay, "A Glimpse into BioWare: An Interview with Ann Lemay."
94. Various, "Diversity in Thedas. ..."
95. Various, "Why No Asian Race?"
96. Stillinger, *Multiple Authorship and the Myth of Solitary Genius*, 186.
97. Manlove, *The Impulse of Fantasy Literature*, 156.
98. Hills, *Fan Cultures*, xii.
99. Hills, *Fan Cultures*, 27.
100. Various, "Race in *Game of Thrones*."
101. Demographics for gamers – such as *Dragon Age* players – are much more readily available than for Fantasy audiences and fans; studies demonstrate that

the assumption of a White male majority is false NB, "Demographics of Adult Gamers." See also Gray, "Intersecting Oppressions and Online Communities: Examining the Experiences of Women of Color in Xbox Live." For the Whiteness of Fantasy fan communities in particular see also Young, "Race in Online Fantasy Fandom."

102. For example, Reid, "The Wild Unicorn Herd Check-in: the Politics of Race in Science Fiction Fandom." I discuss this at length in the final chapter of this book.

103. Stanfill, "Doing Fandom, (Mis)doing Whiteness: Heteronormativity, Racialization, and the Discursive Construction of Fandom," para. 0.1.

104. Newton, "Science Fiction, Fantasy & Minorities."

105. Bury, *Cyberspaces of Their Own: Female Fandoms Online*.

106. Bennett, "Discourses of Order and Rationality: Drooling R. E. M. Fans as 'Matter out of Place,'" 214.

107. Larbalastier, *The Battle of the Sexes in Science Fiction*; Merrick, *The Secret Feminist Cabal: A Cultural History of Science Fiction Feminisms*.

108. Ahmed, "Affective Economies." The piece is also chapter 2, "The Organisation of Hate" (pp. 42–61) in Ahmed, *The Cultural Politics of Emotion*.

109. Ahmed, "Affective Economies," 118–119. SFF is a commonly used abbreviation for "Science Fiction and Fantasy," as I discuss at length in the final chapter, the fandoms are so deeply entangled as to be inseparable.

110. Ahmed writes specifically of hatred in her discussion of White supremacy. Labelling the affect of fan communities collectively in this way here is inaccurate, although there can be little doubt that in specific instances it would be correct. The communities of Fantasy fans based on the White supremacist website *Stormfront.org* is a case in point.

111. Ahmed, "Affective Economies," 118.

112. Ahmed, "Affective Economies," 118.

113. Redding, "Invisibility/Hypervisibility: The Paradox of Normative Whiteness," 233.

114. Dyer, *White: Essays on Race and Culture*, 44.

115. Lentin, "Post-Race, Post Politics: The Paradoxical Rise of Culture after Multiculturalism."

116. Boym, *The Future of Nostalgia*, xi.

117. Marshall, "Neomedievalism, Identification, and the Haze of Medievalism," 30.

118. Young, "Whiteness and Time," 47. This presents significant challenges to theories of medievalism which are beyond the scope of the current discussion.

119. Wolf, *Building Imaginary Worlds*, 179–180.

120. Young, "Approaches to Medievalism: a Consideration of Taxonomy and Methodology Through Fantasy Fiction," 166.

121. Geary, *The Myth of Nations: The Medieval Origins of Europe*; Horsman, *Race and Manifest Destiny: The Origins of American Racial Anglo-Saxonism*; MacDougall, *Racial Myth in English History: Trojans, Teutons, and Anglo-Saxons*.

4   Orcs and Otherness
Monsters on Page and Screen

From 1956, when Edward Wilson squealed in mock fear "Oo, Those Awful Orcs" in his attack on *The Lord of the Rings*, orcs have stood for Fantasy – and its supposed failings – as a genre.[1] For all that boy wizards and vampires have become prominent markers separating Fantasy out from the mass of popular culture in recent times, orcs remain a distinctive marker. They differ from wizards and indeed the other humanoid species conventionally associated with fantasy – elves and dwarves – because they were, from their first appearance, monsters. In this chapter I draw on the theories and methodologies of teratology to take a representational approach to orcs to illuminate the discursive formations by which the identity category of race is produced and re-produced. W. Scott Poole argues that monsters "are meaning machines that embody the historical structures and trajectory of the American nation."[2] In this chapter I explore works produced on both sides of the Atlantic and for a globalized audience to demonstrate that Whiteness is a sustained transnational habit in Fantasy. My interest is not in condemning, or praising, any particular text for a racist or anti-racist message, but in exploring what orcs tell us about the culture which imagines them and its ways of thinking about racial Otherness. That said, many if not most of the works discussed below do perform highly problematic moves and are unable to escape negative racial stereotypes even when they actively seek to challenge them.

Jeffrey Jerome Cohen argues that: "any kind of alterity can be inscribed across (constructed through) the monstrous body, but for the most part monstrous difference tends to be cultural, political, racial, economic, sexual."[3] Fear of racial difference has been embodied through monsters for centuries, and the idea of "monstrous races" stretches back to the Classical Era. Medieval thought "created strong links between physical and non-physical characteristics among different human groups," and used discourses of monstrosity to represent, for example, Jews, Mongols, and Muslims.[4] From the Early Modern era as European powers expanded their imperial holdings increasingly widely, "monsters sustained the ongoing conceptualization of the unknown that was a prerequisite to conquest and colonization."[5] In the nineteenth century, during the height of European imperialism, Gothic monsters such as werewolves at times took on racial dimensions,[6] while in contemporary popular culture vampires,[7] zombies,[8] and aliens[9] have also variously had such discourses attached to them. Postcolonial resistance is also widely expressed through appropriation of monsters and monstrosity, or it re-appropriation where colonial discourses have created monsters where they did not exist before.[10] Vampires, werewolves, zombies, and aliens are mutable, embodying fears around gender, sexuality, class, and politics to name just a few, but orcs are always racial monsters, even on the occasions that they also intersect with other identify constructs.

Orcs in Fantasy came into existence through Tolkien's imagination and have been transplanted into countless worlds outside Middle-earth. In Middle-earth they are a monstrous Other constructed through racial discourses. They are: somatically different to the White Self of the Fellowship; part of a millennium-old Western cultural discourse that Others the East and its people; and the embodiment of racial logics and stereotypes, and the perceived threat of miscegenation. They are the prototypes for the massed armies of evil's foot-soldiers which swarm the worlds of High Fantasy under different names; from the moredhel of Raymond E. Feist's Midkemia to the urgach and svart alfar of Guy Gavriel Kay's Fionavar, and also appear under their own name in a great array of Fantasy.

Humanity and its allies – commonly elves and dwarves – in the High Fantasy worlds in which orcs appear are coded as White. As Tanner Higgin asserts: "the race the reader is meant to identify with ... [is] almost always White, and any racial variations, although providing differences in physiology, rarely add diversity that would remove the characters from proto-European geography."[11] There are, as in any genre, exceptions, but this is a useful summary of High Fantasy convention. Jessica Langer, writing of the massively multi-player online role-playing game (MMORPG) *World of Warcraft* (*WoW*), argues that the game-world is structured "not by virtue of distinctions between good and evil but rather by distinctions between civilized and savage, self and other, centre and periphery."[12] Orcs are always the second half of these pairings in whatever world and medium in which they appear. Fantasy orcs are constructed as non-specifically non-White, often using discourses specifically associated with Blackness,[13] while references to Native American and other indigenous cultures are also frequently deployed. There are four main tropes attached to orcs, some of which stem directly from those of Middle-earth, and others which do not, all are racial. Orcs are commonly Othered by the following: their skin colour, be it green, brown, or black; extreme aggressiveness and irrationality; primitive, disorganized cultures; and homelands which are outside the borders of civilization.

The racialized monstrousness of orcs has lasted more than sixty years from the first publication of *The Lord of the Rings*, although the framing of that racialization has changed. "Monsters," writes Allen Weiss, "are indicators of epistemic shifts,"[14] and orcs are no exception to this. Since early 1970s, sympathetic representations of conventional monsters have become almost *de rigeur* in popular culture. Anne Rice's *Interview with a Vampire* (1976) is often considered the first example of this phenomenon, but John Gardner's *Grendel* (1971) is an earlier example. Gardner's novel problematizes the dichotomous relationship between monster and hero in its Old English source *Beowulf*, his

Grendel: "remains the adversary of human culture, but through his eyes we see a human culture that is ugly and flawed."[15] Vampires, werewolves, and even, recently, zombies, have been habilitated from the realms of horror to those of romance, comedy, and young adult fiction in cultural moves that reflect a diminishing of their monstrous power.[16] The influence of postmodernism with its emphasis on multiplicity and rejection of the concept of unitary truth is discernable in this broad trend, but does not sufficiently account for its specifics in the case of orcs. In modern digital gaming, for example, orcs are as likely to be playable characters as they are enemies to eradicate; in either situation it is still extremely probable that they will be marked as a racial Other to the conventional White Self of Fantasy worlds. This chapter explores the changes and continuities in the representation of orcs across more than six decades as the discourses surrounding their monstrousness have shifted, considering social, cultural, and genre forces that drive that change.

KEY TEXTS AND FRANCHISES

Existing scholarship on orcs tends to address either a single text,[17] or a single medium, usually games or literature.[18] In this chapter I explore the construction of orcs in fiction, films, and different kinds of games; pen-and-paper role-playing; table-top; and digital. This range of media and texts illuminates both changes and consistencies across time and media. I begin here with a brief outline of each text or franchise.

Adaptations of Middle-earth

Peter Jackson's film adaptations of Tolkien's novels, first *The Lord of the Rings* (2001–2003) and then *The Hobbit* (2012–2015) and the franchise which revolves around them, have had a significant influence on the construction orcs in the twenty-first-century popular imagination. This is not least because of their blockbuster status which saw them reach audiences who might not usually consume Fantasy. The films and video-games based on them have garnered significant scholarly attention, including for the ways that they construct race.[19] Chapter two discussed cross-media adaptations in detail, and I do not revisit that ground here but rather explore the ways that representation of orcs in different products across the now decade and a half of the franchise's history.[20]

Games

The first major appearance of orcs outside Middle-earth was in the original 1974 version of *Dungeons & Dragons*, which was followed up quickly by *Advanced Dungeons & Dragons* in 1977.[21] The original or "Basic" version was revised and reprinted multiple times, as was the "Advanced" until 2001 when the two were folded back together and the advanced rules were followed thereafter, under the title *Dungeons & Dragons (D&D)*; it is this thread I follow below. To date there have been five complete editions of *(A) D&D*: the first in 1977; second in 1989; the third in 2000, with an update – known as 3.5 – in 2003; fourth in 2008; and the fifth at the time of writing in 2014.[22] The game was strongly influenced by *The Lord of the Rings*; its world owes clear debts to Middle-earth, so many that details of the first edition had to be changed to avoid a lawsuit for breach of copyright.[23] Multiple "realms," or worlds, in which players could locate their games have been created as part of the franchise.[24] I include some discussion of the "Forgotten Realms," one of the most popular, but focus mainly on the core rules of the games as these are the foundation of play and of the different realms.

Like *D&D*, Games Workshop's *Warhammer Fantasy* (1983) and *Warhammer 40 000* (1987) miniature table-top games construct orcs as primitives living in tribal cultures, emphasizing their violence and brutality, and adding the notion that they are essentially nomadic and migratory in recent editions.[25] The nature of table-top gaming – which requires an active player on both sides of each battle unlike *D&D*-style role-playing in which opponents can be passive non-player characters controlled by the Dungeon Master – means that orcs have always been a playable race in *Warhammer Fantasy*. Their status as monsters thus depends less on the rules and more on the way they are framed within the game-world more than how they are played; in *Warhammer* both sides aim to annihilate the opposing army, creating an inherent dichotomy with less need for active participation in world-building and narrative creation than in RPGs and, as a result, fewer chances for subversion of the received game-world. As with *D&D*, racial discourses are deployed through core rulebooks and supplements.

The *Warcraft* franchise began with real-time strategy (RTS) games, the 1994 *Warcraft: Orcs and Humans (WOH)*, followed by *Warcraft II: Tides of Darkness* (1995), an expansion pack to that game *Warcraft II: Beyond the Dark Portal* (1996), and *Warcraft III: Reign of Chaos* (2002) before the franchise switched to MMORPG in 2004 with *WoW*. As is standard in RTS games players could play on either side from the early games of the franchise. Like *D&D*, *Warcraft* is now a multi-media franchise, including novels, card and table-top games, comics, manga, and a live-action film slated for release in late 2015. *WoW* is to date the most played Fantasy MMORPG, and as noted previously has attracted a great deal of scholarly attention for its constructions of race; by placing it alongside other works in the genre, this chapter provides context.

The final game I consider is the 2012 console-based RPG *Of Orcs and Men*, from Cyanide Studios, which is to date not part of a larger franchise, although a possible prequel has been mooted. The game has strong environmentalist themes,[26] and constructs orcs as freedom fighters opposing a tyrannical human empire. Playing as an orc is an option in many digital Fantasy games, but this is one of the very few where the player-character *must* be an orc.[27] The player characters – gamers switch between the two in combat – are a goblin, Styx, and an orc, Arkail. Orcs had been, however, the protagonists of fiction for two decades before *Of Orcs and Men* was released.

Literature

Mary Gentle's *Grunts!* (1992) was the first novel to feature orcs as its protagonists. The book is in part an anti-war satire and this reading focused principally on the representation of orcs does not have the scope to take up all of its complexities. In it, a small band of orcs come under the influence of a magical curse laid by a dimension-travelling dragon that had collected a vast store of Vietnam-era American military hardware. The curse, "you will become what you steal," gives the orcs discipline, making them act – in some ways – like marines.[28] Stan Nicholls' *Orcs* series, which began with *Bodyguard of Lightning* (1999) and now includes six novels and a graphic novel, also features orcs as protagonists, following the adventures of a small warband across a Fantasy world, and then between dimensions. Terry Pratchett's *Unseen Academicals* (2009) sees orcs make their first entry into the Discworld. Its protagonist, Mr Nutt, is a lone orc in Ankh-Morpork who slowly gains selfhood and agency throughout the story. In other fiction works they remain monsters, constructed as in- and sub-human as well as non-human, and are often referred to as "creatures" or "beasts."[29]

The representation of orcs in all three books is motivated by genre convention, that is, individual authors questioning the inherent and assumed evil attached to them. Nicholls' first trilogy was widely praised for subverting conventional fantasy tropes, and he describes his inspiration as deriving from them:

> Their story had never been told. Orcs were always depicted as a mindless horde fit only to dash themselves against the heroes' blades. I got to pondering how the winners write the history books, and thought, "Suppose orcs just had a bad press?"[30]

Pratchett presents a similar narrative for *Unseen Academicals*:

> Mr Nutt was in a way the seed of the book. Ever since I first read Tolkien at the age of 13, I was worried about the orcs. They were totally and irrevocably bad. It was a flat given. No possibility of redemption for an orc.[31]

Gentle's account in the introduction to the SF Masterworks edition of *Grunts!* is strikingly similar: "Orcs have always had a very poor press … it was obvious to me that Tolkien's orcs got the short and dirty end of the stick, and that this was Not Fair."[32] Habits, as I suggested in the introduction, are not merely matters of repetition, but can themselves initiate change. It is the repetition of habits that I consider first here however.

ORC BODIES

Three common trends delineate orc bodies, separating them from other species and marking them as monstrous: skin colour, strength, and a tendency towards aggression and violence. The combination, found in all of the works I consider here – save only that Pratchett's does not present aggression as an inherent tendency of orcs – racializes their bodies, and often dehumanizes them in the process. These tropes, both separately and in combination, resonate with anti-Black racist stereotypes which developed particularly in the eighteenth and nineteenth centuries to justify colonisation and slavery. I offer here an overview of examples from key texts to demonstrate the trends.

In *Unseen Academicals*, orcs are collectively "grey demons without a hell,"[33] while Mr Nutt, the sole orc character, is marked as different to the humans around him partly by his skin colour. In the 1979 (A)*D&D Monster Manual* orcs are physically "disgusting because their coloration – brown or brownish green with a bluish sheen – highlights their pinkish snouts and ears," and are also dirty and "favor unpleasant colors in general."[34] The description of orcs in each edition of the game's core rulebooks mentions their skin colour as a defining feature, barring only the fourth which gives no general physical description at all, rather relying on a color image of the different classes of orcs (Figure 4.1).[35] Their dark green skin, prominent faces and jaws reflect earlier *D&D* descriptions, while their black plaited or dreadlocked hair, heavily muscled hypermasculine bodies, and the iconography of their armour and weapons which code them as savage, tribal, and not-White bear considerable resemblance to the Uruk-hai of Jackson's *The Lord of the Rings* films.

Figure 4.1 Orcs from the fourth edition of the *Dungeons & Dragons* Monster Manual. © Wizards of the Coast LLC.

Sue Kim observes that the servants of evil in Jackson's first trilogy "exhibit an array of racialized characteristics," orcs "have brown and red faces" and the "Uruk-hai are tall, black, and muscular with long, coarse hair that resembles dreadlocks."[36] The racialized visual coding of the films carries over into other franchise products, notably games.[37] *The Lord of the Rings* films were criticized for their racial codings in the popular press,[38] and some audience members found them troubling,[39] which is likely to have had an effect on later franchise offerings which vary the representation of both orc and goblin bodies. Some goblins in the RPG *Lord of the Rings: War in the North* (2010), for example, have extremely white skin, as does Azog the "pale orc" villain of *The Hobbit* films, while the "Uruks" of the RPG *Shadow of Mordor* (2014) have skin tones which range from green-gray to dark gray and brown. As I have argued elsewhere, however, dark skin is generally a marker of evil in the franchise, and merely changing skin colour does not de-racialize the monstrosity of orcs.[40]

Since the early 1990s green has been a commonly used skin colour for orcs outside the Middle-earth franchise, and is now the norm, especially although not exclusively in games. The second edition of *Warhammer* rules (1984) includes the first detailed physical description of orcs, which emphasizes their size, heavy build, and ugliness, and also has the first mention of their skin colour, which later becomes a defining feature: "skin is often greenish, or a dark olive brown and is covered in warts, scars, dirt and snot."[41] Early editions referred to orcs and goblins, and the various related races, collectively as "goblinoids,"[42] but the 1996 edition of *Orcs and Goblins* refers to them as "greenskins,"[43] an appellation which is now standard in the game. The somatic marker of skin colour connects the racial logics of the Fantasy world with those of the real world where it, more than anything else, stands as the most salient signifier of difference in racial discourses. Parallel to real-world usages which erase in-group difference by applying a single label – Black, White – "greenskin" creates a single Othered mass or army horde out of a "bewildering" array of orcs, goblins, and snotlings.[44] Green-skinned orcs are now the norm in Fantasy. Orcs in Gentle's *Grunts!* are referred to at one point as "damned spear-chuckin' greenies,"[45] and orcs and goblins are also green-skinned in *Of Orcs and Men*. The orcs of *WoW* had green skin when the game was first released, although this was revealed to be due to exposure to evil energies which "turned the orcs' naturally brown skin to a sickly green."[46]

Visual media foreground skin colour in ways that written text and line drawings do not. The visual coding of orcs with skin colour in human ranges – as in *The Lord of the Rings* films – is potentially confronting and uncomfortable to audiences; making orcs green avoids the appearance of directly referencing real-world peoples without removing the underlying logic of difference. Lorenzo DiTomasso argues that:

> The events of this [the twentieth] century and the subsequent sensitivity to race on the part of a significant portion of today's population

have led to a general decline of skin color as a means of blatant ethnic identification in both fantastic and mainstream literature.[47]

The general truth of this statement is called into question by the ongoing use of skin colour as a sign of difference for orcs. The somatic marker connects the racial logics of Fantasy worlds with those of the real world where it, more than anything else, stands as the most salient signifier of difference in racial discourses.

Descriptions of orcs often invoke dehumanizing animal imagery which is reminiscent of colonialist discourses that construct Whites as more evolved than any other people. Comparison to animals, particularly pigs, is common in almost all editions of *D&D* up to the present. According to edition 3.0: "orcs … look like primitive humans with gray skin, coarse hair, stooped postures, low foreheads, and porcine faces with prominent lower canines … they have lupine ears."[48] *Warhammer* orcs are described as having an "ape-like" build and tusks.[49] *Warcraft* orcs also have jutting foreheads and prominent tusks. Pratchett's Mr Nutt has retractable claws, Nicholls' orcs have tusks, as do Gentle's. *Grunts!* opens with a scene that includes various points of description of the orc leader's body; he has "a misshapen skull," and "even to attention he slouches forward; his knuckles hang down beside his knees."[50] The use of animal imagery is generally dehumanizing, but the common use of apes as a metaphor specifically references colonialist discourses of Blackness.

Tolkien's orcs were shorter than humans and those of the early editions of *D&D* were classes as 'medium' sized monsters,[51] but they have grown in size and strength over the years and are now almost invariably larger than humans, with hypermuscled – often hypermasculine – bodies which are extremely strong. The *D&D* image shown previously is a representative example. *Warcraft* and *Warhammer* orcs have similar builds, as do those in *Of Orcs and Men*. Pratchett's Mr Nutt has the strength and capacity for violence associated with orcs in every work in which they appear, but chooses not to use it in destructive ways. As one character comments: "I see 'im around all the time and 'e's never 'olding someone else's leg or head."[52] Ashnak, the orc leader in *Grunts!* has a "muscled" body and a "great fist."[53]

The hypermuscled bodies of orcs are without exception coded as masculine. Players in *WoW* and other MMORPGs can choose to make their avatars female, and there are female orc warriors in both Gentle's and Nicholls' writings, but orc leaders are without exception male. *D&D* orc societies are "mostly patriarchal,"[54] while the images of orcs in *Monster Manuals* are always male warriors. Tolkien says nothing about how orcs breed, but as Kim observes, the Uruk-hai of the *The Lord of the Rings* are shown being "harvested" fully grown from mud,[55] and have no obvious individual gender. The few female orcs which do appear on the page or screen are always warriors, generally slightly smaller but no less strong or violent versions of their male counterparts. Black male bodies are stereotypically associated with strength, violence, and aggression particularly – although not exclusively – in US culture and society, stereotypes which persist not only around race and crime but in "entertainment" spaces around Black athletes.[56]

That orc bodies are violent and belligerent is iterated and re-iterated with each issue of a new edition of *D&D* rules. The most recent edition confirms this pattern: "Orcs gather in tribes that exert their dominance and satisfy their bloodlust by plundering villages, devouring or driving off roaming herd, and slaying any humanoids that stand against them."[57] *Warhammer* orcs "are repulsive monsters who love to inflict pain, cruelty and death ... Orcs are always fighting, if they cannot find enemies to fight they will fight each other. All of Orc technology and culture is geared towards conflict."[58] Gentle's novel presents them as inherently aggressive soldiers, while Nicholls' abandon peaceful existence at the start of the second trilogy to return to the war-torn dimension from which they escaped in the first. *Warcraft* game lore depicts orcs as living in "shamanic clans" with a "peaceful culture" before they fell under the influence of evil, but game-play makes them aggressive fighters. A key racial trait is the "blood fury": orcs can fly into a rage that increases their attack power for a short time.[59] A similar trope is used in *Of Orcs and Men*. The game beings with a "training" sequence in which the player must learn to control Arkail's rage, which can drive him berserk and uncontrolled in battle such that he is a danger to his allies and to himself. Every combat in the game-play – and there are many even for an RPG – involves the same process whereby the player must control Arkail's rage, thus constantly re-iterating the stereotype.

Langer argues that orcs in *WoW*: "seem at times to represent colonial depictions of blackness, and a times to be a sort of sink category, not a specific racial type in itself but a symbolic drain into which all sorts of negative stereotypes seep."[60] Expanding the focus from a single text to take in the continuities in representation of orcs across a broader temporal and textual sweep demonstrates that Fantasy conventions inscribe a habit of anti-Blackness. The monstrousness that orcs embody is always racial, always built on and through racist stereotypes of Blackness, even in works which attempt sympathetic, positive portrayals. Racial logics, which connect physical and non-physical attributes to biology – are, moreover, almost without exception, deployed in representation of orcs, whether they are enemies or protagonists in the narrative.

ORC SOCIETIES AND CULTURES

The places orc bodies are likely to be found and the ways they interact with each other add new and varied layers to constructions of orcs, however, these layers are racially charged. Little is known or shown of orc society in *The Lord of the Rings*, a lack which emphasizes orc Otherness through its contrast with the detailed accounts of elf, dwarf, hobbit, and various human cultures.[61] The early editions of *D&D* show that they are tribal but giving very few details of their way of life. Those which are provided are designed to tell players where they might be encountered, and how to fight them when they are. In the first *D&D* edition, they have tribal cultures, are primitive compared to other races – although they are skilled at mining and building underground, and mainly inhabit wilderness areas.[62] These core tropes have remained in all editions to the present, although they have become less subterranean and more unskilled; the most recent edition has: "orcs ... seldom settle permanently ... [and] build only for defense, making no innovation or improvement to their lairs."[63] A constant and defining feature of orc society in the core rulebooks is that it is uncivilized and static, never progressing technologically or socially.

D&D and other RPGs rely on players' ability to imagine the world in which action takes place. As *D&D* expanded with the creation of new campaign settings, these sparse accounts of orc society and culture became inadequate. Orcs became a playable character race – rather than merely one of myriad possible monsters – in *The Orcs of Thar* gazetteer (1989), one of a series which detailed new parts of the "Forgotten Realms" world, focusing on the homelands of different races.[64] The social structures, religious beliefs, and common foods, as well as physical descriptions of the different tribes that inhabit the Broken Lands are detailed. The publication was revolutionary not only because it describes not only where orcs are from and how they live but also gives them voices to tell their own stories. The booklet opens with a two-page account – told by an orc shaman to young "whelps" – of the legendary deeds of a great orc chieftain who established the laws of the nation of Thar.[65] Orcs cease to be merely the passive foot-soldiers of evil, monsters who are always already enemies who exist only to kill or be killed; they are still Othered,[66] but become more human-like, gaining a much higher level of agency in the game-world as it is imagined, and as it is played. This fleshing-out of orcs and the other inhabitants of the Broken Lands – trolls, goblins, ogres, gnolls, and kobolds – was driven by the *D&D* franchise; the details and backstory made orcs attractive to gamers and enabled them to play as a new race but was also a commercial transaction as they bought the two-part manual.

Even when they are developed as playable characters, however, many of those stereotypes persist and are added to in new and more problematic ways. *The Orcs of Thar* references real-world cultures in combination. The "red orcs," for example, are depicted with Mohawk-style hair, wear "feathers on their heads," and fight with "hatchets and arrows," clearly invoking undifferentiated "everytribe" representations of North American First Nations peoples.[67] The "yellow orcs," meanwhile, are described using pan-Asian referents: they are ruled by "Moghul-Khan," and worship "Hong-Tzu."[68] The races of Thar are constructed using a hodge-podge of cultural references, united only by the fact that the ethnicities to which they refer are not White. The tendency to represent orcs – and other humanoid Fantasy monsters – using somatic and cultural markers associated with marginalized peoples, but to do so in non-specific ways is a sustained one. As Kim observes of the orcs of Jackson's first film trilogy, references are "generally mixed and inconsistent,"[69] they create a generalized image of "non-Whiteness" over the foundations of anti-Blackness that are still attached to orc bodies; Langer's "sink category" is far from unique to *WoW*.[70]

References to real-world indigenous cultures have become common in constructions of orc cultures since they were first used in *D&D*. In Nicholls' books their native world is a romanticized wilderness, and orc life is described in terms closely associated with real-world indigenous peoples, particularly Native Americans:

> The settlement occupied the crest of a low hill. In all directions the outlook was verdant. There were luxurious pastures and dense forests, and the silver thread of a distant river marbling the emerald. In one particular lodge, a female was diverting her offspring.[71]

Orc homes are elsewhere described as "long-houses" with "corrals" for animals.[72] Nicholls' representation of orcs also resonates significantly with historical aspects of the African diaspora and Atlantic slave trade. By the end of the first trilogy, the world the orc protagonists know as home has been revealed to be a place of exile: orcs and dwarves are not indigenous to it but rather were brought there from other dimensions eons previously, and have had their respective cultures largely erased from memory in the process. The orcs are told: "The elder races [all non-human species] came here from other places ... [even though] this place is all you've ever known, and your parents before you."[73] Humans are the only indigenes of that "domain," and the orcs are returned to their original home-world at the end of the first trilogy.

In *Of Orcs and Men* orcs live in tribes in the "Southern Forests," use tattoos to identify group-membership, and worship "Mother Nature." The rainforest scenery with which it begins is reminiscent of that of the planet Pandora in the film *Avatar* (2009). Arkail's green skin blends with the foliage, he appears to be part of the landscape, not just in it. The rainforest setting differs from the kind of barren landscapes usually associated with orcs, such as in *D&D* and much of the *Warcraft* franchise. It evokes a construction of 'wilderness in keeping with contemporary environmentalist thought which sees it as something to be protected, and orcs as its custodians.[74] By doing this the game connects orcs with real-world indigenous peoples, although they have no somatic or cultural markers associated with a particular group. The combination of racial logics and generalized form of indigeneity construct orcs in Nicholls' series and *Of Orcs and Men* in the light of the "noble savage" of colonialist discourse.

Similar constructs apply in *WoW*. Orcs, who have been exiled from their homeland on Draenor, live in "the dry harsh land of Durotar."[75] A new orc player character begins the game in that region, learning to fight/play through tutorials that are framed as quests and initiated by an "elder." Langer argues that:

> Cultural appropriation ... functions as a cognitive link to societal tropes that have been repeated and inculcated into players from when they grew up on fairytales: the use of familiar iconography is as much a marketing decision as an aesthetic and formal one, since players are more likely to find compelling a world that mixes familiarity with novelty.[76]

She shows that these familiar markers "are constructions of power and hierarchy ... colonial subjects and other marginalized peoples ... are cast largely as dirty, disorganized, primitive ... or greedy."[77] Although Nicholls' series, *Of Orcs and Men*, and *WoW* re-cast orcs as protagonists not enemies and portray them in sympathetic ways the racist stereotypes that underpin conventional constructions of orcs in Fantasy are still pervasive in these texts. The layers of non-specific references to real world cultures and histories built over the top of them reinforces rather than challenge the foundational binary of Otherness.

Pratchett avoids overtly attaching real-world reference points to orc culture by not describing it at all. Nutt has been separated from it for his entire life, and at the end of it declares his intention to find and help the remnants of his people recover from the damage inflicted on them by the whips of the Evil Empire.[78] Nicholls' orcs, exiled from their home dimension, similarly have no culture or society beyond that of the army of the evil queen Jenesta before being magically transported back to it, as noted above. These moves gesture towards colonial attempts to erase indigenous cultures, and to the cultural wounds inflicted on African Americans through transportation and slavery. Pratchett and Nicholl's "write back" to the culture-less orcs of convention by highlighting the fact that colonialism and slavery actively seek to erase the cultures and societies of the peoples they dominated. Switching and multi-layering Othering discourses by attaching culture to the monstrous bodies of orcs can at times disguise, but does not remove, underlying racial logics.

WHY ARE ORCS THE ENEMY?

In Middle-earth orcs were created by the evil Melkor, serving his servant Sauron in turn until both had fallen and "the creatures of Sauron, orc or troll or beast spell-enslaved, ran hither and thither mindless."[79] Tolkien's orcs are individually, inherently evil and are given purpose and direction by the imposition of a stronger will. In the 1970s and 1980s as the Fantasy genre became a major market force, with Tolkienian Fantasy at the forefront, motivations for evil were often elided or left unexplored. Orcs in the

1979 *D&D Monster Manual*, for example, are evil because they are evil; according to Alignment, "the moral compass that guides ... [the player's] decisions;"[80] orcs are always "evil," although they switch from "lawful" to "chaotic" in edition 3.0.[81] They are always-already an enemy to be fought, always-already a threat. This simplistic construction, however, has proved insufficient in many Fantasy worlds. In this section, I explore the justifications underlying the construction of orcs as enemies and as former enemies. What kind of threats are attached to their racialized bodies and Othered cultures in the twenty-first century and how have they changed? Alternately, what motivates the threat they always-already pose to be overcome in the imagined world, and what motives the change in the real world?

The orcs of Jackson's *The Lord of the Rings* trilogy and the great majority of video-games in that franchise do not depart significantly from the ways orcs are framed in Tolkien's novels. Orcs in them are driven and directed by the will of powerful evil masters – Sauron and Saruman – but are also inherently vicious and evil themselves. *The Hobbit* film trilogy substantially reworks Tolkien's novel to show Sauron in an active role: he sends an orc force to the Battle of the Five Armies at the end of the tale. The orc leader in the films – Azog, also called "the pale orc" and "the defiler" – is a new character built on one which is referred to but never seen in the novels. The films frame his relentless pursuit of Thorin and the dwarves as a personal vendetta which is far more significant to him than the will of Sauron. The move does nothing to undercut racial logics or change conventional representation of orcs, however, it does suggest that inherent evil is insufficient as a motivating force in contemporary narratives.

As noted above, responses to genre convention and the desire to tell orcs' stories motivated fiction writers to create orc protagonists. Pratchett and Gentle also both mention race directly. Pratchett is slightly defensive about Tolkien, and invokes a narrative of social change: "We are all prisoners in the aspic of our time. But now, I think, people have learned not to think that any race or culture is naturally or irredeemably bad."[82] Gentle, meanwhile, suggests that from her first reading of Tolkien she had "a vague unease about class and race."[83] At the end of the twentieth century constructs of race-as-biology and overt anti-Blackness were less acceptable in the mainstream media than they had once been, although they have not been erased. As Brian Rosebury remarks of Jackson's first trilogy, in an understated fashion: "at the start of the twenty-first century, some may feel that any Eurocentric modeling of peoples in conflict is unacceptable or imprudent."[84] In the first chapter I argued that critiques of racial logics and stereotypes in Tolkien's and Howard's worlds have become more widespread in part as a result of changing social and cultural attitudes to and beliefs about race. The same is true for representations of orcs in the genre broadly. This is not to say that racism no longer exists in either Western society or representations of orcs, but rather to suggest that some discourses around race and difference have changed.

Fear of overwhelming numbers – hordes – of racial Others has been a feature of Western discourses since the Middle Ages. It is visible in the sheer numbers of orc enemies which appear in *The Lord of the Rings* and its film and game adaptations, and is alluded to by Pratchett: "They came in thousands, like lice, killing everything and eating the dead, including theirs. The Evil Empire had bred them in huge cellars."[85] Public discourse and policy in many if not most Western nations in the twenty-first century to date is marked by fears about the integrity of borders, the supposed failure of multiculturalism, and fear of immigration.[86] Orcs, a racialized Other become intelligible as a monster of migration when read against this backdrop, a fantasized enemy who not only can but *must* be fought and defeated.

The shifting construction of orcs in major franchises, like *D&D*, *Warhammer*, and *Warcraft* which have survived in multiple editions and works over decades is particularly illuminating. In early *Warhammer* orcs are described as "dangerous individual foes, but lack the organization or motivation to present any real long term threat to humanity,"[87] and their disorganized methods of fighting remain a constant. The most recent edition calls their armies "fickle and unpredictable," and "hodgepodge."[88] By the mid-1990s, however, as more details about their culture and society were created, they became more of a threat:

> There is nowhere in the Old World where the threat of marauding greenskins is completely unknown … On numerous occasions massive Orc armies have swept down from the north, destroying the towns and cities of Kislev and invading the northern provinces of the Empire.[89]

They live in remote pockets of wilderness area either human realms, or beyond their borders "in areas that are sparsely inhabited or where Men cannot build their homes."[90] The most recent edition of *Orcs and Goblins* (2010), however, develops on the theme of constant threat to frame them as perpetual invaders:

> The more civilized races of the world – Men, Elves and Dwarfs, for example – know that there are greenskins in the wild regions, but whether they are massing for a great migratory invasion or merely drifting by in disorganized packs of unruly raiders is impossible to discern.[91]

The fourteen years between the editions see orcs shift from a literally marginal and ultimately passing threat, to an ever-present menace of mass-migration. A recent digital mobile game in the franchise – *Warhammer Quest* – frames its action in the same way. The player's character is told by an NPC: "I've been monitoring greenskin migrations over the past decade. And, like inclement weather, I'm afraid we're due for an invasion. I've heard terrible rumors."[92] Two seemingly contradictory discourses operate here:

the orcs are marginalized because they lack the organization and purpose to overrun more desirable places; and that they pose an ever-present threat. They are essentially ghettoized within the harshest spaces of human realms, but are also an external Other always on the verge of over-running civilized lands because of their savagery and sheer weight of numbers.

Orcs in the early editions of *D&D*, like those of *Warhammer*, were merely wilderness-dwellers according the core rulebooks (as opposed to the different campaigning realms), threats only if a wandering band of adventurers encountered them. This changed with the 1989 second edition however, which states: "orcs believe that in order to survive they must expand their territory, and so they are constantly involved in war against many enemies."[93] Orcs became a constant threat that could spill over the borders of civilization at any time in an influx of monstrous bodies. *D&D* has linked both the constant aggression and threatened invasion of orcs to orcish religion since the 1989 edition, which states that it is: "extremely hateful toward other species and urges violence and warfare."[94] The significance of orcs religion and the space devoted to it in rulebooks have steadily increased since.

The threads of incursion across borders, hatred and violence towards other beings, and religion are tied together most explicitly in the 2014 fifth edition. After a single-sentence physical description of orcs, the *Monster Manual* entry moves to religion, explaining orcs believe that when the gods divided the world amongst their followers:

> Each place that Gruumsh wanted had already been claimed … Gasping his mighty spear, he laid waste to the mountains, set the forests aflame, and carved great furrows in the fields. Such was the role of orcs, he proclaimed, to take and destroy all that the other races would deny them. To this day, the orcs wage an endless war on humans, elves, dwarves, and other folk.[95]

The passage Others orcs by making them always-already outsiders because the gods of other races had already laid claim to all the lands of the world, so orcs can only ever be invaders and interlopers. The passage, moreover, blurs any line between race and culture: orcs *are* a certain way because Gruumsh decreed it, and the ongoing practice of their religion reinforces that nature. There are several possible reasons for the initial creation of orc religion in *D&D*. One is that as the world developed more detailed accounts of different beings and their societies needed to be created to keep players engaged. A second is that the idea of biological race – even when coded as species – being inherently evil was becoming less socially acceptable. *D&D* moreover, had attracted negative press and moral panic on the grounds that it fostered Satanism, and the second edition removed explicit references to "devils" and "demons." That orcs were made evil because of their religion, as opposed to being evil beings – like devils and demons – was perhaps part of this general re-vamping of the game.

Whatever the reason – or reasons – for the creation of an orc religion, its slow increase in significance as the reason that orcs are a threat to "civilized" peoples resonates with trends in Western culture much more broadly. Orcs in *D&D* have not been de-racialized with the increased role played by their religion, rather culture has been added as another layer to the nature of the threat they embody. Religions perceived as non-Western, particularly Islam, have become increasingly racialized in recent decades in Europe, the US, and Australia.[96] Fear of Muslim migration changing local cultures has become a common discourse in the national politics of many Western nations. There is no resemblance, specific or general, between orc religion and Islam or any other major world religion, but discourses which Other racialized religion and its proximity as a threat to "civilization" resonate between the real world and Fantasy.

Taken over the now twenty-year life of the *Warcraft* franchise, orc-human interactions – those races are constructed as the leaders of their factions, the Horde and Alliance respectively – follow a pattern that is extremely common in High Fantasy: enemies become united by external threats, although conflicts and significant levels of suspicion between them remain. A state of outright war exists in until the end of *Warcraft III* when an uneasy alliance of orcs, humans, and elves unite to defeat the Burning Legion, an army of demons that had corrupted the formerly peaceful orcs. The Burning Legion is the first of many similar scenarios, which see a planetary wide threat force previously hostile groups to band together. Gentle's *Grunts!* performs a similar move. In the second half of the book, the orcs' world is faced with an insectoid alien invader. Peoples aligned, in that world and genre convention, with Good and Evil, unite to defeat a greater evil.

The pattern of historical enemies joining forces to oppose a greater threat than either considers the other resonates with Ulrich Beck's formulation of a "world-risk society," in which global threats – such as terrorism and climate changed, cannot be managed by individual nations. Beck argues that "unity in diversity" can be created "by the experience of a threat," that risk can be "a kind of 'glue' for diversity."[97] Orcs can be such a threat – as they are in *D&D*, and *The Lord of the Rings*,[98] but can also be part of a community that forms to meet one. In Gentle's novel and *WoW* orcs are still racialized, the stereotypes they embody remain and indeed their fighting abilities – strength and aggression – are essential to the success of the new community in meeting and overcoming the risk which brings it together.

The Orc King, a 2008 novel by prolific author R.A. Salvatore which is set in the popular *D&D* "Forgotten Realms" world, posits orcish religion as a "world-risk," but also folds in the capacity for orcs to change into the scenario. The tale, which is summarized in a text box in the fifth edition *Monster Manual*,[99] challenges the racial logics of the world in which it takes place. Obould the orc king of the title, has invaded the Silver Marches – inhabited by dwarves, elves, and humans – and was halted at the dwarven stronghold of Mithral Hall. Orc raids are a feature of that world, happening inevitably if unpredictably according its lore in the manner suggested by the core rulebooks. Obould's raid is different, having gained land, he seeks to hold it by building fortifications and villages. He meets fierce resistance from his own kind who consider the change in their habitual pattern against the will of their god Gruumsh. The dwarven king Bruenor clings to the idea that orcs are simply dangerous beasts to be exterminated. Bruenor finds a ruined city from a time long-forgotten where ruins and ancient scrolls show that orcs and dwarves once lived together in relative harmony. He eventually recognizes that the two peoples – races – are not as dissimilar as had been believed by both for so long, that they have not always been enemies, and that orcs are capable of rational thought and living in "civilized" ways – that is, in a city – as well as in the tribal groups that structure their society in his own time. At the end of the book Obould and Bruenor fight alongside each other to defeat a coup attempt against Obould by orcs who wish to continue raiding and pillaging rather than building a stable kingdom. Racial logics depend on the idea that particular aspects – both physical and non-physical – characteristics of any people are fixed. By creating a world where not only individual orcs but orcish and dwarven societies change, Salvatore works against this construct.

Reading *The Orc King* through the lens of the racialized religious discourses outlined above renders the novel intelligible as a comment on Western, particularly US foreign policy and military intervention in the Middle East. The orcs who stage a coup against Obould are constructed as religious extremists, they invoke the will of Gruumsh to justify their grab for power: "He [Obould] wants the war to be at its end … He defies the will of Gruumsh."[100] Bruenor recognizes at the last moment that a settled, stable orc kingdom on the borders of the dwarven land is preferable to an invasion of fanatics, and prop up his rule helping him defeat the coup. Salvatore's novel ends with a projected future of orc assimilation not into dwarven society directly, but into a normative way of life which will eventually lead to the orc acceptance of the values espoused by the dwarves and their allies.

World-risk narratives that bring orcs into the ranks of civilization generally follow this pattern of assimilation, but it is always imminent, never fully realized within the text. Bruenor and Obould sign a treaty at the end of *The Orc King*, and the final line of the novel is "the world has changed, Bruenor knew."[101] The threat of betrayal hangs over the signing ceremony however, and the changed world is never shown. Even in those worlds which do bring orcs into society, the process is troubled. With each new release of an expansion pack for *WoW* a new threat is revealed to bind the community together,[102] but tensions and at times outright war between the Horde and Alliance factions. *Grunts!* closes with the discovery of portals to "new worlds to conquer."[103] Even Nutt, a lone orc, does not stay in Ankh-Morpork, the great melting pot of the Discworld, but leaves it to find the remnants of his people. Across the span of, to date, forty Discworld novel beings as diverse as werewolves, zombies, vampires, golems, dwarves, trolls, and goblins have been fitted into Ankh-Morpork society, but orcs have no niche in it and even Nutt never reappears after *Unseen Academicals*. No imagined community which includes orcs can sustain their presence without a way of directing them back outside its own boundaries, whether in defense or conquest.

The tension between the desire to assimilate and the inability to form a coherent community which includes the racialized bodies of orcs within its conventionally White borders is explicable at two levels. A stable community, under no threat from within or without, is a poor locale for narrative, much less the kind of adventure narrative that is common to Fantasy. Put simply, if everything is easy, there are no more stories to tell; this negates one of the fundamental purposes of narrative, especially narratives in franchises which depend on constantly expanding and offering new products for consumption. Through a lens of contemporary Western culture, however, the same inability to imagine a unified or cohesive community which includes orcs can be read as a symptom of contemporary fears about migration and multiculturalism.

Playing with Orcs

To this point in the chapter I have focused on orcs in Fantasy texts, that is, on the ways they are constructed games, novels, and films, taking those works as they are created without considering the ways they are received. Audiences can engage actively with any medium, interpreting the scripts offered by texts – literary and otherwise – according to individual inclination and experience as well as cultural habit. Games, however, offer more active and interactive modes of engagement by their very nature than other narrative forms, and although this does not necessarily lead to an increase in pluralistic or oppositional readings of their texts, it can allow space for players to both challenge and change the rules, logic, and nature of an imagined world. This is not equally true for all games however, the computer coding of digital games creates rules which cannot be broken by players. Alexander Galloway argues that the logics of race are "never be more alive, can never be more *purely* actualized, than in a computer simulation."[104] Frans Mäyrä argues of the MMORPG *Lord of the Rings Online* that playing as "monsters" "allows the gamers to play with more complex understanding of power and agency,"[105] but the rules of the digital world imposed by computer coding and by the construction of games as texts, often work against this potential.[106] Physical and non-physical capabilities of any player character in a digital game are circumscribed by its code.[107] *D&D*, *Warhammer*, and other non-digital games where the rules are enforced only by the individual players involved in any given campaign offer significantly more freedom.

Gentle, as noted above, cites a reaction to genre convention as one of the inspirations for *Grunts!* but also foregrounds the influence of games: "I blame gaming ... Gamers, given any concept, tend to fold, spindle and mutilate it, bounce it off the walls a couple of times, and turn it inside out to wear as a party-hat."[108] *D&D* is one of the games she mentions, while "Tolkien and more modern fantasists" are given as the major sources for her Fantasy live role playing. The short account not only provides one example of the inter-connectedness of gaming and Fantasy literature, but also highlights some of the possibilities for resistance to received ideologies inherent in games. Given the length of time *D&D* has existed and the sheer number of players, it is impossible to say how rigidly gamers abide by the rules outlined in each edition, or to count, for example, how frequently they make their characters a specific race. Gauging the resistance to race logics and representations of the millions of *D&D* – and other RPGs – gamers retrospectively would be a mammoth undertaking were it possible at all, and is beyond the scope of this research. Nonetheless, online discussion forums offer significant insights into the different approaches players can take.

A thread asking dungeon-masters how "fantasy racism" – the antipathy of dwarves and orcs for example – affects the design and play of campaigns received a range of answers. One poster said "I have a pretty accepting world. I'm a bit more flexible with alignments than the books suggest ... there aren't *really* any major conflicts on a purely racial basis."[109] Players can change the alignment of individual characters or entire races so that some of the in-world justifications for mutual hatred are removed. One dungeon-master who did this explained that the move was designed to force players not to rely on the "'usually good/evil' tags in the monster manual when encountering a humanoid. Putting racism in the world is one thing, but I wanted the PC's to have to stop and think about their reactions to the random orc versus the random elf." By ignoring the rules of the game as it was designed, this move takes away a key aspects of gaming that sets Fantasy RPGs like *D&D* apart from the real-world and simultaneously draws attention to the constructed nature of racial prejudice.

Other dungeon-masters wrote about the challenges of creating a believable, coherent world where players can still effectively and enjoyably game as non-normative race; such situations can force players to consider the effects of racism beyond direct violence. One suggested ways of non-player-characters expressing bigotry: "maybe they'll charge them more, or give them cheaper drink, or cheat them or lie to them ... maybe they are legally discriminated against." Another responded that in their world the player characters are: "followed by stares and whispers. Merchants mysteriously don't have certain items, or aren't interested in what the PC's sell. Those who will do business charge exorbitant prices." Although this thread was a self-selecting sample in that only players and dungeon-masters who had considered the issue of racism in some depth and were already interested in it responded, their statements demonstrate a level of understanding about both its day-to-day and systemic manifestations.

Players who do not use the detailed campaign settings produced by Wizards of the Coast and other game makers, relying only on the rulebooks and creating their own worlds have a significant level of freedom. One commented that: "in my world I run games in, none of the races are inherently evil ... The orcs have a massive, sprawling capitol city even, and trade regularly with other races. And the humans, of all races, are looked down on by the others." Another was running a game featuring: "an Orc uprising with the intent of building the first ever Orc nation." These decisions demonstrate that gamers are aware of the dominant narratives and constructs around different races and are willing to engage with them in critical ways. The repetition of conventions around orcs – that they are savage, uncivilized, evil and so on – has the potential to engender challenges, refusals to simple accept the habits of Fantasy. As I have argued of Gentle's and Nicholls' novels, however, these types of engagement do not challenge the foundational racial logics that structure the representation of orcs.

Player experiences of pen-and-paper RPGs and table-top games differ significantly in many respects from those in online games like *WoW* because of the relatively high level of control they have.[110] Digital worlds, including those of Fantasy games, nonetheless have significant potential to challenge existing popular understandings of race and difference. Nakamura argues that shared worlds in cyberspace "can enable a thought provoking detachment of race from the body, and an accompanying questioning of race of the essentialness of race as a category" through "a diversification of the roles which get played, which are permitted to be played."[111] The stereotypical representations of races such as orcs in *WoW* and other games, however, prevent this potential from being realized. They lead rather to what Nakamura terms "identity tourism" where cultures marked in the game as non-White are commodified and put on and off by players, giving only the illusion of experience.[112] Players, moreover, come under pressure from game-makers and other gamers to conform to expected behaviors, meaning that both the digital coding of the game and the social codes of playing it work against the kind of diversification that Nakamura argues for.

Orc bodies – rendered digital flesh or merely imagined – are potential sites of pleasurable intimacy with Otherness, the desire for which, as hooks states: "does not eradicate the politics of racial domination."[113] Joseph Packer asserts that player behavior in the *WoW* world over-rides the negative stereotypes attached to orcs: "instead of primitive and disorganized, Orcs embody skill, experience, and dedication because statistically the gamers who choose to play as Orcs demonstrate those characteristics."[114] The reading does not, however, take into account the fact that "primitive and disorganized" are not the only stereotypes attached to orcs, or that those which might be desirable in the game world – notably the capacity for extreme violence – are not necessarily so in the real world. Whether orcs are viewed positively by the majority of players or not, moreover, does not negate the racial logics which are built into the world.

CONCLUSION

When Tolkien's orcs – especially as represented in *The Lord of the Rings*, the piece of his writing which unquestionably has had the most influence on Fantasy – are compared with their descendants in the genre, certain tendencies become clear. The orcs of Middle-earth are racialized monsters, initially inspired by the literary model of medieval Saracens and inflected by nineteenth- and early-twentieth-century colonialist concepts of race and racist stereotypes. The racial logic which attaches physical characteristics – saliently skin colour – to non-physical attributes is sustained across six decades and multiple media, as are the anti-Black stereotypes that are invoked by the particulars of orc bodies. Cultural explanations of orc Otherness do not replace its underlying racial structure, rather they are built on its foundations. The non-specific amalgam of cultural referents attached to orc bodies from the 1990s onward, moreover, are always to ethnicities which are marginalized in the West, most often indigenous peoples. The framing paradigm of a text like *Of Orcs and Men* may construct orcs sympathetically, even positively, but they are still a racialized Other. Susanna Loza argues that the Science Fiction films *Avatar* and *District 9* show that in the twenty-first century: "We have not transcended race. We are still trapped in the coils of colonial logic."[115] The same can be said of orcs when considered across multiple Fantasy texts and franchises. Orcs embody racial Otherness which is always subject to fantasies of control either by extermination or imminent, albeit always unachieved, assimilation. Donna Haraway writes: "to be inappropriate/d is not to fit in the taxon, to be dislocated from the available maps specifying kinds of actors and kinds of narratives, not to be originally fixed by difference."[116] In an ontological sense, orcs are rarely monsters precisely because they are fitted simultaneously into the taxons of genre convention and of racial stereotypes.

NOTES

1. Dragons have also served this function, specifically when attached to the imaginative and transgressive power of the genre as in Ursula le Guin's 1974 speech "Why Are Americans Afraid of Dragons?"
2. Poole, *Monsters in America: Our Historical Obsession with the Hideous and the Haunted*, pt. 649.
3. Cohen, "Monster Culture (Seven Theses)," 7.
4. Strickland, "Monstrosity and Race in the Late Middle Ages," 366.
5. Braham, "The Monstrous Caribbean," 17.
6. du Coudray, *The Curse of the Werewolf: Fantasy, Horror and the Beast Within*, 46.
7. Campbell, "Intersectionality Bites: Metaphors of Race and Sexuality in HBO's *True Blood*"; Halberstam, "Technologies of Monstrosity: Bram Stoker's *Dracula*."
8. McAlister, "Slaves, Cannibals, and Infected Hyper-Whites: the Race and Religion of Zombies."

9. Loza, "Playing Alien in Post-Racial Times."

10. Mitter, *Much Maligned Monsters: a History of European Reactions to Indian Art*. For the destabilizing power of monsters see especially Haraway, "The Promises of Monsters: a Regenerative Politics for Inappropriate/d Others." Caliban, who first appears in William Shakespeare's *The Tempest*, is a key figure of postcolonial resistance.

11. Higgin, "Blackless Fantasy," 11.

12. Langer, *Postcolonialism and Science Fiction*, 88.

13. The Orks of the Science Fiction table-top game *Warhammer 40 000* – a spin-off of the *Warhammer* fantasy game to which I return below – are famously inspired by English soccer hooligans and thus invoke class, but are also constructed using the language of race. They are referred to collective, for example, as "greenskins," referencing the use of skin-colour as a mark of racial difference. Kelly, *Codex Orks*, 3.

14. Weiss, "Ten Theses on Monsters and Monstrosity," 125.

15. Livingston and Sutton, "Reinventing the Hero: Gardner's *Grendel* and the Shifting Face of Beowulf in Popular Culture," 3. *Beowulf* has the earliest usage of a form of "orc": "orcneas," one of a list of evil creatures descended from Cain – in English. Grendel is not one of them.

16. Cohen, "Undead (A Zombie Oriented Ontology)," 401.

17. For example, Packer, "What Makes an Orc? Racial Cosmos and Emergent Narrative in *World of Warcraft*."

18. For the former see Higgin, "Blackless Fantasy." For the latter, Petzold, "'Oo, Those Awful Orcs!': Tolkien's Villains as Protagonists in Recent Fantasy Novels."

19. Kim, "Beyond Black and White: Race and Postmodernism in *The Lord of the Rings* Films"; Redmond, "The Whiteness of the Rings"; Young, "Racial Logics, Franchising, and Video Game Genres: *The Lord of the Rings*."

20. The most complete exploration of its nature and internal workings, albeit one written before *The Hobbit* trilogy was made, is Thompson, *The Frodo Franchise: The Lord of the Rings and Modern Hollywood*. For discussion of the films and games as adaptations see, for example, Auger, "'*The Lord of the Rings*' Interlace: the Adaptation to Film"; Hogset, "The Adaptation of *The Lord of the Rings*: a Critical Commentary"; Randall and Murphy, "*The Lord of the Rings* Online: Issues in the Adaptation of MMOPRGs"; Wallin, "Myths, Monsters and Marlets: Ethos, Identification, and the Video Game Adaptations of *The Lord of the Rings*."

21. As discussed in the second chapter of this book, humans in the early editions of *D&D* were coded as culturally White and depicted as racially so in illustrations in game manuals.

22. For a detailed account of the history of the versions and editions, see Applecliff, "The Long Shadow of *D&D*."

23. For example, following the threatened law suit Hobbits were re-named Halfings, Balrogs became Balor demons. Orcs were not subject to it as the word was not invented by Tolkien. Middle-earth is has had more influence on Fantasy games, both digital and non-digital, than any other Fantasy world.

24. It also includes thousands of novels, as discussed in chapter two, video games, a film, comics, and more. I focus on the games here.

25. The most recent editions of the relevant game books are Vetock, *Orcs & Goblins*. for *Warhammer Fantasy*, and Kelly, *Codex Orks*. for *Warhammer 40*

000. Here I will focus on the fantasy setting rather than the science fictional *Warhammer 40 000* in which "Orks" are a species of fungus and are reputedly based in part on British soccer hooligans.

26. Gander, "*Of Orcs and Men* – the Meanest, Greenest RPG You've Never Played."
27. The only others I have located only feature orcs fighting each other, not orcs fighting humans or other species.
28. Gentle, *Grunts!*, 82.
29. Rivers, *The Guardian of Hope*; Bowyer, *The Impending Storm*; Heitz, *The Dwarves*.
30. Nicholls, "An Interview with Stan Nicholls on *Orcs*." Michael Stackpole's *Once a Hero* (1994) took a similar approach to elves a few years earlier, making them the perpetrators of a genocide against humans.
31. Pratchett, "Guardian Book Club: Terry Pratchett on *Unseen Academicals*."
32. Gentle, "Smarter Than Root Vegetables: an Introduction to *Grunts!*," pt. 38.
33. Pratchett, *Unseen Academicals*, 55.
34. Gygax, *Advanced Dungeons & Dragons Monster Manual*, 76. I use the 2012 reprint of the 4th (1979) printing of the *Monster Manual* throughout. That there are somatic markers of difference attached to orcs are, to some degree, a result of the nature of the game which requires players to use their imaginations within a group to create the game-world; descriptions of the beings their characters encounter in it assist this process. Moreover the tactics they might use when fighting any given monster also depend on its physical attributes. This consideration has little to do with the specific characteristics assigned to orcs.
35. Mearls, Schubert, and Wyatt, *Dungeons & Dragons: Monster Manual*, 205.
36. Kim, "Beyond Black and White," 877.
37. Brookey and Booth, "Restricted Play: Synergy and the Limits of Interactivity in *The Lord of the Rings: The Return of the King* Video Game," 215.
38. For example, Reynolds and Stewart, "*Lord of the Rings* Labelled Racist."
39. Anaesthetized, "The Othering of Orcs: a Post-Colonial Reading of Peter Jackson's *Lord of the Rings* Trilogy."
40. Young, "Racial Logics, Franchising, and Video Game Genres," 9.
41. Halliwell, Ansell, and Priestly, *Warhammer: Battle Bestiary*, 23.
42. Priestly, Halliwell, and Ansell, *Warhammer Fantasy Battle*.
43. Priestly, *Warhammer Armies: Orcs and Goblins*, 4.
44. Vetock, *Orcs & Goblins*, 77.
45. Gentle, *Grunts!*, 268.
46. Blizzard, "Orc."
47. Ditomasso, "Robert E. Howard's Hyborian Tales and the Question of Race in Fantastic Literature," 167.
48. Cook, Tweet, and Williams, *Dungeons & Dragons: Player's Handbook*, 146.
49. Halliwell, Ansell, and Priestly, *Warhammer: Battle Bestiary*, 23.
50. Gentle, *Grunts!*, 21.
51. Gygax, *Advanced Dungeons & Dragons Monster Manual*, 76.
52. Pratchett, *Unseen Academicals*, 282.
53. Gentle, *Grunts!*, 21.
54. Crawford, *Monster Manual*, 244.
55. Kim, "Beyond Black and White," 877.

56. Ferber, "The Construction of Black Masculinity: White Supremacy Now and Then."
57. Crawford, *Monster Manual*, 244.
58. Halliwell, Ansell, and Priestly, *Warhammer: Battle Bestiary*, 22–23.
59. Blizzard, "Orc."
60. Langer, *Postcolonialism and Science Fiction*, 92. For other work on *WoW* orcs as negative stereotypes of blackness see Higgin, "Blackless Fantasy"; Monson, "Race-Based Fantasy Realm: Essentialism in the *World of Warcraft*"; Pace, "Can an Orc Catch a Cab in a Stormwind? Cybertype Preference in the *World of Warcraft* Character Creation Interface"; Rowland and Barton, "Outside Oneself in '*World of Warcraft*': Gamers' Perception of the Racial Self-Other"; Ritter, "Why the Humans Are White: Fantasy, Modernity, and the Rhetorics of Racism in *World of Warcraft*."
61. See chapter one.
62. Gygax, *Advanced Dungeons & Dragons Monster Manual*, 76.
63. Crawford, *Monster Manual*, 244.
64. Not all *D&D* campaign setting include orcs. The *Dragonlance* setting is one of the most popular which does not.
65. Heard, *The Orcs of Thar*, part 1, 1.
66. The Dungeon Master's section of the manual aligns them explicitly with evil, they are: "the reborn souls of evil beings of the world sent back to expiate their crimes," Heard, *The Orcs of Thar*, part 2, 3.
67. Heard, *The Orcs of Thar*, part 1, 10.
68. Heard, *The Orcs of Thar*, part 1, 12–13.
69. Kim, "Beyond Black and White," 877.
70. Langer, *Postcolonialism and Science Fiction*, 92.
71. Nicholls, *Orcs: Bad Blood*, 24.
72. Nicholls, *Orcs: Bad Blood*, 823.
73. Nicholls, *Orcs*, 659.
74. The environmentalist ideology of the game was variously noted by reviewers, for example, Gander, "*Of Orcs and Men*."
75. Blizzard, "Orc."
76. Langer, "The Familiar and the Foreign: Playing (Post) Colonialism in *World of Warcraft*," 90–91.
77. Langer, "The Familiar and the Foreign," 92.
78. Pratchett takes up the challenges of a culturally and socially diverse society in other novels, including *Thud* (2005). *Snuff* (2011) and *Raising Steam* (2013) offer optimistic re-imaginings of colonial engagements with indigenous peoples.
79. Tolkien, *The Return of the King*, 1243.
80. Mearls, *D&D Player's Handbook*, 11.
81. Cook, Tweet, and Williams, *Dungeons & Dragons: Monster Manual*, 2000, 146.
82. Pratchett, "Guardian Book Club."
83. Gentle, "Smarter Than Root Vegetables," pt. 38.
84. Rosebury, "Race in Tolkien Films," 557.
85. Pratchett, *Unseen Academicals*, 54–55.
86. See, for example, Huysmans, *The Politics of Insecurity: Fear, Migration and Asylum in the EU*; Kabachnik, "Place Invaders: Constructing the Nomadic Threat in England."

87. Halliwell, Ansell, and Priestly, *Warhammer: Battle Bestiary*, 22–23.
88. Vetock, *Orcs & Goblins*, 6.
89. Priestly, *Warhammer Armies: Orcs and Goblins*, 4.
90. Cavatore, *Warhammer: The Game of Fantasy Battles*, 174.
91. Vetock, *Orcs & Goblins*, 8. *Warhammer 40 000* uses a similar construct: "should the Orks ever truly unify, they would crush all opposition and drown the civilized races in a tide of gore." Kelly, *Codex Orks*, 4.
92. "Warhammer Quest." It is based on the 1995 board game of the same name.
93. Connors and Thomas, *Advanced Dungeons and Dragons Monstrous Compendium Volume One*. The compendium was issued as un-paginated loose-leaf sheets, so no page numbers are available. Very similar text is found in editions 3.0 (2000) and 3.5 (2003). Cook, Tweet, and Williams, *Dungeons & Dragons: Monster Manual*, 2000, 147; Cook, Tweet, and Williams, *Dungeons & Dragons: Monster Manual*, 2003, 204.
94. Connors and Thomas, *Advanced Dungeons and Dragons Monstrous Compendium Volume One*.
95. Crawford, *Monster Manual*, 244.
96. Dunn, Klocker, and Salabay, "Contemporary Racism and Islamaphobia in Australia: Racializing Religion"; Joshi, "The Racialization of Hinduism, Islam, and Sikhism in the United States"; Meer, "Racialization and Religion: Race, Culture and Difference in the Study of Antisemitism and Islamophobia."
97. Beck, "Critical Theory of World Risk Society: A Cosmopolitan Vision," 4. See also Beck, *World Risk Society*.
98. My reading of cosmopolitanism in Tolkien's *The Lord of the Rings* invokes the concept with orcs forming part of the threat posed by Sauron's power. Young, "Diversity and Difference: Cosmopolitanism and The Lord of the Rings," 354–355.
99. Crawford, *Monster Manual*, 245.
100. Salvataore, *The Orc King*, 317.
101. Salvatore, *The Orc King*, 395.
102. To date there are five: *The Burning Crusade* (2007); *Wrath of the Lich King* (2008); *Catalcysm* (2010); *Mists of Pandaria* (2012); and *Warlords of Draenor*, announced in 2013, and in beta at the time writing.
103. Gentle, *Grunts!*, 429.
104. Galloway, "'Starcraft,' or Balance," 96.
105. Mäyrä, "From the Demonic Tradition to Art-Evil in Digital Games: Monstrous Pleasures in *The Lord of the Rings Online*," 130.
106. Young, "Racial Logics, Franchising, and Video Game Genres," 13.
107. See Monson, "Race-Based Fantasy Realm," 59–61.
108. Gentle, "Smarter Than Root Vegetables," pt. 63." Nicholls, in contrast, says he is "largely ignorant" of gaming in general and of how orcs are represented in Fantasy games. Nicholls, "An Interview with Stan Nicholls on *Orcs*."
109. Various, "Fantasy Racism." Until otherwise indicated, all quotes come from this thread. I have reproduced all quotes as they are given in the original threads without correcting spelling, grammar, etc.
110. Although most companies that maintain MMO spaces have codes of conduct forbidding racial slurs, the failure to enforce those rules is a common topic of complaint on gaming forums and also relies on its victims to report it. Some players do report experiencing face-to-face abuse, see Nakamura, "'It's

a Nigger in Here! Kill the Nigger!': User-Generated Media Campaigns Against Racism, Sexism, and Homophobia in Digital Games," 3.

111. Nakamura, "Race In/For Cyberspace: Identity Tourism and Racial Passing on the Internet," 234. See also Higgin, "Blackless Fantasy," 23.

112. Nakamura, "Race In/For Cyberspace," 229. On identity tourism in *World of Warcraft*, see Langer, "The Familiar and the Foreign," 105; Monson, "Race-Based Fantasy Realm," 66.

113. Hooks, *Black Looks: Race and Representation*, 28.

114. Packer, "What Makes an Orc?" 87. According to Pace, "evil characters like orcs were played bu more hard-core gamers," Pace, "Can an Orc Catch a Cab in a Stormwind?" 2500.

115. Loza, "Playing Alien in Post-Racial Times," 64.

116. Haraway, "The Promises of Monsters," 300.

5   Popular Culture Postcolonialism

The histories of race and racism cannot be disentangled from the histories of colonialism. Robert J. C. Young argues that the idea of Anglo-Saxonism – a key foundation of Whiteness – developed not to explain English identity, but to explain and justify the imperial diaspora of colonisers in North America, the Pacific, and South Africa.[1] Racism, as Frantz Fanon asserts, "was characteristic of the colonial era,"[2] and is, moreover, one of its continuing legacies. The inequalities stemming from colonial practice and ideologies exist to the present day, not only in economic and power disparities between old colonial powers of the First World and developing nations which were formerly colonies, but in systemic and systematically entrenched racisms around the world. Race-based hierarchies were key justifications for colonialism. People who were its targets were constructed as inferior to the colonisers so that ideology and discourse could underpin action. Europe, European culture(s), and Whites were privileged, valued, over all others in a discourse which is still strong today.[3]

Colonisation and its legacies are not widely addressed in the popular Fantasy genre; it is not alone in this failing however. In his exploration of modern media engagements with colonial history, Kent A. Ono remarks:

> Not only is colonialism not commonly recognized as part of contemporary culture, but even U.S. America's colonial past is, at times, mysterious ... processes of forgetting colonialism have taken place in the nation's history that make trying to piece together the history of colonialism difficult.[4]

Western societies fetishize and commodify indigenous cultures, but histories of invasion, dehumanization of native peoples and genocide are largely buried in modern popular culture. Fantasy – despite, or even perhaps because of, its long reception as a genre designed to "serve rather than subvert the dominant ideology"[5] – has considerable power to dig up long-buried histories of colonisation and imperialism and to challenge the assumptions on which their power structures rely by offering new perspectives. This is so despite the ongoing legacy of colonialist ideology which permeates the genre.

The narrative arcs of Science Fiction lend themselves to colonialist and postcolonialist themes. Exploration of the globe, "voyages of discovery," are "a tale the West tells itself" to render non-European lands and people unknown, unintelligible, and uninhabited before European arrival,[6] and this tale is readily re-mapped onto interplanetary travel: the New World becomes new worlds. Scholarly engagements with topics such as empire, colonialism, indigeneity, and diaspora in Science Fiction writing, moreover, are relatively common.[7] The conventional story arcs of epic Fantasy are not so obviously adaptable. Moreover, contemporary popular concepts of the European Middle Ages, and the strong desire for "authenticity" amongst audiences, place significant if not insurmountable difficulties in the way of a medievalist text taking up such themes. As Kim Wilkins argues: "the medievalism in … fantasy fiction makes it almost impossible to represent indigenous stories comfortably because the genre's typical structures and conventions, especially those concerning politics and power, are not equipped to engage with indigeneity as it is conceptualised in contemporary culture."[8] Nonetheless, as this chapter will show, colonialism, imperialism, and the racial logics which underpin them are the target of critique in twenty-first-century Fantasy, although the cultural and social legacies of those same structures still have significant power.

Orientalist eurocentric discourses and colonialist ideologies have been present in the Fantasy genre for as long as it has existed, as the first three chapters of this books demonstrate; this is recognised even in genre journalism intended for fans. In 2011, for example, *SFX* magazine published a "family tree" of the sub-branches of the genre which identified "the Orientalist opium dreams of Sword and Sorcery"; commented that the "Colonial Fantasy" typified by H. Rider Haggard is "pretty iffy according to today's moral standards"; and baldly – and with some accuracy – stated of Steampunk that "this genre venerates empire."[9] Voices of critique of imperialist tendencies in both textual engagements and scholarly analysis, however, have been largely silent until very recently. This is particularly true when it comes to the stories of indigenous peoples, and to scholarship on the stories that are told.

There has been very little scholarly exploration of the representation of indigenous peoples from any part of the world in Fantasy written for adults. One important exception to this is David D. Oberhelman and Amy H. Sturgis' edited collection *The Intersection of Fantasy and Native America* (2009), which examines writing by Native American authors and by White authors who drew on those cultures.[10] Although the collection has a chapter on H. P. Lovecraft, most do not consider mainstream Fantasy works. The general paucity of scholarship is not least because there is very little to write about – few mainstream Fantasy works feature peoples coded as indigenous, and few indigenous authors publish Fantasy.[11] This said, the indigenous peoples of North America have been more widely represented in mass-market popular Anglophone Fantasy fiction than those of other parts of world such as South America and Australia.[12]

Multicultural literature is almost always thought of, and approached, as matter for minorities and thus as irrelevant to a presumed-white majority.[13] This is true of all kinds of writing which are designated as other-than-mainstream: multicultural, Afro-American, postcolonial, cosmopolitan, indigenous, and more. White privilege is inscribed and re-inscribed by marginalizing people and cultures with the assumption that disadvantage is not of concern to the privileged. Marginalization is arguably discernable even in the criticism of post/colonialism in Fantasy writing which does exist. There are two main topics of discussion. The first involves critique of colonialism – or imperialism, orientalism, racism, and related topics – in the genre or the work of particular authors.[14] The second focuses on the work of writers from minority backgrounds.[15] While this is important, and acknowledges the voices of authors of colour, it can re-inscribe marginalization by suggesting that such concerns are theirs alone. This chapter engages with the work of authors of colour and White authors who seek to place critiques of Europe's imperialist past in the centre rather than on the margins of mainstream culture. It begins with a discussion of the marginalization of indigenous authors which draws particularly on interviews with Daniel Heath Justice, a Cherokee man and Fantasy author, and essays by Ambelin Kwaymullina, an indigenous Australian author of Young Adult dystopian fiction.[16] It then examines Namoi Novik's Temeraire series which re-imagines the nineteenth century, tapping into a broad twenty-first-century swell of interest in that era. The chapter closes by exploring the critique of imperialism in N. K. Jemisin's *Inheritance* trilogy (2010–2011); Jemisin discussed the influence of postcolonialism on her world-building for the series on her blog.[17]

INDIGENOUS VOICES

Colonisation and imperialism silence the voices of the colonised, rendering them spoken for and about, to such an extent that one of the foundational questions of postcolonial theory was "can the subaltern speak?"[18] There are a growing number of voices that might be thought of as postcolonial and which identify themselves as such in mainstream Fantasy. Some are those of authors like Nnedi Okorafor and Nalo Hopkinson who, as Brian Attebery observes, are "border crosser[s]" who have "double perspectives" derived from their backgrounds and upbringings: Okorafor was raised in the US by immigrant Nigerian parents and visited that country as a young person; while Hopkinson is of Afro-Caribbean descent, and has lived in the Caribbean, Canada, and the US.[19] In epic Fantasy, Katherine Kerr's Deverry novels (1987–2007) take up questions of colonialism, particularly in the later volumes of the long series. Robin Hobb's work, particularly her Soldier Son trilogy (2006–2007), but also the *Rain Wilds Chronicles* and to a lesser degree the *Live Ship Traders* series, also explores and critiques colonisation.[20] N. K. Jemisin's Inheritance and David Anthony Durham's

Acacia (2007–2011) trilogies highlight the inherently oppressive nature of empire. Voices of indigenous Fantasy authors, however, are extremely difficult to find in the mainstream genre, and indeed are less prominent than those of non-indigenous authors of colour even in the more progressive parts of the genre.

A simple Google search provided results that are indicative of this broad trend: the first result for "indigenous fantasy author" was the Wikipedia article for Patricia Wrightson, a White Australian author of children's Fantasy who drew heavily on indigenous culture and has been strongly criticised for cultural appropriation.[21] In contrast, "author of colour Fantasy" returned a Wikipedia page and a number of Goodreads of lists of speculative fiction by authors of colour. Google, Goodreads, and Wikipedia offer important windows into popular culture, not only reflecting what there is to be found, but also shaping how, and indeed if, that material can be encountered. A further indication, and one which goes further to the heart of the genre community, is that a list of authors and editors whose work inspired marginalized readers, those who felt their stories were "almost never even alluded to" let alone told, in the introduction to the recent anthology *Long Hidden: Speculative Fiction from the Margins of History* (2014), does not include anyone who identifies as indigenous.[22]

Planning the research project that this book is based on, and in the process of writing this chapter, it became increasingly obvious to me that including the work of even one indigenous author in it would be difficult if I did not change my approach. As outlined in the introduction, the research focuses on mainstream, globalized popular culture, on works which are mostly if not all by household names like J. R. R. Tolkien or George R. R. Martin, and which then make regular appearances in the "Fantasy/Sci Fi" sections of generalist bookshops, in the best-seller lists on Amazon, and other similar places. Later chapters explore anti-racist work in the genre-culture which is gradually changing its nature and laying the pathways for more authors of colour, including indigenous authors, to become prominent in the mainstream, but this is an ongoing struggle. I was not able to find an author who identified as indigenous using even the broad criteria I generally applied.[23]

The indigenous authors who do write Fantasy, as Justice observed, "tend not to be mainstream."[24] Celu Amberstone, a Cherokee woman author he mentioned, is an example – as is Justice himself. Amberstone has also published speculative fiction with Kegedonce Press, and was a contributor to *So Long Been Dreaming: Postcolonial Science Fiction and Fantasy* (2004), the first dedicated postcolonial speculative fiction collection.[25] In 2011, Wilkins – herself a successful genre-author – wrote that: "while [Australian] Aboriginal writers such as Sam Wagan Watson Jr have written speculative short stories, none have tried their hand at a full-length fantasy novel."[26] The article in which she makes the comment is concerned with the lack of representation of Australian indigenous characters, rather than of published indigenous authors, but the passing remark begs further discussion. Why are there no Aboriginal Australian authors, and so few indigenous authors globally, with published Fantasy novels?

Structural, systemic inequalities resulting directly from colonialism are a significant factor in the lives and opportunities of indigenous peoples. Globally, indigenous people are more likely to live in poverty, have lower life expectancies, and have poorer access to education and health services and outcomes from these than their non-indigenous peers. They also face significant cultural marginalization and appropriation. The major structural inequalities which impact on the lives of indigenous peoples around the world arguably have a negative impact on the likelihood that any individual will have the economic, social, and cultural capital to become a professional published writer. It is not my intention to downplay the significance of these structural inequalities and injustices by mentioning them as briefly as I have just done, but in-depth discussion is beyond the scope of this study and book.[27] This chapter now seeks to offer some insights into the specific reasons that indigenous peoples are not more visible in Fantasy, particularly among its best-known authors; most of those reasons derive either directly or indirectly from colonialism and its legacies.

One significant issue is the way that colonial societies imagined – and continue to imagine – indigenous peoples, societies, and cultures, speaking for and about them, suppressing their voices while misunderstanding, misrepresenting, and outright falsifying supposedly factual and scientific accounts. In an interview, Justice recounted the story of a friend of his, a Dakota woman, who found the idea of him writing an epic Fantasy story drawing on Native American cultures and experiences troubling. She said to him: "90 per cent of what people have – 99 per cent of what people have written about us is fantasy anyway. Why would you contribute to that?"[28] He acknowledged the validity of his friend's concern, and said: "The nostalgic element of fantasy is so heavily weighted toward colonialist ends. I think that's a particular history that's really problematic for us" and "the nostalgia that we see in fantasy is usually for a golden age of white patriarchs."[29] As Oberhelman writes: "fantastic representations of Native peoples can indeed be hegemonic tools" used by Western culture to claim superiority.[30]

The nostalgic overtones of Fantasy – or better, its overarching habit of referencing the past as opposed to the future, even in works which are not nostalgic – are widely considered not to be present in Science Fiction, arguably making that genre more appealing to indigenous authors. Wilkins observes: "Australian Science Fiction … evidences no qualms about borrowing indigenous material," while Attebery states that "Australian sf writers have long struggled to incorporate native peoples and their traditional stories and ways of life into distinctively Australian futures."[31] Science Fiction appears to be more appealing to indigenous authors as well, although the evidence is scant and the lines between genres are often blurred. For example, the sole collection of speculative short stories by indigenous authors that I have been able to locate is Grace Dillon's *Walking the Clouds: an Anthology of Indigenous Science Fiction*; however this includes a section of stories which fit more closely with the conventions of Fantasy than Science Fiction.[32] Justice remarked in a similar vein about writers that "there are more people who do futurism stuff than do fantasy," and linked this directly to the colonialist nostalgia of the Fantasy genre.[33] He does not, however, feel that the habit of nostalgia should prevent potential authors from writing in the genre.

A second issue related to generic boundaries also comes into play: publication or the reception of a text have significant influence over how any given work is categorised. Sturgis, citing anecdotal evidence, suggests that "fantasy lovers do not devour the novels [of Native American authors ...] simply because [they ...] are not found in the fantasy sections of bookstores or labelled by online sellers as genre-related works," and are rather grouped under "Native American literature" or general fiction.[34] The identity of an author, rather than the nature of her or his writing, can strongly influence the way a text is received. As Sturgis observes: most literary critics and ethnologists today who study such texts [by Native American authors] label them as "magical realism," a habit which, she rightly argues, threatens to leave them "forever marginalized, historicized, and untasted."[35] Not all works that see the supernatural touch or encroach upon the natural, fit within the Fantasy genre, but presuming that one does not because of the identity of the author means that the genre's habits of Whiteness are inscribed and re-inscribed at its boundaries. There is more than one factor to be considered here: Fantasy has a particularly low status in academia, while that of Magic Realism – considered to be literature and not merely popular culture – is relatively high; scholars who work on texts which *can* be classified as not-Fantasy may do so to protect their own work, reputation, and status.

Kwaymullina raises a significant point for concepts and definitions of Fantasy more broadly: "Eurocentric genre categories are difficult to apply to works that were not created out of a Eurocentric worldview, because the very notion of what is speculative and what is not relies on assumptions about the real."[36] Western concepts of reality in the post-Enlightenment period emphasize rationality and scientifically explicable and observable phenomena, and it is against this backdrop that the "not real" of Fantasy is generally and generically defined. Colonial attitudes devalued and dismissed indigenous knowledge and ways of knowing. Indigenous worldviews draw lines between "real" and "not real" in multiple different places and ways. As Kwaymullina writes elsewhere, "the centre ground of 'truth' is claimed by Eurocentric knowledge traditions, while ancient Indigenous understandings are labelled myth and legend."[37] If a Fantasy narrative must include some element of the "not real" by definition, then a story told from a worldview which does not share same concept of real and not real may not be easily or casually fitted within the boundaries of the genre. Dillon asserts that "writers of indigenous futurisms ... invariably *change* the perimeters of sf."[38] Including a work of Fantasy written from an indigenous worldview necessarily does the same for that genre. However, those changes may not always be recognized or accepted.

Dominic Alessio provides concrete examples of two indigenous authors – Witi Ihimaera and Albert Wendt – who were not included on the fan-sourced list of New Zealand/Aoteroan authors on the website of the Science Fiction and Fantasy Association of New Zealand (SFFANZ). He suggests that this, while probably an "oversight" and not a deliberate exclusion, is a case of "life imitating art imitating life," given that both have written works in clearly speculative fiction modes that "deal overtly with postcolonial themes."[39] Fantasy, so widely considered a White genre, in this sort of process is marked as "off limits" to indigenous authors and voices. At one level this valorises their work by classifying it as literature, but it simultaneously marks the work as Other.

Although the Fantasy's habits of Whiteness tend to re-inscribe colonialist ideologies, perspectives, and narratives, those habits can be broken by telling different stories in different ways. Justice said: "one of the challenges that any colonised people has is having our imaginations diminished so that we start to imagine that the colonial state of affairs was an inevitability and that's the only way it could be." Dillon similarly comments that indigenous authors must "confront the possibility of internal colonization" when writing in speculative genres implicated in colonialism.[40] Both, however, argue that this should not stop them from doing so; as Justice said: "It's not so vexed that we can't get some good out of it and it's not so vexed that we can't retell those stories or challenge them."[41] He asserts that no part of culture should be off limits to the imagination of indigenous people: "We shouldn't have to give up anything in terms of our imaginations; we shouldn't have to give up any territory."[42] Challenging the dominance of colonialist structures involves, in postcolonial theory, "writing back" to dismantle them; Justice advocates this kind of move as a way of reinventing Fantasy and claiming it as a space where indigenous people can tell their own stories.

His own work exemplifies this idea by reimagining a colonial struggle. Ania Loomba's characterisation of colonialisation is a useful starting point for reading the trilogy: it is "the takeover of territory, appropriation of natural resources, exploitation of labour and interference with political and cultural structures of another territory or nation."[43] In Justice's series, the Kyn are a forest-dwelling people who, along with other "Eld-Folk" live in the Everland, a wilderness world which was "Melded" with that of Humanity a millennium or more before the action of the series takes place. Humans trade with the Kyn, and some are adopted into their culture and "accepted as kith,"[44] but the Dreyd, the dominant power in their society, generally view the Everland as a potential source of resources and wealth. At the time of the series, the Shield, an assimilationist group which sees traditional "*wyr*" power and ways as merely savagery, is gaining power within Kyn society. The Dreyd seek to appropriate *wyr* power for their own gain, and to force the Kyn to leave their traditional lands in order to achieve this. The trilogy, with its story of a battle between good and evil, sits firmly within the borders of epic Fantasy, a point that is invariably commented on by both critics and readers reviewing it.[45]

Justice draws on Native American culture and the history of British colonisation of North America for inspiration; the Trail of Tears and broken treaties are evoked by the events of the narrative, "demonstrating how Indigenous fantasy can provide new insights into the unfortunate clash of civilizations that took place."[46] The Folk are aligned with indigenous peoples and humanity with colonisers with explicit references to real-world historical beliefs and events. Some of these relate directly to constructions of racial difference, including anthropological approaches and phrenology. Humans rob the graves of the Folk, and one Kyn character remarks: "Some of their more learned types measure the bumps and dips of the skulls they dig up to tell how capable we are of thinkin' … Ye can figure we never rank too high 'gainst Humans … It's all just another way of provin' that Humans is better than everybody."[47] The Western tendency to dismiss non-Western religions and beliefs as mere legends is also pilloried.[48]

The trilogy subverts the conventions of what Farah Mendlesohn terms "portal-quest" fantasy which is "about entry, transition, and negotiation" on the part of the protagonist.[49] One of the central characters, a Tree-Born she-Kyn Tarsa'deshae is a newly trained Redthorn Warrior at the beginning of the narrative, which is in part a coming-of-age for her. Her development parallels that of conventional heroes in some ways as she inherits power unexpectedly and is a key figure in the salvation of her people. The use of this convention is one element of the trilogy that makes it intelligible as Fantasy despite its unconventional setting and anti-colonial ideology. Mendlesohn argues that "this kind of fantasy is essentially imperialist: only the hero is capable of change; fantasyland is orientalised into the 'unchanging past.'"[50] It is this convention that the series works against. In Justice's series Tarsa's people undertake parallel physical and spiritual journeys to her own as they are forced to leave their homeland, and create a new one with new social structures that are inflected by traditional ways – some of which had been lost and are remembered as a result of her individual trajectory – but not solely dependent on them. She says in the epilogue: "We will change, as all things change, and our future will be no better or worse for it. We will simply be. The Folk will continue."[51] The Folk, marked as like-but-not-like Native American peoples, are emphatically not the dying and/or perpetually primitive and unchanging colonialist fantasy but are a people and culture who can change with the world around them.

Their relationship with the land is key to this capacity. The Melding of their world with that of humanity – the human world is not our own but rather one that has its own magic, albeit of a different kind to the *wyr* – intrudes into the relationship between the Kyn and the land, and seems to cause a breach in it, rendering them alien to each other. Tarsa realizes that this is not the case at a key point in the action: "This is no Melded world. It has always been out own. *This* is the Eld Green, all of it. They wanted us to forget, to believe that we didn't belong here."[52] A second central character, the Beast-Clan he-Kyn Tetawa Tobhi shares her realisation:

> The whole of this world … were the homeland of the Folk. [The Melding] hadn't brought the world of the Folk into the world of men. It had simply brought Men into the Eld Green, and they'd laid claim to it. And over the years as the Folk fell to the tyranny of Men and the lands beyond their Thresholds grew harsh and hostile, many forgot the truth and came to believe the lies men told to assure themselves of the right of conquest.[53]

When all the Folk remember the truth of how they and their land came into contact with humanity, they are able to defeat Vald, the Dreyd leader, and thwart his desire to destroy them all, while simultaneously forging a new home for themselves. The passage quoted above is one of the clearest anti-colonial statements in the trilogy; substituting real-world names for those of the Fantasy world makes the passage applicable to any colonised space.

Justice's series is arguably an example of what Bill Ashcroft characterises as postcolonial interpolation of history as it works towards establishing a "counter-discourse" to the colonialist nostalgia of Fantasy convention.[54] This occurs in part through anti-colonial statements and storylines as discussed above. The books also challenge the lie described by Justice: "part of the great lie of colonialism is the singular narrative, the singular vision."[55] There are many different peoples who have different relationships with the land and other beings among the Folk, including both not limited to the Tree-Born like Tarsa, Beast-Clan Tetawi like Tobhi, and the Gvaerg who are related to stone. The narrative, moreover, follows the stories of several different characters, and provides multiple different perspectives reflecting the diverse experiences of individuals and peoples in any colonial situation, including central characters who are female and queer. Tarsa forms a three-way loving relationship with the he-Kyn Daladir and the she-Kyn Jintadi,[56] while another character, Averyn, realises at the moment of remembering mentioned above: "The zhe-Kyn, like all the other zhe-Folk, was a between-worlder, neither male nor female, something other than both."[57] Justice says: "Anything that's intended to be anti-colonial, if it's going to be at all effective, has to take up the complexities and the multidimensionality of our lives."[58]

Justice is very positive about writing into Fantasy with indigenous perspectives and voices, but has also experienced first-hand some of the challenges of publishing such work. In a 2008 interview, he spoke about his unsuccessful attempts to find an agent for *The Way of Thorn and Thunder*: "One agent said to me, 'This is interesting and good, but I don't have any idea how I would market it.'"[59] He decided to approach a publisher specialising in indigenous writing – Kegedonce – instead of a mainstream genre press directly, even though it had not previously published speculative fiction. That agents would not represent the book, and could not conceive how to market it, demonstrates how extensively marginalized indigenous voices are in mainstream genre publishing, and popular culture more broadly. Justice's trilogy was published as an omnibus volume by the University of New Mexico Press in 2011, making it available to a wider audience than the resources of Kegedonce, a small press, could allow. He described the process of finding the new press: "I was at a conference and I was chatting with an acquisitions editor at University of New Mexico Press and she showed interest and I just followed it up from there."[60] It is worth noting that Dillon's *Walking the Clouds* collection was likewise not published by a genre-specific press, but with the University of Arizona Press.

While postcolonial writings of some authors of colour who are not indigenous – Jemisin with Orbit, and Saladin Ahmed and Okorafor with DAW/Penguin – have found outlets with major genre presses, indigenous authors have not yet had their work taken up. Crowd-funding, through websites such as Kickstarter, has enabled marginalized voices to be heard within the genre in recent years, with collections such as the previously mentioned *Long Hidden: Speculative Fiction from the Margins of History*, the forthcoming "Women Destroy Fantasy" special issue of *Lightspeed* magazine, and the cross-genre website *Strange Horizons*. I have been able to find, however, no similar ventures dedicated to indigenous voices either launched or funded at the time of writing.

One factor in Justice's decision to publish his trilogy with a small press in the first instance was that he was concerned a mainstream press would require changes:

> By adapting my work so that it would be accepted by a publisher like DAW, I might also run the risk of diluting the cultural content of my writing to the point that it wouldn't speak to anybody … there were certain things in my writing that I wasn't willing to compromise about.[61]

The prospects of finding a mainstream genre publisher for a new series he is currently writing, moreover, do not seem high to him:

> Women-centred queer-affirming people of colour fantasy, even though there's a huge market out there and a huge audience, publishers are less enthusiastic about that kind of weirdness. It's still white is right and patriarchs rule. So there are some publishers I think would be interested, but I'm not enthusiastic about my chances in terms of finding publishers that are really open to decolonial anti-racist work.[62]

The active silence about and forgetting of colonisation and its legacies that Ono, as cited above, finds in the United States' culture extends into realms of mainstream Fantasy publication even if they are being challenged at grass-roots level in the genre.

NAOMI NOVIK'S TEMERAIRE SERIES

Authors who are not indigenous have, in the past decade or so, begun slowly to engage in critical ways with colonisation and imperialism in Fantasy. Such moves can be fraught, and risk erasing or ignoring the traumas of the past by seeking to imagine alternative histories, and of committing inappropriate and counter-productive acts of cultural appropriation when indigenous perspectives or cultures are included in the narrative. As Wilkins says, "borrowing from indigenous culture cannot but be a political act."[63] Here I explore some of the ways in which Novik, a contemporary White American author, critiques colonialist ideologies and practices in her alternate world Temeraire series. At the time of writing, Novik's series is comprised of eight books, with a further novel planned.[64] It is set in a world like ours, but where dragons are real, sentient, and generally friendly to humans. The action takes place during the Napoleonic Wars, with Britain and France both possessing draconic air forces.

The series challenges nineteenth-century eurocentric assumptions about racial difference and White superiority by creating a world in which colonisation and imperialist expansion was much less successful than it was historically. Novik's works ask a "what if" question: What if European technology did not facilitate global domination? Technology was not the only factor in the success of European colonisation and imperial success, but it had a significant role, facilitating travel, communications, and military superiority.[65] Dragons in Novik's imagined world play a key role in all three areas, changing global power dynamics significantly and seeing some attempts at colonisation and imperialism completely defeated, others halted, and enabling the direct intervention of non-European powers in European internal politics. The "what if" question at the heart of the series gestures towards Alternate History, a sub-genre which "aligns itself with the science-fictional traits of the plausibility of its extrapolation and its scientifical approach to mimesis."[66] Novik's series is not, strictly speaking, Alternate History because that sub-genre centres on what arguably *could* have happened in the world in which we live, had one event in in history changed. The dragons she inserts, however, are natural not magical beings and the works follow the logic of Alternate History in their extrapolation of how a draconic presence might have affected historical events; the history rendered in the series can be termed an Alternate World.

It is extremely rare for Alternate Histories to change the history of European imperialism and colonisation, the legacies of which continue to affect the lives of nations and individuals around the globe.[67] The nature of the genre itself works against such a narrative being written. Alternate History "supports the Great Men theory of history" in which the actions of particular individuals, such as Adolf Hitler, at the very least, a major event, like a battle lost or won, provides the turning point. [68] The history of European imperialism provides, however, no convenient pivotal moment.[69]

Multiple series change *which* power builds an empire, including some which make that power non-European, but the domination itself remains constant.[70] The extreme paucity of works which imagine the world without a history of European domination shows just how firmly entrenched the ideologies which underpinned it remain in the modern day world. French victory in the Napoleonic War, the South winning the American Civil War, and even the sustained dominance of the Roman Empire are all conceivable, but a world *not* dominated by Europe is almost unthinkable. Doing so requires an entirely separate world to be imagined, as Novik does in her series, and as Hobb does in the *Soldier Son* trilogy. Fantasy thus offers the chance for the fetters of History to be broken in ways that Science Fiction forms seem unable achieve.

In Novik's series, dragons can – although do not always – form strong emotional bonds with humans if the right person is present when they hatch. The novels trace the adventures of one such pairing: Captain William Laurence, originally of the Royal Navy, and Temeraire, a rare Chinese breed of dragon whose egg was aboard a French vessel captured by Laurence's ship at the beginning of the first novel. The pair help to repel a French invasion of England during *His Majesty's Dragon*, and sail to China in *Throne of Jade*. They return overland by way of Turkey to collect a dragon egg the government has bought, and are caught up in the French invasion and defeat of Prussia before finally reaching England in *Black Powder War*. They discover that British dragons are infected with a fatal flu-type disease and are sent to South Africa to find a cure in *Empire of Ivory*. While there they encounter a sophisticated African civilization, the Tswana, in the parts of the continent hitherto unexplored by Europeans. The Tswana have been heavily impacted by the slave trade and are actively seeking to stop it and take revenge for its depredations. They destroy the colony at Cape Town doing so. Laurence and Temeraire return to England with the cure but Laurence is convicted of treason after they share it with the French, whose dragons were deliberately infected with the disease by the British.

Victory of Eagles sees them win a reprieve when they are instrumental in ejecting Napoleonic forces after a second, successful invasion attempt of England; they are exiled to the struggling colony of New South Wales. In *Tongues of Serpents* they unsuccessfully try to recapture a dragon egg stolen from the British by indigenous Australians. During their failed attempt to regain possession of the egg, they find that the Chinese have been trading into the northern parts of Australia, and that their influence spreads as far as the colony at Sydney. In *Crucible of Gold* they are sent to South America to help the Portuguese colony in Brazil against the Tswana who have arrived there in force seeking their enslaved peoples. They attempt to negotiate with the Inca – Spanish colonisation of South America was attempted but unsuccessful in this world, although diseases they brought have more than decimated the human population – but discover that they are allied with Napoleon, who has travelled there himself to marry the widowed Incan

ruler. In *Blood of Tyrants*, they lead a force of Chinese dragons overland to
help defeat Napoleon's invasion of Russia.

Temeraire and Laurence serve the British Crown throughout the series.
Even when Laurence has been dismissed from the military after being convicted of treason, they continue to action the interests of Britain. One of the
central challenges Novik faces, as a result, is the need to avoid valorizing
Britain's historical imperial ambitions.[71] Some explicit criticisms are voiced
in the text. A Chinese character remarks:

> From your small island you come to our country, and out of kind-
> ness you are allowed to buy our tea and silk and porcelain ... But still
> you are not content; you forever demand more and more, while your
> missionaries try to spread your foreign religion and your merchants
> smuggle opium in defiance of the law.[72]

Temeraire, hearing that the British claim sovereignty over the north coast of
Australia demonstrates the hollowness of the grounds on which the claim
is made, says:

> I do not see how this is reasonable: after all, it is stuff for the Regent
> to say we have claimed the country when the Larrakia are right here
> and have been for ages. Why, what if I were to land in London and say,
> "Very well, because I am the first Chinese dragon to land in London,
> now I will claim it for the Emperor," that has as much sense as this
> does.[73]

The most extended critique, however, is expressed through the alternate
vision of global history that the series constructs, based on the presence of
sentient, human-friendly dragons in most continents.

Making European powers less successful than they were historically is
a key move. The British colony at Cape Town is destroyed and Portuguese
holdings in Brazil are threatened by the Tswana, who also reach Gibraltar
in a proposed invasion of Europe before turning their attention across the
Atlantic. The protagonists do not travel to North America, so a detailed
re-imagining of colonisation there is not given, although there are clear
indications that it developed very differently to real-world history:
a Native American, Tecumseh, is president of the United States in *Blood
of Tyrants*. Australia is the sole site of successful colonisation by Britain in
the Temeraire series and even that colony is under threat: the colonists are
threatening to secede, in much the same manner as the US did historically,
over taxation without representation at the end of *Tongues of Serpents*.
The only dragons indigenous to Australia are bunyips which, far from
being friendly to humans, prey on them. Australia is the only continent on
earth where this is the case, and the lack of draconic resistance enables the
success of White settlement.

The indigenous peoples of Australia are almost completely absent; Laurence and Temeraire do not encounter them at the colony in Sydney, nor during the time they help expand it across the Blue Mountains to the west. They fly the length of the continent, passing major landmarks such as Uluru, during which time the indigenous people are not so much as glimpsed until they finally reach the northern shores. Nor do they encounter indigenous peoples on their trip back to Sydney. While several tribes are named as part of the trading network between Sydney and the Chinese outpost, none of them is more than peripheral to the narrative. No indigenous person, moreover, has a speaking part in the book; the dragon which hatches from the stolen egg speaks for them. Their theft of the egg from the British is designed to allow them to trade with the Chinese, and in narrative terms, serves largely to draw Laurence and Temeraire into an encounter with Chinese expansion. Representing the indigenous humans principally through their absence re-inscribes the domi- nant historical view of Australia as *terra nullius*, land belonging to no one, a construct which justified colonisation and an ideological and legal principle which still has a significant presence in Australia today.

The newly hatched dragon explains to Laurence that the local people are just one of the many indigenous nations which inhabit Australia and that the egg was stolen in part to facilitate transport, but chiefly for communication. Dragons learn language in the shell; the egg was passed through the hands of the many indigenous peoples so that its ability to speak to and understand all of them – as well as the English and Chinese – would overcome practical barriers to trade. The indigenous nations form a trading network, or better, a trading conduit, between the Chinese outpost, near to what is Darwin in this world, and the English colony in Sydney and its surrounds. Both land and people form a bridge, a crossing place between Orient and Occident in a fantasy of the smooth, and benevolent, spread of capitalism. The situation in the colonies is unresolved in the series at the time of writing, but there is an implication that the ability of the Australian indigenous peoples to buy and sell desirable goods will lead to less damaging and violent events than historically occurred. The retention of language is a particularly poignant re-writing of history; more than a hundred of the 250 indigenous languages of Australia were lost as the result of British colonisation, and most of those which remain are critically endangered.[74]

Not only are the indigenous humans absent, but the local dragons/ bunyips are represented principally through colonial-era stereotypes which construct the landscape of Australia as threatening. Their man-eating hab- its make them a constant threat, and they do not possess territory in the way that dragons on other continents do. Temeraire and Laurence literally colonise the land, considering it empty because they do not yet know of the bunyips, when they find a place to build a home. Temeraire says: "While it *is* strange there are no dragons here, it is very convenient not to always be wondering if something you happen to look at it already some-one else's territory, and they will be upset that you have taken one of their cows."[75]

There are bunyips – and indigenous humans – in the region they claim, but this fact makes no difference; even once they are aware of it, they take possession and impose their own rule on it by force in conventional colonising practice. At the beginning of *Crucible of Gold*, bunyips living in the valley they colonise are driven away by the threat of Temeraire's superior strength. Laurence says: "That is enough: be off, the lot of you, or we will clear your nest out to the bare rock."[76] Bunyips are decidedly unfriendly to humans, but they understand Laurence and Temeraire enough to show that they have some degree of sentience. Temeraire and Laurence have no better claim on the valley they settle in than that of the British Crown to the whole continent, which Temeraire dismisses as "stuff" in the passage quoted above; he fails to realise that he has performed the very act he considers absurd in taking the valley for his own.

Novik does not, however, fall into all of the pitfalls that face non-indigenous authors who write about indigenous cultures. Where the peoples and cultures that were subject to settler colonialism are explicitly referenced in Fantasy, they largely fulfil very limited roles in White-centred narratives. Brooke Collins-Gearing's insights into the ways that Australian indigenous peoples are commonly constructed in children's Fantasy resonate however; they "propagate the idea of dying race and/or a people in a timeless, remote past."[77] The "traditional" – read primitive – indigenous character, whatever people he or she is written to represent, is not the protagonist of any given story but is a helper to them, almost always a variation on the spirit guide trope, one who has access to magic and arcane knowledge which enables the protagonist to grow and complete their story-arc successfully.[78] Whiskey Jack in Neil Gaiman's *American Gods* (2001) is one example; a number of Charles de Lint's Urban Fantasy works also feature characters of this type. Novik's Aboriginal peoples collectively fit into this type. Their story – such as it is given their absence – exists only to further that of Laurence and Temeraire, although she does not represent them as having access to magic or spirituality that her other peoples do not. However, as active participants in the commercial transactions and merchant networks that structure international relations in that world, the indigenous peoples of Australia are shown as modern, not "primitive" or "timeless."

In addition to re-imagining history to disrupt the trade in human slaves across the Atlantic as noted above, the series also deploys slavery as an extended metaphor for human-dragon relations, particularly in England. *Throne of Jade* and later works see British ways challenged: Chinese dragons are fully integrated with human society, they live in the cities, earn wages, and are valued for their skills and intelligence as well as size and brute strength. In Incan and Tswana society alike, dragons are the protectors of humans, rather than being dominated and controlled by them. In contrast with China, in Britain and indeed most of Europe dragons are feared by most humans, permitted to live only in sequestered wilderness areas and kept as breeding stock if they are not actively serving in the military.

Temeraire recognises the injustice of such treatment, and remarks: "We are just like slaves; only there are fewer of us, and we are much bigger and dangerous, so we are treated generously where they are treated cruelly; but we are still not free."[79] The metaphor works strongly against racial logics that link physical characteristics with the non-physical; dragons possess the mental and emotional faculties of humans, Temeraire has "all that we believe is good about ... being human."[80] Dragons kept in chains – both literally and figuratively – and then being freed is a repeated motif throughout the series, notably in *Blood of Tyrants*. The extended metaphor speaks to racial prejudices and inequalities.

Ramón Saldívar argues that "the goal of ethnic writers is to imagine a state of achieved social justice." Further, he argues that the intrusion of fantasy into realist texts "compels our attention to the gap or deficit between the ideals of redemptive liberal democratic national histories ... and the deeds that have constituted nations and their histories as public collective fantasies."[81] While Saldívar is not concerned with the Fantasy genre specifically, his argument speaks to Fantasy's potential when it engages purposefully with received history as Novik's work does. Despite its problematic re-inscription of some aspects of colonialism in its account of Australia in particular, the series implies a state of achieved – or at least improved – social justice for the present of its Alternate World by imagining a past which would have fostered such an outcome, with a particular view to the colonisation of the globe by European powers. The gulf between received history and imagined histories highlights injustices of the past, but also of the present, in our own world, as close as it is to Novik's imagined one.

N. K. JEMISIN'S INHERITANCE TRILOGY

Where Novik's work problematizes the creation of Empire, a small but significant number of recent Fantasy works focus rather on its destruction and the challenges of escaping its legacies. These include Brandon Sanderson's Mistborn series (2006–2011);[82] Durham's Acacia trilogy (2007–2011);[83] and Jemisin's Inheritance series (2010–2014).[84] All three are set in premodern Secondary Worlds ruled, at the beginning of the series, by a long-established empire which is constructed not as the Othered empire of genre convention, but as what happens after a conventionally "good" victory. That is, the global rule of a dynasty whose power seemingly cannot be challenged, but which portrays itself as benevolent. The first book of all three series reveals the inherent oppression of empire, and sees the power upholding that of each world destroyed; the later two books explore the formation of a new and more just world order, ending with the hope of decentralised and relatively democratic government. All three explore the role of social and cultural institutions in maintaining political and ideological power, and include specific rejection of constructs of race-as-biology and racial superiority, which are woven into the structure of the empires. A detailed exploration of all three is beyond the scope of this chapter, so I focus on Jemisin's Inheritance trilogy – a Hugo, Nebula, and World Fantasy Award nominated work – as an illustrative example.

The trilogy takes places several millennia after a war between divinities has seen the god of the sun, order, and stability, Bright Itempas, kill one of his peers, Enefa, enslave others to the family of his chief priestess, the Arameri, and banish the rest from mortal realms. Able to command the enslaved gods, the Arameri have created a global theocracy in which only Itempas may be worshipped. In *The Hundred Thousand Kingdoms*, Yeine, the half-blood granddaughter of Dekarta, the head of the Arameri, by a "barbarian" Darren man from the northern kingdoms, is brought to the capital Sky and named one of the heirs. Brought into the vicious and sometimes deadly family power struggles, her presence and actions lead to the freeing of the enslaved gods, and Yeine herself becomes a god, taking on the power and role of the slain Enefa.

The Broken Kingdoms is set against the backdrop of attempts by the Arameri to maintain order and control when they can no longer command the formerly enslaved gods. Itempas has been forced to take on human form by those he had once enslaved, and all the gods have returned to mortal realms while humanity is slowly regaining some of the cultural and religious diversity it lost under the monotheist Arameri rule. Through the protagonist, Oree Shoth, who finds and cares for the human Itempas, details of the gods' war are slowly revealed, demonstrating the falsehoods that the Arameri had spread to justify their monotheistic rule. *The Kingdom of Gods* explores themes of change, vengeance and forgiveness through the character of Sieh, one of the gods who had been enslaved by the Arameri, as he becomes mortal and dies. *The Awakened Kingdom* is a novella, set decades after the events of the trilogy in which Shill, the first new godling for more than a millennium, discovers her name and nature while learning about the ways that gods and humans now interact in the mortal realms.

The theocracy of the Arameri is an empire, although it is only so named once in the trilogy, after the destruction of a continent at the hands of an enslaved god when one of the Arameri gives imprecise orders to suppress a rebellion. The Arameri's lost home was: "a beautiful country, the perfect seat for the capital of a global empire."[85] They maintain the pretence of only advising a council of nobles from the myriad kingdoms of the world after which the book is titled, but maintain social, political, and economic control through both the threat of violence and social institutions. Power is centralised in the capital, Sky. Both Justice's and Novik's works discussed above invoke settler colonialism – the "planting" of colonies and supplanting of local populations – but this is not the pattern in Jemisin's world.

In a 2010 interview, Jemisin remarked that "the way we write traditional epic fantasy now is making the whole genre look bad ... There's no reason for medieval Europe-based fantasies to be as boring as they are. It's time to shake things up."[86] The Inheritance trilogy subverts many of the tropes of epic Fantasy, writing back into many of them in ways which both reveal and critique colonialist ideologies within them. Empire, as discussed in the first and second chapter of this book, is always marked as Other in the medievalist worlds of epic Fantasy. The ultimate trajectory of conventional narrative, however, is of good triumphing over evil and ushering in an implied sustained era of stability and peace under the rule of a single realm. Aragorn's rule in Gondor at the end of *The Lord of the Rings* is one example; David Eddings' Belgariad and Malleorean series reveal that Eriond – once the boy Errand – is the rightful god of all humanity and will one day replace all the others. Jemisin's trilogy – like Durham's and Sanderson's – is situated millennia into such a regime, and demonstrates the oppression inherent in the imposition of imperial rule, even when its own ideologies work to present it as benevolent.

The Arameri circulate an account of the gods' war which casts Itempas as the rightful ruler of the universe and a benevolent saviour of humankind from the chaos of the other gods. According to their version of the gods' war, Itempas was the rightful ruler of creation, but his sister Enefa and brother Nahadoth conspired with some of their children to overthrow him, but:

> Itempas, mightier than both His siblings combined, defeated them soundly. He slew Enefa, punished Nahadoth and the rebels, and established an even greater peace – for without His dark brother and wild sister to appease, He was free to bring true light and order to all creation.[87]

In the first novel Nahadoth reveals to Yeine that this is false, that it was Itempas who was jealous of Enefa because Nahadoth loved her and not just him, an account Itempas confirms in the second book.[88] The ideological justification for the rule of the Arameri, known as the Bright because Itempas' status as the god of the sun, is exposed as a lie which had been specifically designed to justify their rule. This references the way in which racial hierarchies developed in the eighteenth and nineteenth centuries largely to justify European imperialism and the domination and acquisition of land, resources, and labour by claiming White racial superiority over all other peoples of the world. The story, moreover, still circulates and has power in the second novel after the freeing of Nahadoth and the other enslaved gods takes away the core of the Arameri's power, echoing the ongoing power of racist ideologies in contemporary society, decades after the end of official colonial rule.

The rule of the Arameri is revealed as inherently hypocritical and corrupt. It maintains stability, stasis, and a veneer of global peace only through the threat, and occasional act, of violence. Any rebellion against their rule is met with destruction and genocide: "There are strange and new plagues. Occasionally the population of an entire city will vanish overnight."[89] The Bright erased diversity, particularly religious diversity. Before the gods' war, "there were many temples but few holy texts, and no persecution of those with differing beliefs."[90] A strict monotheism is maintained under the Bright, although a certain level of cultural difference is permitted. Yeine's people the Darre are matriarchal for example, unlike their neighbours, but they are forced to change their sacred places and modes of worship. This monotheism crumbles and reverts to polytheism, once the gods return to mortal realms; and people are no longer forced to worship or pay tithes to Itempas' temples and priests. The second and third books in the trilogy are deeply concerned with the disorder that follows the toppling of a dominant rule and political system, even when that rule is not as benevolent as it claims to be.

In the Inheritance trilogy, the logic of race-as-biology is distilled and attached to the Arameri family; individuals have power and privilege in the world because of their membership of this related group. Yeine's first hours in the palace Sky, from which the Arameri rule the world, reveal that merely being a blood relation, even a close one, does not however grant her access to the source of their power – the ability to command enslaved gods. Rather, that is given through the application of a "blood sigil" which all recognised members of the family have on their foreheads in various forms that indicate their place within it and their level of power. The mark itself is literally a sign of privilege, signifying not only access to power, but safety from the violence that lies under the surface of the apparently peaceful Arameri rule. Before Yeine has her mark drawn, one of the rival heirs sets an enslaved god to chase her through the corridors of Sky and kill her, a command that can only be countermanded by another fullblood. Another character, T'vril, explains to her: "Lord Dekarta has decreed that you are to receive a fullblood mark. You are of the Central Family. I am a mere halfblood."[91] He, like Yeine, is closely related by blood to Dekarta, but has not been assigned a place in the inner circles of the family and serves as a steward. The contrast between their situations reflects the arbitrary and inherently unstable nature of racial divisions.

The Arameri, and indeed all the peoples of Jemisin's world, do not align precisely with the phenotypes of the real world; they are members of the Amn race, and described as "tall and pale" and generally dark haired.[92] The nature of their rule, which is designed to reflect the core nature of Itempas, is aligned in multiple ways with the Western colonialist thought and values even though they are not somatically White. A statue of Itempas "in one of his most famous poses, the Appeal to Human Reason" overlooks the meeting room of the powerless council of nobles.[93] Control over the emotions, meanwhile, is a core tenet of the Arameri's values, and they are trained to maintain it in all situations. Shahar, their last ruler remarks, for example, "By my training, I should never have smiled."[94] The Itempan privileging of rationality and order resonates with colonialist paradigms that constructed Whites as rational and people of colour as inherently irrational and uncontrolled.

The Arameri construct the order they impose as being a duty for them: "All descendants of Shahar Arameri must serve," T'vril tells Yeine.[95] The concept of "the White man's burden," which in Rudyard Kipling's eponymous poem represented colonisation and imperialism as a duty and the imposition of Western ways and values as a service to the colonised, underlies this. Usein, a rebel leader in *The Kingdom of Gods,* says bitterly, "Even the history taught to our children in the White Hall schools glorifies them and denigrates everyone else. *All civilization*, every bit of it, is made to keep the Arameri strong."[96] She later tells Remath, then the head of the Arameri, that "Peace is meaningless without freedom"; Remath responds, "I doubt the children who starved to death, before the Bright, would agree." The hypocrisy of Remath's position does not go unchallenged however, as Usein retorts: "And I doubt the races and heretics your family have destroyed would consider the Bright *peace*."[97] The comments can be read as reflections on real world discourses which construct Western society and culture as civilized, and all other ways of life as barbaric or underdeveloped, but gloss over the violence inherent in colonial and imperial rule.

The action of *The Broken Kingdoms* pivots on the offspring of humans and gods, known as demons, which are "neither one or the other, possessing the greatest gifts of both," including mortality.[98] The blood of demons can kill gods; as Nahadoth tells Yeine, "it was the only poison that could harm us."[99] The gods sought to destroy them all, and Nahadoth believed that only one survived, hidden by Itempas who used its blood to kill Enefa. Their attempt at genocide was not successful, as Oree Shoth, the protagonist of the second novel and herself a demon, is told by another: "It was foolish for them to fight, really, given the gods' power. Some of the demons no doubt realised this, and hid instead."[100] This is precisely what Oree herself does, with the help of the Arameri who have taken some of her blood as insurance, at the end of the novel, along with a child she bears to Itempas. The danger that results from the miscegenetic mixing of mortal and immortal blood could be read as indicative of fear of hybridity and impurity. The attempt by the gods to destroy the demon hybrids of god and human, however, is presented as not only unsuccessful but disastrous for them because it leads ultimately to their war amongst themselves. In the final book, moreover, Sieh uses a dagger coated in demon blood to kill the god of Vengeance and save both the mortal and divine realms from destruction,[101] while in *The Awakened Kingdoms* the demons play a key role in managing interactions between mortals and gods.

The second and third books in the trilogy, and the novella which follows it, are chiefly concerned with the slow collapse of the Arameri hegemony once they no longer command divine power, and with the challenges of creating a social and political order, first among humanity and then including the gods. In both novels, a single being seeks to become a god and claim power, but is foiled, leaving the peoples of the world – humans and gods alike – to negotiate a way forward. The last head of the Arameri family announces at the end of *The Kingdom of Gods* that they will abdicate power:

> Not to be distributed among the nobles, however, which would only invite chaos and war. Instead, we would give the bulk of our treasury, and management of our armies, to a single new governing body ... [comprised of] the priest, the scriveners, the godlings, the merchants, the nobles, the common folk. All of them.[102]

This is a strikingly unconventional in Fantasy terms precisely because political, economic, and military power is transferred to a group that is, if not democratically elected, nonetheless representative of the diversity of peoples in that world. Genre convention would suggest a single ruler, but the logic of Jemisin's world rejects this. All three books work against the imposition of a single rule and ruler, human or divine.

Jemisin blogged in 2011 about the influence of postcolonial thought on the published version of *The Hundred Thousand Kingdoms* compared to the first version of the novel she wrote more than a decade previously, citing among other influences Hopkinson and Meehan's anthology *So Long Been Dreaming*. She writes: "I didn't make a conscious choice to tackle the subject of colonialism" in the trilogy, but "developed the worldbuilding in a way that made sense to me."[103] The changes she mentions are largely at the level of world-building, and make the series, darker and more "gritty." A key change she lists as having been made in the light of postcolonial approaches to Science Fiction and Fantasy is increase in the level of racial and cultural diversity among humans after two millennia of Itempan rule. The new form of government, named the Aeternat, to which the Arameri devolve most of their economic, military, and political power, includes the leaders of multiple different nations with very different cultures.

The vision of the post-imperial future Jemisin offers at the end of her trilogy is essentially a cosmopolitan one in which a global community values its own diversity. The threat of chaos if the rule of the Arameri is destroyed hangs over the final book. Sieh, one of the formerly enslaved gods tells Usein, "I remember when Darre infants starved in their cribs because enemies burned your forests. I remember rivers with water tinted red ... Is that really what you want to return to?"[104] The binary opposition of order and chaos – facets of the natures of Itempas and Nahadoth – is invoked by multiple characters throughout the trilogy; but at the levels of world building and narrative the dichotomy is revealed to be fundamentally meaningless. Justice, as quoted above, says "the great lie of colonialism is the singular narrative, the singular vision;"[105] Jemisin's trilogy, and the novella that follows, work against singularity of narrative and being.

CONCLUSION

Postcolonial theorist Homi Bhabha states that: "postcolonial criticism bears witness to the unequal and uneven forces of cultural representation involved in the contest for political and social authority within the modern order."[106] Critiquing real-world history through a popular genre, at the same time as critiquing the history of that genre's conventions, is a contest enacted at the heart of Western popular culture. The turn away from medievalist conventions that is a feature of such works – even Jemisin's pre-modern world is decidedly not in the Middle Ages – reflects the depth of colonialist and racial logics that structure much of the genre. If imagining the future a *raison d'etre* for Science Fiction, the popular culture postcolonialism evinced in these and other Fantasy texts re-imagines the past not only to reflect on its violent injustices, but to gesture towards a more equitable future in the process.

NOTES

1. Young, *The Idea of English Ethnicity*.
2. Fanon, *The Wretched of the Earth*, 162.
3. "White," as discussed in the Introduction, changes its precise meaning with time and place. In the British empire and its colonies, for example the Irish were generally not considered White during the nineteenth century and the term was usually equated with Anglo-Saxonism.
4. Ono, *Contemporary Media Culture and the Remnants of a Colonial Past*, 4.
5. Jackson, *Fantasy: The Literature of Subversion*, 175.
6. Shohat and Stam, *Unthinking Eurocentrism: Multiculturalism and the Media*, 68.
7. For example, Attebery, "Aboriginality in Science Fiction"; Csicsery-Ronay, "Science Fiction and Empire"; Dillon, "Diaspora Narrative in *Battlestar Galactica*"; Hoagland and Sarwal, *Science Fiction, Imperialism and the Third World*; Rieder, *Colonialism and the Emergence of Science Fiction*.
8. Wilkins, "'Cutting off the Head of the King': Sovereignty, Feudalism, Fantasy," 140.
9. Haley, "Fantasy Family Tree," 46–49.
10. Sturgis and Oberhelman, *The Intersection of Fantasy and Native America: From H. P. Lovecraft to Leslie Marmon Silko*.
11. I discuss the coding of orcs as indigenous in a range of games and novels in chapter four.
12. Fantasy writers have drawn on and appropriated Native American cultures since at least Charles de Lint's 1984 novel *Moonheart*, although not generally to engage with colonisation and its impacts.
13. Glazier and Seo, "Multicultural Literature and Discussion and Mirror and Window?"
14. For example, Balfe, "Incredible Geographies? Orientalism and Genre Fantasy"; Knaus, "More White Supremacy? *The Lord of the Rings* as Pro-American Imperialism"; Sturgis and Oberhelman, *The Intersection of Fantasy*

and Native America; Winegar, "Aspects of Orientalism in J.R.R. Tolkien's *The Lord of the Rings*."

15. For example, Alessio, "From Body Snatchers to Mind Snatchers: Indigenous Science Fiction, Postcolonialism, and Aotearoa/New Zealand History"; Ramraj, "Nalo Hopkinson's Colonial and Dystopic Worlds in *Midnight Robber*."

16. I am grateful to Assistant Professor Kwaymullina for sharing her thoughts and directing me to a number of published essays, and to Dr Gillian Polack for putting me in touch with her.

17. Jemisin, "Considering Colonialism."

18. Gayatri Chakravorty Sivak's essay of this title is one of the foundational works of postcolonial theory. Spivak, "Can the Subaltern Speak?" It is available at http://www.mcgill.ca/files/crclaw-discourse/Can_the_subaltern_speak.pdf.

19. Attebery, *Stories about Stories: Fantasy and the Remaking of Myth*, 170–173.

20. Young, "Critiques of Colonialism in Robin Hobb's *Soldier Son* Trilogy."

21. Bradford, *Reading Race: Aboriginality in Austrsalian Children's Literature*, 130. Attebery defends Wrightson, arguing that she actively tried not speak for indigenous peoples, in "Patricia Wrightson and Aboriginal Myth." The books in question, however, are now out of print in Australia despite being very successful at the time of publication in the 1970s-1980s, suggesting some discomfort with them amongst publishers.

22. The full list is: "Octavia E. Butler, Diane Duane, Gael Baudino, Tobias S. Buckell, Nalo Hopinkson, Ellen Kushner, Samuel R. Delany, Caitlín R. Kiernan, Lawrence Schimel ... N. K Jemisin ... Sheree Renée Thomas ... and M. Christian." Fox and Older, "Introduction," i. The biographies for contributors to the collection generally do not specify an author's backgrounds, and there are none who state that they identify as indigenous.

23. See page 4 in the introduction.

24. Interview with Daniel Heath Justice, conducted via Skype, 24th October 2014. He mentioned Blake Hausman and Celu Amberstone, both Cherokee authors.

25. Hopkinson and Meehan, *So Long Been Dreaming: Postcolonial Science Fiction and Fantasy*.

26. Wilkins, "'Cutting off the Head of the King,'" 138.

27. For a detailed discussion of the historical, current, and future challenges facing indigenous peoples around the world, see Carino et al., *State of the World's Indigenous Peoples*.

28. Interview.

29. Interview.

30. Oberhelman, "'Coming to America': Fantasy and Native America Explored, an Introduction," iv.

31. Wilkins, "'Cutting off the Head of the King,'" 133; Attebery, "Aboriginality in Science Fiction," 387.

32. Dillon, *Walking the Clouds: An Anthology of Indigenous Science Fiction*.

33. It is telling that the only collection of speculative stories written by indigenous authors to date, Dillon's *Walking the Clouds*, is specifically titled as "Science Fiction."

34. Sturgis, "Meeting at the Intersection: The Challenges Before Us," 11–12. For an author's account of this kind of categorization, from an African American perspective, see Jemisin, "Don't Put My Book in the African American Section."

35. Sturgis, "Meeting at the Intersection," 12.

36. Kwaymullina, "Guest of Honour Speech, from Continuum X."

37. Kwaymullina, "Edges, Centres, and Futures: Reflections on Being an Indigenous Speculative Fiction Writer," 23–24.

38. Dillon, "Imagining Indigenous Futurisms," 3.

39. Alessio, "From Body Snatchers to Mind Snatchers," 259.

40. Dillon, "Imagining Indigenous Futurisms," 5.

41. Interview.

42. Interview.

43. Loomba, *Colonialism/Postcolonialism*, 11.

44. Justice, *The Way of Thorn and Thunder*, pt. 2008.

45. For example, Oberhelman, "Review of Daniel Heath Justice *The Way of Thorn and Thunder*," 119; Washburn, "*The Way of Thorn and Thunder: The Kynship Chronicles* by Daniel Heath Justice," 401. See also the Goodreads and Amazon review pages for general readers' responses.

46. Oberhelman, "Review of Daniel Heath Justice *The Way of Thorn and Thunder*," 119.

47. Justice, *The Way of Thorn and Thunder: The Kynship Chronicles*, pt. 3031. Skull measurement was a key tool for "proving" White superiority over colonised peoples in the nineteenth century, Sussman, *The Myth of Race: The Troubling Persistence of an Unscientific Idea*, 31.

48. Justice, *The Way of Thorn and Thunder*, pt. 18248.

49. Mendlesohn, *Rhetorics of Fantasy*, xix.

50. Mendlesohn, *Rhetorics of Fantasy*, 9.

51. Justice, *The Way of Thorn and Thunder*, pt. 22015.

52. Justice, *The Way of Thorn and Thunder*, pt. 20881.

53. Justice, *The Way of Thorn and Thunder*, pt. 20905.

54. Ashcroft, *Postcolonial Transformation*, 109.

55. Interview.

56. Justice, *The Way of Thorn and Thunder*, pt. 17944.

57. Justice, *The Way of Thorn and Thunder*, pt. 20905.

58. Personal interview.

59. Amberstone, "Interview With First Nations Fantasy Author Daniel Heath Justice."

60. Interview.

61. Amberstone, "Interview With First Nations Fantasy Author Daniel Heath Justice."

62. Interview.

63. Wilkins, "'Cutting off the Head of the King,'" 136. This is true of all marginalized identities, not just racial ones. The question of cultural appropriation is taken up further in the following chapter.

64. *His Majesty's Dragon* (2006); *Throne of Jade* (2006); *Black Powder War* (2006); *Empire of Ivory* (2007); *Victory of Eagles* (2008); *Tongues of Serpents* (2010); *Crucible of Gold* (2012); *Blood of Tyrants* (2013); and the forthcoming *League of Dragons* (2015).

65. Headrick, *The Tools of Empire. Technology and European Imperialism in the Nineteenth Century*. Technology is still a critical aspect of its legacies, and neo-colonialism in the twenty-first century.

66. Ransom, "Warping Time: Alternate Histories, Historical Fantasy, and the Postmodern Uchronie Quebecoise," 260. The Amazon "Alternate History" set is located in both "Fantasy" and "Science Fiction," demonstrating the difficulties of critical, audience, and marketing overlap.

67. Eric Flint's *1812: The Rivers of War* and *1824: The Arkansas War* are one exception. They reimagine parts of American history - the Trail of Tears and

the Civil War specifically – but find ways to ameliorate and avoid only some of the worst excesses of American colonialism and slavery.

68. Ransom, "Warping Time," 261.
69. Orson Scott Card's *Pastwatch: The Redemption of Christopher Columbus* (1996) is the only near exception I have found to date, but is a time travel story not an Alternate History; the future intervenes in the past via a time machine rather than a past event occurring differently.
70. S. M. Stirling's *The Domination* (1988–90) sees the British take over from the Dutch in South Africa during the American War of Independence rather than in 1802, for example. Steven Barnes' *Insh'Allah* series makes Islamic Africa not Christian Europe the centre of global technology and power in the nineteenth century, but re-inscribes the colonisation of the Americas, changing the perpetrators but not the process.
71. Scheurer and Scheurer, "The Far Side of the World: Naomi Novik and the Blended Genre of Dragon Fantasy and the Sea Adventure," 579.
72. Novik, *Throne of Jade*, 162.
73. Novik, *Tongues of Serpents*, 294. Scheurer and Scheurer observe that Temeraire acts as a "foil" to Laurence's and other conservative views throughout the series, providing "modern perspectives that validate contemporary reader values and expectations" in "The Far Side of the World," 587.
74. AUSTLANG, "Frequently Asked Questions."
75. Novik, *Tongues of Serpents*, 114–115.
76. Novik, *Crucible of Gold*, 6.
77. Collins-Gearing, "Imagining Indigenality in Romance and Fantasy Fiction for Children," 32.
78. There is much in common with the "magical negro" trope pilloried by Okorafor in her short story "The Magical Nero" in the collection *Kabu Kabu* (2013).
79. Novik, *Throne of Jade*, 496.
80. Scheurer and Scheurer, "The Far Side of the World," 587.
81. Saldivar, "Historical Fantasy, Speculative Realism, and Postrace Aesthetics in Contemporary American Fiction," 593–4.
82. *Mistborn* (2006), *The Well of Ascension* (2007), *Hero of Ages* (2008), and the novella *The Alloy of Law* (2011) which is set several centuries after the trilogy, published by Tor Books, a division of MacMillan Publishers.
83. *The War With the Mein* (2007), *The Other Lands* (2009), and *The Sacred Band* (2011), published by Anchor Books, a division of Random House.
84. *The Hundred Thousand Kingdoms* (2010), *The Broken Kingdoms* (2010), *The Kingdom of Gods* (2011), and the novella *The Awakened Kingdom* (2014), published by Orbit, a division of the Hachette Book Group.
85. Jemisin, *The Hundred Thousand Kingdoms*, 55.
86. "N.K. Jemisin: Rites of Passage."
87. Jemisin, *The Hundred Thousand Kingdoms*, 117.
88. Jemisin, *The Broken Kingdoms*, 128–129.
89. Jemisin, *The Hundred Thousand Kingdoms*, 14.
90. Jemisin, *The Broken Kingdoms*, 134.
91. Jemisin, *The Hundred Thousand Kingdoms*, 17. The mark also prevents those who bear it from acting directly against the head of the family.
92. Jemisin, *The Hundred Thousand Kingdoms*, 7.
93. Jemisin, *The Hundred Thousand Kingdoms*, 5.

94. Jemisin, *The Kingdom of Gods*, 565.
95. Jemisin, *The Hundred Thousand Kingdoms*, 19.
96. Jemisin, *The Kingdom of Gods*, 266.
97. Jemisin, *The Kingdom of Gods*, 514.
98. Jemisin, *The Broken Kingdoms*, 134.
99. Jemisin, *The Hundred Thousand Kingdoms*, 117.
100. Jemisin, *The Broken Kingdoms*, 213.
101. Jemisin, *The Kingdom of Gods*, 560.
102. Jemisin, *The Kingdom of the Gods*, 561.
103. She cites the influence of Hopkinson and Meehan's *So Long Been Dreaming* anthology mentioned above. Jemisin, "Considering Colonialism."
104. Jemisin, *The Kingdom of Gods*, 265.
105. Interview.
106. Bhabha, *The Location of Culture*, 131.

6 Relocating Roots
Urban Fantasy

The rise of Fantasy as a major publication category and the development of medievalist European worlds from inspiration into convention was attended, like all such habits, with the desire *not* to conform. As Brian Attebery states, one of the key motivations for seeking different inspirations is "the desire to avoid simple imitation."[1] Gritty Fantasy, as discussed in chapter three, repeatedly asserts its own difference from Tolkienian imitation, while the modern settings of Urban Fantasy seem to reject the medievalist mode altogether. A third clear trend which also had its beginnings in the late twentieth century but has emerged more strongly in the twenty-first, is the creation of settings which are pre-modern, but not European. Some, like Guy Gavriel Kay's novels and N. K. Jemisin's *Dreamblood* (2012) books, are Secondary Worlds inspired by real world historical cultures. Others have some resemblance to Urban Fantasy in that they are historical versions of our world in which magic, gods and other mythical beings exist alongside humanity. Kij Johnson's *The Fox Woman* (2000) and *Fudoki* (2004), both set in Japan, are early examples. More recent ones include Aliette de Bodard's *Obsidian and Blood* novels (2010–2011) set in the Aztec empire, and Saladin Ahmed's *Throne of the Crescent Moon* (2012) and Howard Andrew Jones' *The Desert of Souls* (2012) set in the medieval Middle East.[2]

The ways in which such works are grouped together illuminates the habits of Whiteness that still structure Fantasy even at times when active attempts are being made to break them. One recommended reading list, compiled in 2013 by author Juliette Wade, titled "Beyond the Same-Old Fantasy Culture," was made for readers who are looking for something "outside the tried-and-true Tolkien-inspired fantasy model" and lists works with specifically "non-Western" settings.[3] The settings are described as: "fantasy-Africa" (Nnedi Okorafor); "ancient Egypt" (Jemisin); "cultures of the Islamic world" and "Islamic-inspired" (Jones and Ahmed); "dreamy fantasy alt-China" (Daniel Fox); "Russian culture" and "Russian inspired" (Brad Beaulieu, Leigh Bardugo, and Jane Kindred); and "Japanese culture and mythology" (Johnson). The framing of these settings as collectively "non-Western" – even though some detail is given for each – illustrates that a binary division is assumed to be in place within the genre, one where the medievalist Western setting – which stands for Whiteness – is the norm, the Self, defined against the collective Otherness of diverse temporal and cultural locations. "Non-Western" and "non-medieval" are frequently used to label such lists.[4]

In the previous chapter I explored works which critiqued European colonialism and imperialism, all of which avoided medievalist conventions. Here I consider further the ways in which moves away from those conventions – some of which have been concerted enough as to create their own set – impact on Fantasy's habits of Whiteness, working variously to strengthen or break them. I begin with an exploration of Urban Fantasy, a sub-genre which developed first in the 1980s and 1990s but has burgeoned in the twenty-first century, considering American television first before expanding to include novels from both sides of the Atlantic, comparing and contrasting media forms and locations. I then turn to the politics of writing the kinds of diverse settings mentioned above to consider questions of identity and cultural appropriation.

URBAN FANTASY

Alienation – the absence or loss of identity – in modern society as both felt in and caused by city spaces has a long history in Western literature and thought. The metropolis is understood as both symbol and manifestation of the problems of modernity: "loneliness, isolation, fragmentation, alienation"[5] – all of which might be characterized as identity trouble. Tolkien and his followers turned to the medieval in search of authentic identity, while Urban Fantasy also looks to the past in search of identity, but brings that past forward into the present, populating the streets of small towns and cities with the beings of folklore and mythology. Siobhan Carroll argues that Urban Fantasy has a "preoccupation with place," and that by locating folklore within modern cities, it "assert[s] continuity with a historical past,"[6] and seeks to heal some of the identity troubles resulting from urbanization.

There are two major trends in the very broad field of Urban Fantasy: imagined, fantastic cities such as Terry Pratchett's Ankh-Morpork which are usually part of a Secondary World; and "a more or less recognizable city," such as London, Portland, or Hong Kong, which is "in contact with the realm of Faerie, or some magical realm."[7] The first has a very long history reaching back to Plato's *Republic* and Thomas More's *Utopia* (1516), and Samuel R. Delany's Nevèrÿon series in the genre. The second is newer, it became an identifiable trend in the 1980s and 1990s. Early examples included Emma Bull's *War for the Oaks* (1987), the novels of Charles de Lint, and Neil Gaiman's *Neverwhere* (1996). In this chapter I am interested in the latter kind, that is, in works which are set in approximately contemporary versions of the real world, which I term Suburban Fantasy to delineate it within the broader sub-genre.

Suburban Fantasy is not limited to works which have city settings and engage more or less with the nature of the metropolis. It also includes the literally suburban, but also the sub-urban – what lies beneath – both literally and figuratively. Thus, the supernatural might come from underground – as it often does in *Buffy the Vampire Slayer*, one of the early and influential television texts in the set – but might equally be a product of the history of a place, be it migration, colonisation, indigenous history, war, famine, the past of the protagonist, or some combination of these. Suburban Fantasy, with its intrusions of the supernatural, can be understood as the suppressed history of modernity resurfacing. If the metropolis – the urban – always signifies modernity, the sub-urban explores what lies beneath and beyond it in the sewers, suburbs, and small towns of modern Western nations.

The common elements of Urban Fantasy also characterize the sub-set of Suburban Fantasy: "a city in which supernatural events occur, the presence of prominent characters who are artists or musicians or scholars, the redeployment of previous fantastic and folkloric topoi in unfamiliar contexts."[8] To this list of occupations I would add the broad "detective," meaning police officer, private investigator, and occasionally a spy.[9] All create meaning from chaos and disorder: artists and musicians manage emotions and creative forces;[10] scholars systematize information; detectives reveal the unknown. They are all agents of different kinds of order: the artist of the personal; the scholar of cultural and scientific information;[11] and detectives of social order. Suburban Fantasy always fits into Farah Mendlesohn's rhetorical category of "intrusion fantasy" which:

> takes us out of safety without taking us from our place ... it has at its base the assumption that normality is organized, and that when the fantastic retreats the world, while not necessarily unchanged, returns to predictability – at least until the next element of the fantastic intrudes.[12]

In Suburban Fantasy, the intrusion – disorder – comes at least initially from the presence of "the re-deployment of previous fantastic and folkloric topoi" in literal form – usually but not always corporeal form at that. Gods, monsters, and Faerie of various kinds are real. A common conceit is that a given work is revealing the hidden truth behind folklore and mythology. This becomes a way of managing the threat posed by the intrusion through fitting it into an existing body of knowledge; scholars and books play a key role here, while scientific frames are also increasingly employed.[13] That the unknown becomes known is a key difference from Horror, particularly that of the Lovecraftian kind in which the "weird" is frightening precisely because it is incomprehensible by rational faculties.

PORTABLE STORIES

Angela Carter writes "stories have seeded themselves around the globe not because we all share the same imagination and experience but because stories are portable, part of the invisible luggage people take with them when they leave home."[14] This is true, but it is not the whole truth. The people who tell stories – particularly the orally transmitted tales that Carter collected in her book – are individuals, but in the global movement of peoples, individuals rarely move strictly alone but are more often part of a diaspora, voluntary or forced, comprised of hundreds, thousands, and hundreds of thousands of other individuals from a similar background going to the same place. When they take shared stories – folktales, legends, myths, history – with them, that invisible luggage changes the nature of their home when it is unpacked, maintaining a connection with the old, but also reshaping the new. The folkloric traditions which are characteristically reworked in Suburban Fantasy are precisely these portable stories.

America on the Small Screen

Since the last years of the twentieth century, a significant number of Suburban Fantasy television programs have been produced in North America and principally for that market, although most have also been shown elsewhere. They feature the motif of a protagonist – or more than one – who, as a teen or adult, is made aware of their magical heritage and the existence of a supernatural world which overlaps with the mundane one in which they have been raised: *Buffy the Vampire Slayer* (1997–2003) and its spinoff *Angel* (1999–2004);[15] *Charmed* (1998–2006); *True Blood* (2008–2012); *Lost Girl* (2010–2015); *Once Upon a Time* (2011–current); *Grimm* (2011–current); and *Sleepy Hollow* (2013–current) are among the best known.

Whiteness is a dominant feature of casting in almost all of these programs; only *Sleepy Hollow* features a majority of characters of colour in leading roles. The Whiteness of the characters and cast of *Buffy* has been variously remarked on.[16] Placing Black characters in supporting roles is by far the most common way of attempting to include some racial diversity, such as in *Angel*, *Grimm*, *Lost Girl*, and *True Blood*. Compared with cable television more broadly, this overall pattern of Whiteness does not stand out as notably bad or good, but rather reflects the much broader picture. A 2013 report, based on evidence conducted in the US in 2011–2012 when all but the earliest three of these programs were showing, found that minorities collectively comprised 36.3 per cent of the population, but only 15 per cent of lead roles in cable television programs, and 11 per cent in broadcast programs.[17] Decisions about casting and character – and all other aspects of production – in commercial television programming are widely understood to be driven primarily by what will generate a profit, which, in television terms, equates to audience numbers. The same report, however, shows that median household ratings for both cable and broadcast television were highest for programs which "reflect the nation's racial diversity" of 30–40 per cent of minority character, and significantly lower for programs with 10 per cent or less.[18] Market forces, which neoliberal societies like the US and much of the Western world claim drive the production of culture, have not corrected the imbalance of racial representation on American commercial television.

Suburban Fantasy television presents identity as a fraught category, and explores to some degree the different forces that act on an individual – biological, social, familial – in the process of identity construction. As Buffy says: "I'm cookie dough. I'm not done baking. I'm not finished becoming whoever the hell it is I'm gonna turn out to be."[19] They also, however, present identity as inherent, and often inherited. The protagonist must integrate the different aspects of their nature – the mundane and the supernatural – into a coherent whole. The NBC website describes *Grimm* in terms of a conventional crime drama, and emphasizes the competing forces pulling at the protagonist: "after Portland homicide detective Nick Burkhardt ... discovers he's descended from an elite line of criminal profilers known as 'Grimms,' he increasingly finds his responsibilities as a detective at odds with his new responsibilities as a Grimm."[20] Identity is not just a matter of inheritance, but Nick is always still a Grimm, and Buffy is always a Slayer. The supernatural identity which intrudes into their mundane lives is, in this sense, essentialized; a given and inescapable part of their being. It is suppressed for their early lives, but once revealed, cannot be escaped.

Matthew Frye Jacobson argues that in contemporary American culture, ethnicity may be suppressed – sometimes defensively – but not lost, it "is essentialized and stable" as a category of identity.[21] The same is true for these television protagonists: their difference from the rest of humanity is only ever newly *known* or understood, never newly acquired. Essentialized identity constructs are not inherently racial in the contemporary popular imagination any more than all struggles with identity formation are. Some Suburban Fantasy engages with "identity" in a generalized way, while others – notably *Charmed*, *Buffy*, and *Lost Girl* – are particularly interested in female gender and sexuality. Overt engagements with race and ethnicity are rare. Nonetheless, the underlying structures are arguably racialized. Most of the protagonists, as noted above, inherit their supernatural identity components biologically, that is, through their family.[22] Race, in twenty-first-century Western society is the category of identity most closely linked to descent by far: neither gender nor sexuality, for example, are generally considered to be carried through multiple generations of a family line even when they are constructed as essentialized and biological. Moreover, the inherited powers, while sometimes specific to the protagonist's family, always force him or her to engage with a much wider supernatural world with its own rules and mores. The family is not alone in its identity, but is one of many which share it. Thus, even those programs which do engage with identity constructs like sexuality and gender, do so through a racialized lens.

The storylines of Suburban Fantasy television add a layer of meaning to the White-centric casting and characterisation of the majority of these programs. The supernatural is always dangerous, not just to the protagonist's sense of identity and being, but to their very life, and almost invariably to the mundane human world – often although not invariably to the extent of Apocalypse. The protagonist is variously charged with controlling that danger and protecting humanity and are always exceptional: the Halliwell sisters of *Charmed* as the most powerful witches ever to live; in *Sleepy Hollow* Ichabod Crane and Abbie Mills are the two "witnesses" who can avert the coming of the Apocalypse; Buffy saves the world so many times that her once boyfriend Riley Finn comments, "I suddenly find myself needing to know the plural of Apocalypse."[23] As these programs represent it, averting the Apocalypse always requires not just the presence but the active participation of a White person. There are various helpers of colour, but only Abbie Mills is exceptional enough to be fundamentally necessary to saving humanity.

Beings marked as indigenous to the American landscape are always threatening monsters in Suburban Fantasy television. The vengeance-seeking Chumash warrior Hus of the *Buffy* episode "Pangs" is one example. Although "Pangs," the episode in which he appears, was intended by its makers to engage critically with America's violent colonial history and treatment of indigenous peoples, the negative and stereotypical representation of Hus made this largely a failure. [24] The Djieine, a spider-like creature said to be native to America, from the *Lost Girl* episode "ArachnoFaebia," is another.[25] It is an "Under Fae," the Fae equivalent of an animal and not part of their organized, human-like society. The novels of de Lint offer a different construction of First Nations stories, as Carroll states, in his *Moonheart* and many later novels, "the spirit world is revealed to be a space shared by creatures from both Celtic and First Nations mythology."[26] No similar multicultural or cosmopolitan space has been created for the small screen, however, and First Nations peoples are marginalized at best; monsters at worst.

Returning to Carter's portable stories demonstrates that cultural Whiteness supports that of the casting and characterisation as the supernatural world in Suburban Fantasy television is dominated by the folktales and mythologies of Western European cultures. The "Fae" of *Lost Girl* are largely those of Irish legends, a connection made explicitly on multiple occasions. The *"wesen"* – German for "creatures" – of *Grimm* are represented by the show as the truth behind the Brothers Grimm's *Kinder- und Hausmärchen* (Children's and Household Tales) usually known as *Grimm's Fairy Stories* in English translation,[27] while *Once Upon a Time* has the same underlying conceit. While there are vampire-like beings in the tales of multiple world cultures, those of *True Blood* and the *Buffy*-verse are very much those of Western European tradition. As W. Scott Poole states, "the folklore of Eastern Europe and China viewed the vampire as a bestial creature, barely if at all human," but in the nineteenth-century West it "became a dark lover,"[28] more human than animal, even if monstrous. It is this type of vampire, filtered through popular culture, that occupies the American landscape. Some monsters are represented as coming from beyond the borders – the "Inca Mummy Girl" of the eponymous episode of *Buffy* is one of multiple examples in that program – as are some few indigenous beings as discussed above. The vast majority, however, are European in origin.[29]

Suburban Fantasy is, as discussed above, deeply concerned with connections between race and human identity. As Carroll argues of Urban Fantasy, it "assert[s] continuity with a historical past."[30] When that historical past is constructed chiefly through the portable stories of European peoples, it is a form of cultural colonisation which repeats that of earlier years. From the late eighteenth century on, while the racial discourses of Anglo-Saxonism "justified the dispossession of indigenous peoples by white settlers [in North America, Australia, and other colonies and former colonies], medieval provided narratives of European cultural identity and progress" which could be transported to new geographical locations.[31] As Whiteness reformulated following the decline of scientific racisms in the early-to-mid-twentieth century, the final dissolution of colonial rule by the former British Empire, the Civil Rights Movement and related social changes around the globe,[32] Anglo-Saxonism and medievalism lost some of their cultural power. European folklore, collected and printed in the nineteenth century as part of the same kinds of ethno-nationalist projects that shaped modern medievalisms performs similar moves, but with even greater effect because the corporeal forms it takes in Suburban Fantasy link contemporary human identities with the historical past of place in ways that medievalisms – which could only cross the Atlantic (or other oceans) as cultural artefacts – could not. Medievalism in America traces a past back to another land, but the beings of folklore trace it "here." This is true not just in television programs, but in novels and all other forms of media as well.

Whiteness has never been a stable category of identity, a result of two main factors: that the race to which it refers is scientifically non-existent and thus cannot be accurately defined; and that, as a socially constructed sign, its significance and what it signifies necessarily change as society and culture do, across space and time. In the US, the social and cultural changes wrought by the Civil Rights movement made earlier constructions of "White Anglo-Saxon Protestant" American-ness less tenable. Jacobson argues that the resulting shift in identity:

> Bolstered the racial whiteness that had long held the key to American belonging and power relations, though it did generate a new set of popular narratives about who these "Caucasian" Americans were and where they have come from. It relocated that normative whiteness from what might be called Plymouth Rock whiteness to Ellis Island whiteness … there arose a new national myth of origins.[33]

That myth centred on migration and the reclamation of ethnicities – "ethnic revival" as Jacobson terms it.[34] The re-construction of American identity moved away from medieval Anglo-Saxonism, and resulted in a diffusion of Whiteness into constituent parts that detached the overarching label without erasing the privilege of normativity that attends it. Reclaiming folklore, understood for centuries as the repository of racialized culture, is an essential aspect of this process of identity construction; populating the American landscape with it is a way of recolonising in a new – but still monochrome – image. Attebery argues that "one motivation [for turning away from medievalist Fantasy convention] was an interest in exploring one's own cultural roots, especially for the many US and Canadian writers whose ancestors did not come from the British Isles."[35] This move, however, can merely diffuse the Whiteness of genre rather than refracting it into greater diversity.

Close consideration of the currently running series *Grimm* illuminates patterns that occur throughout Suburban Fantasy. The reclamation and reconstruction of identity occurs at both personal and social levels, and depends significantly on connections with Europe – inherited identity – being remade for a specifically American context. Nick's individuality and personal freedom to choose what is "right" in any given situation is paramount in the series, reflecting the essentially liberal discourses that pervade American society and culture. As discussed above, Nick's identity as a Grimm is essential: it was suppressed but has always been inherent in him. Grimms are the enemies of *wesen*, their purpose is to hunt and kill them, nominally to protect the human population. It is this legacy that Nick inherits, but he is consistently said and shown to be "not like the other ones."[36] Nick has the abilities of the Grimms, but not their attitude, that is, he does not treat *wesen* as mortal enemies merely because they are *wesen* and is willing to protect weaker ones from stronger – although he is also willing to kill them without compunction. Nick cannot escape his inherited identity, but in his struggles to reconcile it with his humanity, he reconstructs it to suit his own position.

Nick's attitude to *wesen* and their place in human society is essentially assimilationist, that is, he is willing to allow them to live in Portland as long as they fit in with its mundane inhabitants. He also, however, becomes actively involved in policing *wesen* society in Portland, often actively disrupting their traditional ways of life – which are almost invariably depicted negatively – in the process. In the episode "Bad Moon Rising,"[37] an extended family of Coyotl – canine *wesen* whose name suggests they are native to North America – come into conflict with each other over a traditional coming-of-age ceremony in which the females are initiated to the tribe through a ritual which involves pack rape. A Coyotl girl, Carly Kampfer, is abducted by her male cousins who plan to conduct the ritual. One of them tells her: "Your daddy brought shame down on us when he took your mama and you away … we're gonna take you back into the pack."[38] When her father, Jarold, also a Coyotl, reports the kidnapping to the police, Nick becomes involved, rescuing her and arresting the pack.[39]

The Coyotls are constructed using an amalgam of racist stereotypes which combine to effectively construct them as Other. They are described as: "the street gangs of the *wesen* world," invoking the gangster stereotype especially associated with Blackness in American culture. Carly's uncle, Hayden Walker, who is the pack's leader, is a violent criminal who is known to the local police despite having only been in Portland for a few months. The family members who abduct Carly are from Texas, the entries about Coyotls in the Grimm diaries are written in Spanish, and the name of the ritual – "aseveracion" – is given in that language, which constructs them as Latino.[40] The ritual itself is a fertility rite, which Carly's father calls "barbaric." Their pack culture is represented as vaguely tribal through its superstitions and insistence on the violent fertility rite. The Coyotl pack is thus constructed as criminal, dangerous, and backward using stereotypically racialized discourses.[41]

Carly and Jarold, in contrast, are integrated into human society and upstanding members of the Portland community. Carly is a good and reliable school student, and god-daughter to Nick's partner Hank, who went to school with Jarold. He also tells Nick that he and her mother left the pack – and Texas – because they "wanted to raise Carly in a more normal environment." They, like Nick, exercise their personal liberties in choosing to separate themselves from the other Coyotl. They retain their essential *wesen* nature, but have been assimilated into "normal" human society, as Jarold terms it, by choosing to give up – fleeing – their traditional way of life. Nick, acting in his role as a detective and agent of social order, literally polices the racialized *wesen*, enabling those who are assimilated to maintain their place in human society.

Other *wesen*, such as the beaver-like Eisbiber who appear in multiple episodes, involve Nick in their disputes, but are able to retain their traditional ways of life because they do not disrupt human society. *Wesen*, like Nick, cannot give up their essential nature – race – and must face arrest or death at Nick's hands if their traditional ways – cultures – do not conform with "normal" human ways. Some, moreover, have natures which are inherently inimical to humanity: spinnetods, spider-like creatures, for example, "are plagued by a condition that causes rapid ageing. The only way to reverse it is to kill and suck the lives out of young men."[42] When Nick encounters one – in the first season in which the nature of the world of *wesen* is principally established – he arrests her, preventing her from performing the acts that will keep her alive. The woman is otherwise a functioning and productive member of society. Thus, most *wesen* can integrate with reasonable levels of success, retaining their essential nature but conforming to contemporary American identity, while others are fundamentally unable to do so. The construction of *wesen*-human integration reflects Jacobson's "Ellis Island Whiteness:" some cannot take on this "human" identity completely, no matter how well they perform it, because of their essential nature – race; those whose race does allow them to do so, can only retain their cultural identity as well if it is not in conflict with normative ways.

A core conceit of Suburban Fantasy television, as noted above, is that it reveals the hidden truths behind folklore and mythology, a trope which is also reminiscent of Jacobson's "ethnic revival" which constructs itself as revealing what was already there – migration and ethnicity – in American history.[43] This is particularly true for works which, like *Grimm*, engage overtly with the folklore of a particular people – always White – at length.[44] *Grimm* clams as its source not the translated, often abridged and bowdlerized American printings of *Grimms' Fairy Tales*, much less the Disney animated film versions, but the nineteenth-century collection of folktales by the Brothers Grimm: *Kinder- und Hausmärchen* (Children's and Household Tales). The tales, often in abridged volumes, were widely read in the United States in translation and the original German in the nineteenth century and into the twentieth, while new editions are still being published in the twenty-first.[45] In the early nineteenth century, there was a strong "feeling that American nationalism had little strong soil to root itself in, no historic past or ancient traditions."[46] European folktales – particularly those of the Grimms' which were held to be the cultural inheritance of all Germanic peoples, including the Anglo-Saxons from which White America held itself to descend – became widely accepted as repositories of values and the essence of the American people.[47] Donald Haase shows that, "de-historicized and de-nationalized, they are appropriated as American myth" and retained "no specifically German cultural identity" in the twentieth-century United States.[48] *Grimm* works hard to revive that ethnicity and to place it in present day America, re-connecting that place and its people with Europe, particularly Germany and Austria.

The show is littered with markers of German-ness: the name of the protagonist – Burkhardt; *wesen*, pronounced "vesen," is German for creature, and the names of many different kinds are also rendered in that language.[49] The only one of the seven royal *wesen* houses to be named in the program is the House of Kronenberg, headed by King Frederick, and its members and their retainers speak in snatches of German. Portland was selected as the location because it reminded the producers of the Black Forest in Germany.[50] Some references are to places outside the current borders of Germany, but identifiable as Germanic nonetheless: in season two, one character moves back and forward between Vienna in Austria and Portland, while at the end of season two Nick is kidnapped in an attempt to take him to Germany. Nick is not just a member of "elite line of criminal profilers," as the show's website claims,[51] he is a member of a markedly German line, which predominantly hunts German *wesen*, even in America.[52] *Grimm* thus revives the ethnicity of the folktales that it constructs as its source.

Grimm establishes a particularly close relationship with the *Kinder- und Hausmärchen*, as Kristiana Willsey discusses at length. She argues that the selective process of adaptation that the Grimm's stories – selectively edited by the Brothers – undergo results in: "an overly simplified, Romantic reading of literary source material to offer an allegedly authentic alternative – the television show's gritty realism."[53] The project of adaptation/reclamation of truth mirrors that undertaken by the gritty medievalism discussed in chapter three precisely, down to the "villain" of the piece – Disney – which has bowdlerized and stripped the meaning from the originals – folktale or history – in the service of modernity and capitalism.[54] Both, moreover, seek authenticity and identity in cultural spaces which have been associated with Whiteness – and Germanic Whiteness at that – since at least the nineteenth century. *Grimm*, moreover, performs at fulfilling precisely the purpose that the Brothers' Grimm attempted with their original collection: locating/creating the mythology of the Germanic peoples which, they believed, had been suppressed by conversion to Christianity and the rationalism of the Enlightenment. In reviving/revealing the "truth" of their tales, *Grimm* participates in the "Ellis Island Whiteness" of contemporary American identity – the essence of the people is in its stories.

Sleepy Hollow offers an illuminating counter-point, not least but also not only because three of the major characters are African American: Abbie Mills, her sister Jennifer, and Captain Frank Irving. The series draws on Washington Irving's story "The Headless Horseman" (1820) and to a lesser degree his "Rip Van Winkle," as well as Christian mythology – particularly the Biblical book of "Revelation" which prophecies the apocalypse – as well as some European legends. "The Headless Horseman" has achieved the level of folktale through its popularity and myriad adaptations and re-tellings. Irving works to create this feeling in his tale, which was first published in 1820, and set in 1790, just seven years after the end of the Revolutionary War. He invokes folk versions of local, oral history in his account of the "drowsy, dreamy influence" that pervades Sleepy Hollow: "some say that the place was bewitched by a High German doctor … other, that an old Indian chief … held his powwows there."[55] The story was thus framed specifically as a folktale, that is, as a recorded version of orally transmitted narratives. The project of the Brothers Grimm and their contemporaries in the other countries of Europe was approximately contemporarily with Irving's work.

In *Sleepy Hollow*, the "nameless battle during the Revolutionary War"[56] which killed the (probably non-existent) Hessian trooper who became the headless horseman is a real skirmish, including a mutual mortal combat between Ichabod and Death – one of the Four Horsemen of the Apocalypse. The local legend becomes global in scale, escalating in a way that is common to televised Suburban Fantasy. The American Revolution becomes not just a struggle against the British, but a defense of the world – one which is repeated in events of the television series as the returned Ichabod and Abbie struggle first with the Horseman and other demons. *Sleepy Hollow* reflects the problematic paradoxes of mass American culture in the twenty-first century. The casting of people of colour in leading roles makes it stand out in a positive way against the habit of Whiteness that dominates the televisual landscape as well as much of the Fantasy genre. The bodily presence of African Americans is significant because of its rarity, but elides the realities of slavery during the Revolutionary War – which is still foundational to American ethno-national identity, and likewise has little to say about contemporary inequalities and injustices. It offers, as a result, a vision of America which is post-racial, that is, a world in which an individual's race does not significantly affect his or her life.

The monsters of history and mythology that intrude into the present and must be defeated are rarely those of the race-based injustice and inequality that marked the late eighteenth century, and when they are, they are not American. The most brutal figure out of the past is Tarleton, the British officer who orders Ichabod to torture an emancipated slave and is actually a demon. Tarleton is the epitome of everything that the Patriots reject in *Sleepy Hollow*'s re-write of history. In the first episode, Abbie tells Ichabod, "slavery has been abolished 150 years. It's a whole new day in America," suggesting that racial inequality is a thing of the past.[57] Race, and racisms, are history in *Sleepy Hollow*, and are constructed as the business of the enemy of America in the early episodes of the show. The situation becomes more complex as the seasons progress.[58]

In the first season some negative stereotypes of African Americans are present in Abbie's account of her past, notably that of the absconding father: "Dad bailed when we were kids. Mom had a nervous breakdown a few years later … The state dumped us in foster care."[59] Episode nine of the second season, "Mama," however, reveals that their mother saw real demons, as opposed to having paranoid delusions. Abbie and Jennifer both have criminal pasts, although these are explained as the direct result of their encounter with a demon as children, and – in Jennifer's adult life – preparation for the war against evil which she believed was coming. Abbie and Jennifer, moreover, are not on speaking terms in the early episodes, stemming from Abbie's refusal to support Jennifer when she told police about the demon they saw as children. They reconcile after Jennifer escapes from a psychiatric hospital and becomes an ally in the struggle with evil. Their absent father, to date, has not returned, but they shared a father figure in the late Sheriff August Corbin, although he hid his involvement in Jennifer's life from Abbie, not wanting her to know he believed the story of a demon.

Abbie and Jennifer meet the ghost of their mother in the episode "Mama," discover that she knew Abbie was a Witness destined to fight evil and try to prevent the Apocalypse, and that there is "a journal that belongs to me, passed down form the ancestors" which will aid in the fight against evil.[60] They locate it among her personal effects, which are still stored in the basement of the Tarrytown psychiatric hospital, and discover that it was not only passed down from but written by one of their ancestors, a Black woman named Grace Dixon, who was the housekeeper at nearby Fredericks' Manor during the eighteenth century. In it they find "a West African invocation to expel witch doctors who had risen from the dead," which they use to exorcise an evil ghost from the hospital.[61] In the final episode of the second season, Abbie, who has travelled back in time to the eighteenth century, meets Grace, who casts a spell that returns Ichabod and Abbie to the present.

The episodes are highly significant for several reasons, particularly when read against the habitual Whiteness of genre-programs such as *Grimm*, because they establish that the historical fight against evil – like the present one – was not just the preserve of White men like the Founding Fathers. Not only are Black women present throughout, but Grace's journal takes the magic back across the Atlantic to Africa. Books containing magic and information, as noted above, are a staple of Suburban Fantasy, but they are exponentially more likely to be written in language of the Western intellectual tradition – Greek or Latin – if they are ancient, than to include an African spell. *Sleepy Hollow* places not only African American women at the centre of a long struggle against evil, but also a lasting intellectual tradition that represents authority within that struggle, an authority which is generically much more likely to be associated with White men.[62] Placing Black women in an apocalyptic struggle across centuries moves them to the centre of history from the margins to which they are all too frequently pushed, when they are allowed any presence at all.

Sleepy Hollow, like many other Suburban Fantasy works – especially television – reflects the strong tradition of exceptionalism that has shaped American national myth-making for centuries by placing not one but two struggles to avert the Apocalypse on US shores, and linking the first directly to the Revolutionary War. Abbie, Jennifer, and Frank Irving's presence in contemporary times is significant, but the centrality of Black people in the historical struggle is even more so because of the strong links between history and identity not only in Suburban Fantasy, but in culture much more broadly. Although *Sleepy Hollow* elides the violence of slavery in its eighteenth-century episodes, and does not engage in detailed ways with the inequalities and injustices in modern society which are its legacies, what it does is create an image of American identity which includes the active presence of people of colour from the founding conflict of the nation. The diffuse Whiteness of returning to European ethnic roots to mythologize American identity, as evinced in *Grimm*, is rejected in *Sleepy Hollow*.

SPIRITS OF PLACE

One category of supernatural being that is not mobile in the way of the folktale beings of Carter's portable stories, or the people who tell them, are the spirits of place, *genius loci*, personifications of features of the landscape, whether human-made or natural. The idea that supernatural beings inhabit and protect given geographical locations, whether urban or rural, natural or manmade, has a long history in Western culture – and many others. The Romans sacrificed to the *lares familiarias*, protectors of the house and family, and the *lares compitalicii*, protectors of local neighbourhoods and communities, for example. After the spread of Christianity in Europe, saints replace local gods and spirits as the patrons of cities and nations. Spirits *of* place, as opposed to those which are merely *in* places, are particularly illuminating in the current discussion. They represent not just the inhabitants, the beings that have taken possession or taken up habitation and might equally move on to somewhere else, but the essence of the place itself. They are a staple of Suburban Fantasy, and exemplify its concern with anthropological place.

The first episode of season two of *Lost Girl* features the spirit of the local land, the unnamed North American "Everycity" in which the action takes place. The Ash, the leader of the local Light Fae court, is critically injured in the finale of the first season and lies in a coma. A band of wandering Fae – the Sluagh – who are cursed to never be able to settle, attempt to exploit the resulting power vacuum and seize control of the area through a mystical ceremony in which, as Dyson explains to Bo, The Ash "marries the land ... the soul of the land takes on corporeal form with which The Ash will mate."[63] The leader of the Sluagh invokes the spirit of the land and attempts to take the place of The Ash in the ceremony, but Bo foils him at the last moment, telling him, "I know exactly what it is like to be an outcast, to have no home. But this one is spoken for."[64] The spirit of the land, who has few lines and plays no active role in the episode, is played by Sarah Jurgens, an English-born Canadian actress with pale skin and blond hair. The land itself is White, which reflects – although the show does not explicitly comment on – the power structures of North American society and culture in the twenty-first century. The accreted past of North America is personified by Whiteness. Whether *Sleepy Hollow* will inspire a wider shift away from the largely tokenistic representation of characters of colour on the small screen as has been predicted remains to be seen.[65]

In recent years, in contrast, London, first established as a city – a "place" under the colonial rule of the Roman Empire – has been inhabited in Aaronovitch's *Rivers of London* books, by the Black Mama Thames and her daughters. As the name of the series and first novel suggest, the *genii loci* are spirits of rivers, the two most important being Mama Thames and Father Thames. The protagonist, police constable Peter Grant – a mixed-race man whose mother is a Fula woman from Sierra Leone – meets them in the first novel, where Mama Thames explains their origins, and how there came to be two spirits of what is ostensibly the same river. Mama Thames was, as a human, a Nigerian woman who came to London in 1957. She tells Grant that after failing in her studies to become a nurse and being abandoned by her lover, she went to London Bridge to commit suicide:

> London was still a port back then, dying but like an old man with a long, exciting life, full of stories and memories. And terrified that he was going to be old and frail with no one to look after him because there was no life left in the river, no Orisa, no spirit, nothing to care for the old man.[66]

She speaks to the river and agrees to become its spirit, sacrificing her human self whose name she has forgotten. Mama Thames, who came to London three years before Nigeria officially gained independence from the crumbling British empire, represents postcolonial, post-imperial London, and the two-way relationship between colonial metropolis and margins.[67]

The Thames once had another guardian spirit, Father Thames. She critically explains to Grant that he had abandoned the lower river when she came to London:

> When he was a young man he stood where I stood, on the bridge, and made the same promise I did. But he hasn't been below Teddington Lock since the Great Stink of 1858. He never came back, not even after Bazalgette put the sewers in. Not even for the Blitz, not even when the city was burning.[68]

Friction over territory between the two and their offspring – the lesser rivers and streams of the Thames Valley and London – is the source of some narrative tension and drive throughout the series, although it does not break into open conflict. As a human, Father Thames was not a migrant, but one Tiberius Claudius Verica, "an aristocratic Briton who lived around the time the city was founded," a magistrate during Roman times.[69] A native Briton, he nonetheless represents colonial power – that of Rome – and is framed that way explicitly.[70] The essence of London has always been dependent on the global movement of people and power; before the coming of the Romans, there was no "place" and the river neither needed nor had a spirit.

In the first four books of the series, the race of the river spirits is divided along rural/urban boundaries. The rivers of the country are White and descended from a man indigenous to England, while those of London are Black and the daughters of a migrant. In the most recent book, *Foxglove Summer*, Peter Grant travels to Herefordshire, near the English border with Wales, an area drained by the River Lugg. Beverly Brook, one of Mama Thames' daughters, follows him there, encountering the White female spirits of the Rivers Teme and Corve, who are suspicious of her initially, *genius loci* who claim Welsh roots to go with the Welsh sources of their rivers. The River Lugg, however, does not have a resident spirit; Beverly says he "was done in by the Methodists in Victorian times."[71] She initiates a sexual encounter with Peter in the water, which she later tells him was intended to awaken a new spirit for the Lugg, a plan she had agreed to with the local Welsh rivers. She tells him "there were no genes involved whatsoever, no transfer of information, we were strictly catalytic in the process."[72] Race in the human sense is irrelevant to the river spirits, although Beverly and the other daughters of Mama Thames are all physically coded as Black, while Father Thames' sons are physically coded as White. Beverly says "I think this is going to be a boy river … but you never know – it might have its own view."[73] Its racial coding, like its gender, is left uncertain, nonetheless, the involvement of a bi-racial human and a spirit who is coded as Black in the ensouling of place moves Blackness outside the boundaries of London.

There are multiple factors underlying the different racial coding of *genius loci* in *Lost Girl* and the *Rivers of London* novels, many of which go beyond the matter of authorial or directorial choices which are, in any case, not completely autonomous. North American mass-market television screens, as discussed above, feature disproportionately White casting and character compared to the population, and for the most part Suburban Fantasy television does not break this habit. The pages of Suburban Fantasy novels are often similarly dominated by Whiteness. Jim Butcher's *The Dresden Files* series, for example, were criticized in 2011 for "whitewashing" the population of Chicago.[74] Nonetheless, it is a great deal easier to find protagonists of colour in Suburban Fantasy literature than television, including in works published by major international houses.[75] Despite the move towards niche markets in television broadcasting driven by pay-TV (cable or satellite) and the proliferation of channels, there are far more books published than television programs made in contemporary culture, while books also cost less to produce. Publishers may therefore be more willing to produce works which, because of their characters of colour, are often assumed to only appeal to readers of colour. Urban Fantasy novels with protagonists of colour, furthermore, have a much longer history of demonstrated success than similar television, given that *Sleepy Hollow* is the first of the latter. In contrast, Nalo Hopkinson's multi-award winning and nominated novel *Brown Girl in the Ring* appeared in 1999.

Suburban Fantasy's deep concern with history and identity, mediated through anthropological place, is also a significant issue, one which sheds light on the different challenges faced by the US and the UK. Historically, London has been – and been understood as – the central metropolis of the British Empire – not as a former colony of the Roman – and thus as a source of White settler colonists. Although throughout the colonial period there was a complex "interplay of the metropolis and imperialism,"[76] and London was a site of significant resistance to empire in the nineteenth century,[77] London's history of immigration, particularly by people from the former colonies, is relatively recent in its approximately 2 000 year urban past. The US although it suppressed the diversity of its immigrant population for a long period, began its history as a nation as a colony much more recently.[78] North America, moreover, has been understood as a destination for migrants for centuries longer than London. The anxieties of history that are managed by anthropomorphizing place into *genius loci* are, as a result, significantly different.

American Whiteness asserts its own legitimacy, refracting into multiple migrant ethnicities, but its underlying anxieties can be discerned in the exclusion of people of colour from the small screen in general, and from manifesting as *genius loci* in particular. American spirits of place cannot be First Nations, African American, or Latino because this would undermine the legitimacy of the White domination of both history and the present. Britain, with a medieval past so strongly associated with Whiteness, is arguably too secure in its own legitimacy *in place* to be troubled in the same way. The history that it must manage in contemporary society is not that of migration, but of imperialism and colonialism. Father Thames may have deserted the estuary leaving a place for the Nigerian nursing student to become its spirit, but the sixty or so years she has dwelt there do not compare with the almost two thousand he inhabited it. Immigration, particularly by people of colour, is a source of social and cultural anxiety in the present in Britain, but this does not extend to its history which remains – if anachronistically – White.

PRESENCE AND AGENCY

In her essay "Eating the Other: Desire and Resistance," bell hooks argues that "subject to subject contact between white and black which signals the absence of domination ... must emerge through mutual choice and recognition."[79] The presence of people of colour in a genre-culture space does not in and of itself work to change its habits of Whiteness when they do not have agency – the ability to act autonomously, to choose to act or not act, to not be acted upon. In *Sleepy Hollow* and the *Rivers of London* series, characters of colour are agential protagonists, sometimes at the mercy of supernatural forces they cannot resist, but nonetheless able to choose how and when to act. Their actions, significantly, impact not only in them as individuals, but on the society in which they live. They are active presences, moreover, not just in the imagined worlds they inhabit, but in the genre-culture of which those worlds are a part.

The multiple spaces – literal and conceptual – in which the presence of agential people of colour can work to break the habits of Whiteness of Fantasy genre-culture can be illuminated through an exploration of Hopkinson's novel *Sister Mine* (2013). Hopkinson, who was born and raised in the Caribbean before moving to North America in her teens, is a woman of colour who has had a significant presence in speculative fiction genres as an author, editor, speaker, and teacher for almost two decades.[80] Until very recently, she was one of "a short list" of authors of colour working in Fantasy and Science Fiction.[81] Her success as a genre author is arguably in and of itself agential because, like that of other well-known authors like Samuel R. Delany and Octavia E. Butler, it makes a lie of the assumption that people of colour are not interested in either genre. As Delany argues, inspired in part by being placed in a signing session with Hopkinson, the exclusion or marginalization of people of colour in Science Fiction and Fantasy cannot be changed without an increase in the proportion of authors of colour.[82] Hopkinson fosters diverse voices through her work as an editor,[83] and speaker,[84] while her novels draw significantly on Afro-Caribbean mythologies and feature protagonists of colour. Although diversity of inspiration and character are arguably becoming more common, Hopkinson's works were among the forerunners of both.[85]

Sister Mine is a Suburban Fantasy novel set in the Canadian city of Toronto. Makeda, the protagonist, is the child of a demi-god and a Black human woman who was separated at birth from her conjoined twin sister Abby. Abby has inherited magic from their father and is a professional singer, while Makeda, who moves out of their family home at the beginning of the novel, has neither magic nor the ability to support herself through an art form, although she makes small sculptures. Makeda is pursued throughout the novel by a "haint," a small monster which takes various forms, and physically attacks her at any opportunity:

> I felt the scrape of claws slicing through the fabric of my jeans as I pulled away. My haint was upon me. Its small hairy body scrambled, quarrelling, up my side … One of the haint's searching thumbs pushed brutally past my teeth into my mouth.[86]

The narrative does not, unlike those discussed above, contain an imminent global apocalypse that threatens the survival of humanity which must be averted, but focuses rather on the individual and family.

Divisions within the self and the family, and healing them to create coherent and unified identity, are central themes in *Sister Mine*. The keys to healing are the revelation and acceptance of truth. The intrusion of the supernatural which characterises Suburban Fantasy is not the presence of magic in mundane space as such, but the haint, which is eventually revealed to be the physical manifestation of Makeda's magic. Its physical attacks are attempts to reconnect itself with her. It is only once she is told the true story of how she was separated from her twin sister and why she is able to recognize their unified and mutually dependent nature and integrate the magic which was taken from her at that separation. Working together Makeda and Abby are able to do magic which allows their father, who was trapped in a human body unable to access his celestial power as punishment for transgressing laws of nature when the twins were separated, to unify his soul and power once more and prevent him being killed by a jealous brother.

The main characters in *Sister Mine* are all of colour, including those who are not members of Makeda's family, while those with celestial powers choose to appear in ways which are racially coded as Black. The human side of the family have served the celestial side for generations: for "centuries her family had been in charge of the hoodoo tree. It was their old guys' branch of the eternal tree, the spine of the world's soul."[87] Makeda's Aunt Suzy encounters several generations of family ghosts living beneath its roots, all of whom are also coded as Black, although, significantly, not through their appearance. The text, for example, describes the clothes the ghost of her mother is wearing but does not mention her bodily markers such as skin and hair which are commonly racialized. Rather, when she criticizes the name Suzy has given her daughter, Suzy replies: "that Black Power stuff was from your time, not mine."[88] Another ghost does not appear at all: "from the hole came a drawn-out, echoing kiss-teeth of vexation. Suzy had to smile. She'd never met a black person who didn't make that noise when they were exasperated."[89] The novel is not interested in how the family came to Toronto in the first place,[90] but like *Sleepy Hollow* it establishes their long history in that location, laying claim to it through their continued presence in the real-world place reimagined in the text.

While the narrative is framed through familial connections and does not threaten a global apocalypse, the celestial side of Makeda's family are not merely local spirits: "his quantumate selves could be here, there, and everywhere people were borning and dying, every millisecond of every day, world without end, amen."[91] The individual identity work that Makeda does in order to be able to heal the spiritual separation from Abby, and their subsequent joint rescue of their father has implications and impact far beyond the personal. *Sister Mine*, like *Sleepy Hollow*, features characters of colour who are not only agents in their own right, but are agential and exceptional on a much larger scale. Both works turn away from genre convention which puts White characters almost exclusively in those positions. In the network of genre-culture the works themselves are thus agents of change.

CULTURAL APPROPRIATION

In the past five years or so, an increasing number of authors of colour have had success in the Fantasy genre – I explore the impact of their presence and some dedicated efforts to increase diversity in the following chapter. Breaking habits of Whiteness, however, is not merely the business – or in the interests of – members of minority groups. A significant number of the authors whose work is included in the list of books with "non-Western settings" discussed at the start of this chapter write about cultures and societies of which they are not a part, and create characters from races which they themselves are not members of. This usually takes the form of White authors writing about people of colour and their cultures, but this is not invariably the case. Aliette de Bodard, a French national of Vietnamese ancestry who grew up between the US and France, and whose first novels were the *Obsidian and Blood* series (2010–2011), is one example not mentioned in that particular list, although her work often appears on them.[92]

There are multiple motivations for moving away from Fantasy convention, including "the desire to avoid simple imitation ... the desire for new sensations" as Attebery puts it.[93] Nisi Shawl writes: "readers looking for something 'different' in fantastic fiction, and authors who attempt to supply them with it, often turn to mythologies, religions, and philosophies outside the dominant Western paradigm."[94] Many now working in the genre have transitioned from reader to writer, and been influenced by its habits in the process. De Bodard comments of *Obsidian and Blood*: "I wanted a non-Western culture because I'd read far too many medieval fantasies and mysteries and wanted to go further afield."[95] The desire for newness, hooks argues, can result in cultural appropriation and reinscribe existing power differentials when it is directed towards an Other – racial and cultural – which is understood as fundamentally different to the Self. The same desire, however, also has the potential to do the opposite: "Desire for contact with the Other, for connections rooted in the longing for pleasure, can act as a critical intervention challenging and subverting racist domination, inviting and enabling critical resistance."[96] In light of hooks' comments, authorial identity is significant because race is a socio-economic marker as well as a matter of personal identity, and individuals are socially positioned and privileged – or not – no matter what their intent, beliefs, or attitudes.

Writing about characters and cultures to which one does not belong, particularly for White writers who cannot escape their privileged positions in both wider society and genre-culture, is complex and requires significant levels of mindfulness and care to avoid merely reinforcing the status quo. The same acts, however, also have significant potential to change Fantasy's habits of Whiteness. hooks argues that "ethnicity has become spice" in contemporary popular culture;[97] the racially marked "indigenous" monsters of television discussed above, are such seasonings. For Fantasy genre-culture, not just individual authors and creators, the challenge is to make newness the substance not the spice. At what point then does writing about a culture with which one does not identify or a character whose race one does not share become appropriation?[98]

A theoretical critique of the concept of cultural appropriation argues that it relies on constructed categories of race and thus unavoidably re-inscribes essentialized understandings: "what this … relies on, however, is a set repertoire – or what may pass for a belief in 'blackness' … – that resides in the realm of 'culture.'"[99] For something to be appropriated, moreover, it must necessarily belong to another party in the first place. Although Carter and many others argue that any story, particularly a folktale, belongs to the individual who tells it in any given iteration,[100] the concept of cultural ownership is still a very strong one in twenty-first-century culture, and extends beyond folktale in to the arena of legends and mythologies as well. When Fantasy works reimagine real world cultures and societies, either in historical settings or contemporary ones, they necessarily represent the lives of the people who are part of them, whether the author intends that the work speak for authentic experience or not. The issue of ownership and appropriation is an especially charged one in a popular culture genre like Fantasy in which commodification is a goal of the capitalist industrial processes which underpin it.

One way of understanding the issue of cultural appropriation, and of untangling it without the slippery meanings of "ownership" and "belonging" is to consider cultures as semiotic systems akin to languages. Any aspect of culture however big or small is thus a sign – stories, hairstyles, items of clothing, tattoos and so on. What any given sign signifies, means, or stands for, is arbitrary; there is no underlying reason why a sound or series of written letters means what it does, no fundamental connection between "dog" – written or spoken – and the animal itself.[101] Any word, however, "is fixed, not free, with respect to the linguistic community that uses it."[102] A sign – be it a word, hairstyle, tattoo, physical gesture, sound etc – only has meaning because it is understood to do so by a community of people. Removing a sign from the system in which its meaning was originally assigned thus necessarily changes that meaning, especially when it is relocated without surrounding context and the members of the community that use the new system into which it is inserted have little or no knowledge of the original. So, a kanji character written in a Japanese book means one thing to a person who reads Japanese, but nothing to someone who does not understand that semiotic system. When the same character is tattooed onto the arm of a White person living in Australia, the original meaning is not known to the majority of people who will see it, but the character takes on entirely new meanings; it might tell them, for example, that the person on whose skin it appears is interested in Asian culture. Stories can function in similar ways: that of Christ's resurrection is a sacred tale to Christians but a myth to others. Any act which moves a sign from one system of meaning to another, creating new meaning in the process, is potentially one of appropriation.

Some further points can be drawn from this method of approaching the issue of an individual author writing about cultures of which she or he is not a part, even if that author understands some of the meaning that are made within them. Taking signs – even multiple signs – from a culture and recombining them in ways which suit the needs of the story or imagined world but do not reflect their significance in the culture from which they derive is one kind of appropriation. As Shawl puts it, an author – or other creator – who does this, "take[s] whatever they want for use in whatever way they see fit."[103] This happens most frequently when a culture is designated as Other within an imagined world, whether or not the signs of Otherness all come from a single real world culture or are an assemblage. Shawl gives an example: "in one unpublished story I've seen, the writer took a sacred song here, a tattoo there, snapped up a feast featuring roasted pig and manioc root from somewhere else and presto! South Pacific Island culture at our fingertips."[104] The use of cultural references loosely drawn from Native American cultures to attach a sense of Otherness to orcs, such as in *Dungeons & Dragons* worlds,[105] is another example.

Racial stereotypes can be understood as collections of signs attached to particular bodies, on the basis of how they appear, by the dominant culture – which is Whiteness in Western society and Fantasy genre-culture alike. Thus, if an imagined world includes characters of colour, which are constructed using the same stereotypical signs as in dominant culture, that imagined world reinforces the structure of the culture in which it was created, and as a result does not work to break Fantasy's habits of Whiteness. The signs which are used might be cultural – ways of life, types of dress – or phenotypical signs such as skin colour, facial features or hair, or a combination of both. Orcs, again, are a significant example of this occurring, even in works like Mary Gentle's *Grunts!* or the game *Of Orcs and Men* which seek to do so. The longest, most widespread, and one of the bitterest online debates about race in Fantasy and Science Fiction genre-cultures was sparked by a reader who found the stereotypical construct of a male character of colour in Elizabeth Bear's *Blood and Iron* (2006) profoundly disturbing and distasteful.[106] Known colloquially in as "The Great Cultural Appropriation Debate of Doom," or "RaceFail 09," it involved unprecedented numbers of people in discussions about cultural appropriation – and ranged into multiple other facets of Science Fiction and Fantasy's habits of Whiteness; I explore some of the dynamics of the discussions in the following chapter.

Considering the question of authorial identity and cultural appropriation through a semiotic lens demonstrates that the core issue is not who moves a sign from one system to another, but how it is done and to what effect. Whoever does the moving, a new significance will be produced by the new context. To return to one of my earlier examples, a kanji tattoo on the arm of a White person takes on new significance in Australia where the cultural system is different to Japan and thus most of the people in the community cannot read its original meaning, just as the same tattoo on a Japanese person's arm would have different meanings in those two communities. Extrapolating, a Black author is equally capable of writing a stereotypical Black character in a Fantasy world as a White author. Thus, a person who is not a member of the community that uses a particular system of signs needs to do more work to re-code a sign or series of signs appropriately – without creating contradictory or arbitrary new meanings – when shifting them into a new system. In Okorafor's *Who Fears Death* and *Zahrah the Windseeker* the protagonists are born "dada" – with natural dreadlocks – which in the novels indicates that they have magic. This echoes a tradition in southern Nigeria which takes being dada as a sign of mystical ability, but such children are often viewed negatively in contemporary Nigerian society. Okorafor – fluent in both traditional and modern Nigerian cultures, and in Fantasy – moves the sign of dada hair from the real world to her imagined ones maintaining meaning and nuance. Both book protagonists are powerful, positive female characters but are viewed with suspicion by the societies in which they live. A White author could arguably have done the same, but would have needed to be fluent in the different cultural "languages."

CONCLUSION

In his discussion of the desire for newness and resulting turns away from medievalist Fantasy inspirations, Attebery argues that the sacred stories of living cultures, as opposed to the mythologies of long dead cultures like the gods of ancient Greek, are "tempting to the writer, for ... they are alive in oral tradition and religious practice and thus powerful, [and] dangerous."[107] The same is true for living cultures and peoples as well, particularly those which are understood as Other to the dominant Whiteness of both Western society broadly and the Fantasy genre more specifically. Newness simultaneously comes from and drives change but of differing kinds. Exploring the roots of diffused Whiteness, as occurs in *Grimm*, has no impact on the racial habits of Fantasy. Attebery suggests that "opening up the genre itself to new voices and perspectives" is an essential aspect of engaging with "living myth;"[108] the same is true of living cultures. The presence of people of colour in both the real world and textual elements of Fantasy is crucial to breaking its habits of Whiteness.

NOTES

1. Attebery, *Stories about Stories: Fantasy and the Remaking of Myth*, 120.
2. These are illustrative examples but by no means a representative list of such works.
3. Wade, "Beyond the Same-Old Fantasy Culture: Nine Authors Worth Reading."
4. Other examples include Various, "Fantasy Novels in Non-Medevial Settings?"; Various, "Non-Western Mythology Based Fantasy Novels ..."
5. Wirth-Nesher, *City Codes: Reading the Modern Urban Novel*, 17.
6. Carroll, "Place and National Identity in Neil Gaiman's *American Gods*," 312.
7. Irvine, "Urban Fantasy," 200–201.
8. Irvine, "Urban Fantasy," 200.
9. Irvine's list is based almost exclusively on an exploration of works which were published in the twentieth century. The latest he considers is from 2006, which may explain why the detective – a relatively recent addition – does not feature in it.
10. Irvine characterizes this as "aesthetic rationale" in "Urban Fantasy," 203.
11. The scholar is supplemented by books – like the librarian and later magic-book seller Rupert Giles in *Buffy the Vampire Slayer* – or even replaced by them as in Aunt Marie's trailer archive in *Grimm*.
12. Mendlesohn, *Rhetorics of Fantasy*, xxii.
13. This is particularly true of works which feature detectives, such as *Grimm*, *Lost Girl*, and Ben Aaronovitch's Rivers of London series.
14. Carter, "Introduction," xvi.
15. The pattern of the protagonist acquiring supernatural powers does not occur in this program, but is rather reversed as the title character – a vampire with a soul – learns to manage human society as well as the non-human.
16. Gill, " 'Cuz the Black Chick Always Gets It First: Dynamics of Race in *Buffy the Vampire Slayer*"; Kirkland, "The Caucasian Persuasion of *Buffy the Vampire Slayer*."
17. Hunt, *Hollywood Diversity Brief: Spotlight on Cable Televison*, 3.
18. Hunt, *Hollywood Diversity Brief*, 6.
19. Whedon, "Chosen."
20. NBC, "About *Grimm* & Cast Bios."
21. Jacobson, *Roots Too: White Ethnic Revival in Post-Civil Rights America*, 122. This also applies to race, even though in a supposedly post-racial society, the word is often avoided.

22. Buffy is an exception, but the program uses the language of descent to frame the way that Slayer abilities are transmitted, the "Slayer line" (genealogy) is mentioned frequently. That Willow disrupts this construct in the final episode by giving power to all the "potential" Slayers undercuts but does not negate the framing up to that point.
23. Gershman, "A New Man."
24. Episode eight of season four. There has been some scholarly debate over the representation of Hus and colonial history. See Alessio, "'Things Are Different Now'?: a Postcolonial Analysis of *Buffy the Vampire Slayer*"; Wilcox, "'Let It Simmer': Tone in 'Pangs.'"
25. Season one, episode seven.
26. Carroll, "Place and National Identity in Neil Gaiman's *American Gods*," 313. *Moonheart* and de Lint's other works have been at times criticized for cultural appropriation, and for his invention of a purely fictional First Nations tribe. I return to the issue of cultural appropriation at the end of this chapter.
27. Although they were published as part of a German nationalist project, the tales quickly came to be considered the cultural inheritance of all the Anglo-Saxons as well, including the English and Americans.
28. Poole, *Monsters in America: Our Historical Obsession with the Hideous and the Haunted*, pt. 1412.
29. This is true even when they are played by Black actors, for example the character of detective Hale in *Lost Girl*.
30. Carroll, "Place and National Identity in Neil Gaiman's *American Gods*," 312.
31. Young, "Whiteness and Time: the Once, Present, and Future Race," 42.
32. See, for example, Barkan, *The Retreat of Scientific Racism: Changing Concepts of Race in Britain and the United States between World Wars*; Jacobson, *Whiteness of a Different Color: European Immigrants and the Alchemy of Race*.
33. Jacobson, *Roots Too*, 7.
34. Jacobson, *Roots Too*, 8.
35. Attebery, *Stories about Stories*, 120.
36. Nick's wesen helper, the vegan blutbad (werewolf) Monroe says this in episode five of season one, Solomon, "Danse Macabre." The same sentiment is repeated by multiple other characters throughout the show.
37. Episode three of the second season.
38. Solomon, "Bad Moon Rising."
39. The existence of wesen, and Nick's role as a Grimm, are revealed to his police partner Hank in the process.
40. They are not cast as Hispanic, and are not named in ways which obviously invoke that culture: Hayden Walker, and Todd are two of them.
41. Racialized discourses of monstrosity are also used in *Buffy*. Ono, "To Be a Vampire on *Buffy the Vampire Slayer*: Race and (Other) Socially Marginalizing Positions on Horror TV."
42. Werner, "Tarantella."
43. Jacobson, *Roots Too*, 8.
44. Others include *Lost Girl*, in which the Fae are those of Celtic mythology, and are linked to Ireland in multiple ways throughout the series.
45. A new translation by Jack Zipes of the first edition has just been released at the time of writing. Grimm and Grimm, *The Original Folks and Fairy Tales of the Brothers Grimm: The Complete First Edition*.

46. Poole, *Monsters in America*, pt. 1387.
47. Haase, "German Fairy Tales and America's Culture Wars: From Grimm's *Kinder- Und Hausmarchen* to William Bennett's *Book of Virtues*," 17.
48. Haase, "German Fairy Tales and America's Culture Wars," 23. This was not the case in other countries, the Grimms' work was favoured by the German Nazi party for its ethno-nationalist aspects, see Kamenetsky, "Folktale and Ideology in the Third Reich."
49. "Blutbad," meaning "blood-bath" are the first kind Nick encounters.
50. Executive Producer David Benioff makes the comment in the short documentary film *The World of* Grimm, included in the DVD box set of season one.
51. NBC, "About *Grimm* & Cast Bios."
52. A few are marked as having other ethnicities, including La Llorona from episode nine of season two.
53. Willsey, "New Fairy Tales Are Old Again: *Grimm* and the Brothers Grimm," 212.
54. The nationalist myth-making purposes of Disney are ignored.
55. Irving, *The Legend of Sleepy Hollow*.
56. Irving, *The Legend of Sleepy Hollow*.
57. Wiseman, "Pilot."
58. The second season had recently concluded at the time of writing.
59. Edwards, "The Lesser Key of Solomon."
60. Stanzler, "Mama."
61. Stanzler, "Mama."
62. The Founding Fathers, as noted above, are also deeply involved and create a variety of artefacts that Abbie and Ichabod use.
63. Lieberman, "Something Wicked This Fae Comes." The episode invokes negative stereotypes of nomadic peoples, and of the Roma in particular, as thieves and murderers.
64. Ibid.
65. The series was optioned for television in 2013, but no casting has been announced to date.
66. Aaronovitch, *Rivers of London*, 113.
67. For discussion of similar moves in non-genre literature see McLeod, *Postcolonial London: Rewriting the Metropolis*.
68. Aaronovitch, *Rivers of London*, 115. Teddington Lock is at Ham in the western suburbs of London. It is the upper limit of the tidal flow of the river.
69. Aaronovitch, *Rivers of London*, 359.
70. The construction of the character in this way evokes the opening of Joseph Conrad's *Heart of Darkness*.
71. Aaronovitch, *Foxglove Summer*, 144.
72. Aaronovitch, *Foxglove Summer*, 233.
73. Aaronovitch, *Foxglove Summer*, 233–234.
74. See, for example, Various, "Customer Discussions: Jim Butcher Drama"; Broaddus, "Putting the Urban in Urban Fantasy."
75. A few recent examples include: Lauren Beukes' *Broken Monsters* (2014), published by Harper Collins; Nalo Hopkinson's *Sister Mine* (2013), published by Grand Central, a division of Hachette; G. Willow Wilson's *Alif the Unseen* (2012) from Corvus, an imprint of Atlantic Books; and Daniel José Older's *Half-Resurrection Blues* (2015) from Roc, a Penguin's Fantasy imprint. There are also numerous small press and self-published examples.

76. Chrisman, *Postcolonial Contraventions: Cultural Readings of Race, Imperialism, and Trannationalism*, 22.
77. Schneer, *London 1900: The Imperial Metropolis*.
78. This is not to dismiss or ignore the presence and history of the First Nations peoples, but to emphasize that the US – and Canada – were both founded in their modern forms by the violence of colonialism.
79. hooks, *Black Looks: Race and Representation*, 28.
80. Hopkinson says: "I, while phenotypically and culturally black, also have Scottish, Jewish, South Asian, and possibly Arawak ancestry," in "Maybe They're Phasing Us In: Re-Mapping Fantasy Tropes in the Face of Gender, Race, and Sexuality," 100. Her first novel, *Brown Girl in the Ring* was published in 1999 and won the Locus Award, while she won the John W. Campbell Award for best new novelist for it.
81. David Anthony Durham makes the comment in Jernigan, "Writing About Race in Science Fiction and Fantasy (Part 2 of a Roundtable Interview)." See also Rutledge, "Futurist Fiction & Fantasy: The 'Racial' Establishment Author(s)."
82. Delany, "Racism and Science Fiction."
83. For example, Hopkinson and Meehan, *So Long Been Dreaming: Postcolonial Science Fiction and Fantasy*.
84. Hopkinson, "A Reluctant Ambassador from the Planet of Midnight," 350. Hopkinson also advocates actively through both her speaking and writing for what might be termed intersectional inclusion, that is, of all marginalized groups including women, and the LGBQTI community as well as people of colour, and particularly those individuals who identities intersect across more than one of these identities. Hopkinson, "Maybe They're Phasing Us In." See also Enteen, "'On the Receiving End of the Colonization': Nalo Hopkinson's 'Nansi Web.'"
85. Her early novels are generally considered Science Fiction however they also have elements of Fantasy.
86. Hopkinson, *Sister Mine*, 57.
87. Hopkinson, *Sister Mine*, 43.
88. Hopkinson, *Sister Mine*, 46.
89. Hopkinson, *Sister Mine*, 47.
90. Other of Hopkinson's works engage with the movement – often forced – of Black people around the globe. Boyle, "Vanishing Bodies: 'Race' and Technology in Nalo Hopkinson's *Midnight Robber*."
91. Hopkinson, *Sister Mine*, 200.
92. Her more recent writing is largely set in an alternate history world in which the Chinese discovered America before Europeans did, resulting in very significant changes in history, the present, and future which make all of them far less Eurocentric than genre convention – either Fantasy or Science Fiction. The stories set in it so far have occurred in the recent past, but mainly in future Science Fictional settings. For details see Bodard, "The Universe of Xuya."
93. Attebery, *Stories about Stories*, 120.
94. Shawl, "Appropriate Cultural Appropriation."
95. de Bodard, "The Big Idea: Aliette de Bodard."
96. hooks, *Writing Beyond Race: Living Theory and Practice*, 22.
97. hooks, *Black Looks: Race and Representation*, 21.
98. I do not attempt to teach authors how to avoid cultural appropriation here. A myriad of online sources offer insights into this and have done so for more

than a decade. The essay by Nisi Shawl I quote in this section is just one example.

99. Shiu, "What Yellowface Hides: Video Games, Whiteness, and the American Racial Order," 117.
100. Haase, "Yours, Mine, or Ours."
101. Translating from one language to another illustrates the point. The same "dog" would be *"un chien"* in French.
102. de Saussure, *Course in General Linguistics*, 71.
103. Shawl, "Appropriate Cultural Appropriation."
104. Shawl, "Appropriate Cultural Appropriation."
105. See chapter four, page 98.
106. Avalon's Willow, "Open Letter: To Elizabeth Bear."
107. Attebery, *Stories about Stories*, 127.
108. Attebery, *Stories about Stories*, 139.

7 Breaking Habits and Digital Communication

The winners for best novel at the three most prestigious awards in fantastic literature – the Hugos, Nebulas, and World Fantasy Awards – provide a useful snapshot of the Science Fiction and Fantasy (SFF) communities historically. Awards, which necessarily are won by a tiny minority of writers, do not represent the whole of any genre community, but they are an indication of whose work is valued and who is prominent within it. The different awarding bodies of the three mean that combined they represent multiple sections of the genre-culture: the Hugos are voted on by members of the annual World Science Fiction Convention; the Nebulas by the members of Science Fiction and Fantasy Writers of America; and the World Fantasy Awards by a small panel usually composed of authors, editors, and academics, and despite its name it is not exclusively for genre fiction.[1] At the time of writing, no author who identifies as a person of colour has won a Hugo award for best novel. Only two have won for best novel at the Nebulas: Samuel R. Delany for *Babel-17* and *The Einstein Intersections* in 1967 and 1968; and Octavia E. Butler for *Parable of the Talents* in 2000. The World Fantasy Award was won by Japanese author Haruki Murakami for *Kafka on the Shore* in 2006. Nnedi Okorafor was the first woman of colour to win with *Who Fears Death*, while Sofia Samatar won for *A Stranger in Olondria* in 2014.

Awards are "instruments of authority … which announce every year that a few select works represent the best of the genre."[2] Of the few novels listed above, only two – Okorafor's and Samatar's – are widely considered to be, or are marketed as, Fantasy. That only one person of colour won any of the three major SFF awards for best novel before the twenty-first century, and that only the two authors of colour to have won for Fantasy novels did so in the past three years, are very strong indications that the genre's habits of Whiteness extend far beyond imagined worlds and into the genre-culture. Controversy attached to the 2014 Hugo nominations likewise give an indication that the habits are not being broken without a fight. Theodore Beale, known also by his online handle Vox Day, and infamous not least for referring to a people of colour, and N. K. Jemisin in particular, as "half-savage," led a successful campaign to have his own and various works, mainly by authors who share his views, nominated; neither he nor they won.[3] Beale is widely perceived as representing the "old guard" of white, male authors, albeit as being at its most extreme edge.[4] None of the works on Beale's campaign ticket won awards, however all but one of the winners was White; Asian American author John Chu won for the short story "The Water That Fall on You From Nowhere." The episode is an illustrative example of the ongoing struggles over the identity of SFF.[5]

This chapter moves beyond the primary focus on representation I have taken thus far to focus on aspects of genre-culture which are not primarily textual and which drive the changes evinced by awards and nominations. I am particularly interested in the role of digital communication technologies in shaping genre-culture in the past fifteen years or so, and their affordances for activism which seeks to break its habits of Whiteness. Web 2.0 is a term that was fashionable for only a few years in the 2000s, but the key features of the kinds of digital technology for which it stood remain salient: "participation, interactivity, collaborative learning, and social networking."[6] SFF fans were "early adopters" of the internet, creating fan fictions archives and mailing lists from the early 1990s,[7] but the changing web infrastructure post-2000 has moved fandom from these relatively centralised forms to vast numbers of overlapping participatory networked spaces. The effects of digital communication technologies on participatory fandom have been widely discussed by scholars;[8] the changing dynamics of fan-producer relationships and roles is a major theme in such work.[9] In this chapter I build on this work, and the theorisation offered in the introduction of this book, to further explore the nature of genre-culture and the communities that comprise it, and the ways in which their nature shapes attempts to change the genre-culture.

FAN COMMUNITIES AS AFFECTIVE NETWORKS

The specific characteristics of genre-culture, and digital fandom in particular, shape any discussion which happens in the spaces of genre communities, whether on- or offline. Genre-culture, as theorised in the introduction, is a network in which influence circulates among texts and "discursive agents."[10] Two major kinds of influence flow along connections: affective and financial, that is, feelings – both positive and negative – and money. Any genre-culture is both affective and financial, in the simplest terms, because audiences buy products that they like, critics recommend them, and authors are influenced by them, resulting in similar works which audiences might also be expected to like and buy. Digital technologies have impacted significantly on the circulation of both affect and money – influence – in the twenty-first century, further exploration of the nature of genre-culture is necessary before I turn to an examination of that impact however.

Genre-culture has always had multiple communities – fan or otherwise – within it: "different spaces meet different needs and attract different types of fans,"[11] and others.[12] Countless communities of varying sizes and kinds exist within genre-culture, and any individual is highly likely to be a member of more than one at any given time. They may exist on or offline, or in a combination of the two. Even within the fandom of a given author or text there are myriad communities, participating in varied ways, and with diverse attitudes to and relationships with the object of their fandom. Social media has created a "perception of proximity" between fans and producers – celebrities – throughout popular culture,[13] while connection with one's readers – and expressing affection for them – is one of the hallmarks of popular fiction.[14] In SFF genre-culture, moreover, there is an extremely high likelihood that authors, editors, and publishers are also fans who grew up reading, watching, and playing Fantasy, and have not stopped doing so on becoming professionals working in the industry. Thus affect is a key aspect of genre-culture broadly, and of the communities within it, and there are likely to not only be individuals who are members of multiple other communities within any given group, but also those who either have or have had multiple agential positions: author, editor, fan and so on.

Digital technology, with its capacity to bring together diverse, disparate, and otherwise separated individuals has vastly increased the capacity of people with shared interests – including but not limited to fans – to form communities. Fan communities still police their boundaries more or less rigorously,[15] and the democratising power of decentralised communication has not erased hierarchies within them.[16] Nonetheless, web technologies have enabled the proliferation of genre spaces, and the formation of communities of colour and activist communities in SFF. Reid observes: "fans of color have established communities in all iterations of the web, including blogs and social networking sites dedicated to antiracist activism, education, and support."[17] Genre-culture, thus, can be best considered as a network of networks. With its in-built multiplicity, the accuracy of the perception that SFF is by, for, and about White people is necessarily called into question. Further exploration of the ways that affect flows within and between communities, however, illuminates how a seemingly monolithic identity can be produced and re-produced.

In her theorisation of blogging communities, Jodi Dean writes that "every little tweet or comment, every forwarded image or petition, accrues a tiny affective nugget;" social networks and blogs, she says, "produce and circulate affect as a binding technique."[18] In the light of this, genre communities – whatever mix of fans and producers belong to them – can be considered, to use Dean's phrase, "affective networks," not only because they are centred on the affect generated by engagement with a text in this first place,[19] but because acts of communication – which form the connections in networks – have their own attendant affect for participants. Dean writes specifically of digital fans and communication, but the same insights obviously also apply to non- and pre-digital forms of communication. Writing a letter to a pulp magazine, producing a fanzine, or going to a convention also helps to create affective networks. Digital communication media may make the formation of affective networks easier, but it is not a causal or a necessary condition, nor are such networks a new phenomenon.[20]

Communicating as part of an affective network, however, does not in and of itself equate to membership of a given community as it is conceived of by its members. Fan communities in particular are always-already undergoing continual processes of creating collective identity, defining themselves in opposition to other fandoms,[21] negotiating "correct" behaviours within their own community,[22] and separating themselves from mere consumers.[23] These processes like other iterations of Selfhood, coalesce around the creation of Otherness, and occur not just in fan-specific communities but across the various spaces of genre-culture. The nature of that Otherness can vary; fan community struggles around gender, for example, have been variously documented,[24] while chapter three demonstrates that race is another locus of difference.[25]

As noted in that chapter, Sara Ahmed's concept of "affective economies" offers insights into the dynamics of genre communities in the light of the shifting locations of Otherness.[26] Genre communities are always-already structured by a narrative of affective connection – usually figured as love – for a text, corpus, or genre. In White nationalist narratives of Self, "it is the love of white, or those recognizable as white, that supposedly explains … [the] shared 'communal' visceral response of hate."[27] In SFF communities, similar structures become intelligible with the substitution of a few words: "it is the love of genre [or author or text], or those recognisable as fans, that explains shared visceral responses of negative affect. Those who are not recognizable as fans – defined by love of genre – are excluded, open to and even deserving of hatred when they intrude into social spaces of genre communities." When members of a community which coheres around positive affect question or critique its focus – liking (or loving) a text, author's corpus, or genre for example – that community reconstitutes itself by directing negative affect towards them, constructing that criticism as a sign of Otherness.

In the discussion threads on *Westeros.org* and the Bioware Social Network examined in chapter three – and many others besides – that Otherness is located in race. The communities which constituted themselves as White, are part of the much larger genre-culture, but while similar debates and formations of identity occur repeatedly within it, many if not most have little impact outside the spaces in which they occur. The individual threads on *Westeros.org* are a case in point, although the various discussions of *Dragon Age* have impacted on representation in that franchise, and have potential to do so in gaming more broadly although I have found no direct evidence this has occurred to date. Many communities within genre-culture, however, overlap with each other as noted above, either because of the membership of individuals or because of common interests. When this occurs, identity may be constituted, reconstituted, and contested across multiple spaces as affect and communication move between them. To explore this further, I turn now to a period when issues of race, representation, and identity became heated topics of debate across a large proportion of SFF genre-culture, moving from one community – largely but not exclusively online – to another and back again: the debates now commonly referred to as RaceFail 09.

RACEFAIL 09

RaceFail 09, also sometimes known as "The Great Cultural Appropriation Debate of Doom" as noted in the previous chapter, is to date the biggest and most long-lasting flare up of the ongoing discussions and debates about race and representation in SFF genre-culture history. Sarah N. Gatson and Robin Anne Reid point out, in one of the very few pieces of scholarship which engage with it, that RaceFail 09 differed from previous online discussions on similar topics because it lasted longer – approximately 3 months from January to March 2009, and it involved authors and editors as well as fans.[28] Much of the discussion took place in the blogging site LiveJournal, which was – and to a lesser degree still is – the location of multiple genre communities.[29] Over the three months, more than 1000 posts and uncounted comments on them were written, and over 500 individual usernames have been identified.[30] Five years later at the time of writing of this book, approximately 75 per cent of the original posts identified in the most comprehensive contemporary list are still extant.

Here I do not attempt to provide a definitive account or commentary on RaceFail 09. Rather, I first outline how the debates moved between existing spaces, generating both positive and negative affect as they did so. My discussion then turns to discursive constructs of race and difference within the overlapping debates, showing that they reflect with those that circulate in wider society, and demonstrating how they resonate and align with strategies fans in multiple communities – SFF and otherwise – use to create and maintain normative identity. I use Eduardo Bonilla-Silva's frameworks of colour-blind racism[31] and fan theory in tandem in that section of the argument.

There are more than 750 RaceFail 09 posts, including some with hundreds of comments, still online, and an in-depth analysis of all of them was beyond the scope – temporal and financial – of the research project on which this book is based. For this reason, the discussion below is based on 25 of the most extensively commented on and linked-to posts. To conduct the analysis, all comments were expanded so that discussion threads following each post were maintained, and the original posts and comments were saved as PDF files so that all comments could be seen in context. Discourse analysis using Bonilla-Silva's concepts was then performed on the files utilising the qualitative analysis program NVIVO© to identify themes and patterns. All material was read and analysed in this fashion at least twice, by myself and at least one research assistant.[32]

At the time of writing, RaceFail 09 occurred five years ago, but its effects are still felt in the genre community, and many of the participants are still active fans and professionals working in the field. The exchanges which took place were at times extremely heated, and at others outright abusive. Some posts were deleted quickly; others were removed and then put back up; still others are no longer extant. Given that most people who contributed to the vast array of blogs, LiveJournal posts, and comment threads did so using screen-names, first names only, or otherwise unidentifiable names, it would have been impossible to seek permission to quote individuals. In an endeavour to respect the privacy of participants, I have quoted only from posts which are still publically available at the time of writing in early 2015 – and have not quoted from any which require membership of a particular site or mailing list to access. In an attempt to keep the reference list of this chapter to a manageable length, and to direct readers not already familiar with RaceFail 09 to a reasonable number of entry points to the vast network of posts, I have quoted directly from a very limited number of the posts in my analysis sample. At no point do I identify the real name of any person whose identity was not a matter of public knowledge at the time the posts and comments were originally written.

A significant aspect of the anti-racist praxis which occurred during Race-Fail 09, and continues in fandom today, involves individuals – often but not always people of colour – observing and discussing the discursive constructs which support racism, colour-blind or not. As Reid recently commented:

> The real work being done on critical race and intersectional issues in theory and praxis in SF communities is being done by people of color in a number of fandom communities, online and offline, some public and some closed to or invisible to white members of the SF communities.[33]

RaceFail 09 involved theoretically and critically sophisticated meta-analyses of what was happening, as it happened,[34] as well as retrospective views.[35] My purpose here is not to replicate what is already being done within SFF communities, or to co-opt or simply report on the work of others. My discussion seeks to draw together many threads in order to demonstrate the connectedness of what can appear to be disparate and unrelated discursive strategies. It illuminates the ways that media fan communities, SFF in particular, struggle with habitual Whiteness on a large scale and to offers new ways of understanding those struggles.

Linking Communities

RaceFail 09 was sparked by posts by White authors about writing characters from backgrounds other than their own in early January. The late Jay Lake wrote one, titled "Another shot at thinking about the Other,"[36] closely followed by Elizabeth Bear's "Whatever You're Doing You're Probably Wrong."[37] The discussion on Lake's post foreshadowed, and overlapped, many of the topics and debates which later dominated RaceFail 09, although Bear's is generally considered the catalyst for the broader debates because it sparked two direct responses from readers of colour: "I Didn't Dream of Dragons," by Deepa D.,[38] and "Open Letter to Elizabeth Bear," by Avalon's Willow.[39] Both expressed their anger and frustration with stereotypical representation of characters of colour by White writers in SFF. Issues relating to cultural appropriation and ownership of culture – who can and should write about cultures which are not their own, and how – were the focus of initial discussions in RaceFail 09, and remained a theme throughout, as noted in the previous chapter.

Although SFF genre-culture is strongly networked, the conversations happening in one community or set of connected communities can take some time to move to new spaces, if they do at all, and this was arguably a significant issue in RaceFail 09. Social networks, although they connect people, can also create communities which are relatively closed or invisible to each other; the niche spaces of like-minded individuals that digital communication enable are not always easily permeable. Mary Anne Mohanraj, who wrote two long posts during RaceFail 09 on John Scalzi's blog commented in hindsight:

> There were these long intense complicated conversations happening in LiveJournal. There was a real frustration that what the participants thought that the writers, the professional writers and editors were deliberately ignoring and were essentially on the side of the people they were perceiving as problematic and/or racist. From my point of view it was entirely invisible to me ... when it finally came out into the blogs and this became visible I think a lot of us were very horrified that we had missed all of this.[40]

She pointed to Scalzi's initial reaction to the debates when they entered his space as evidence of this. He was dismissive not of the need for a discussion of race and representation, but of the manner in which it was being conducted in the first instance – in early March – describing the debates as "flinging spittle" and saying that he "stayed out of it until I was dragged into it by people pulling discussion-related shenanigans on my site."[41] He posted an apology "for that inaccurate characterization, and the various offense it caused" after having the ongoing situation explained both on and off his blog, and invited Mohanraj to contribute "something on the topic of race and science fiction and fantasy" on his blog; her two posts are among the most commented on in the wider RaceFail 09 discussions.[42]

As the discussions extended into – and moved backward and forward between – multiple different spaces, the affective communities centred in them constituted their identities in response. With habits of Whiteness so deeply ingrained in SFF genre-culture that they often shape, as I have variously shown throughout this book, even works which actively seek to be progressive and inclusive, it is perhaps not surprising that many did so along racial lines and using racial discourses. The immediate result was a ripple effect of visible Whiteness that spread – albeit not unchallenged – through the genre-culture; what had once been largely transparent to many became much clearer to see.

Examining the responses to Bear's early posts illuminates the nature of genre blogging communities and the ways that they construct identity. The comments on Bear's 12th January post were very positive, and she was thanked there multiple times for writing it and for generating discussion of what was agreed to be an important issue – framed as "writing the Other."[43] The readers – and commenters – on Bear's blog established it as a community of people concerned with improving racial representation in SFF writing. On this post the comments generated affect through the discussion and general agreement, while a thread of the discussion also established that Bear and her readers did *not* take the same approach as Guy Gavriel Kay; negative affect directed outward accompanies the positive affect generated by agreement.

Two days later, Bear posted again, framing her comments as a direct response to Avalon's Willow,[44] it began: "You're right. You're pretty much right categorically and without exception." The first comment on that post was titled, in bold "seems an overreaction," and this set the tone for the great majority of comments which followed.[45] The change in tone exemplifies the economic nature of affect as Ahmed theorises it: Otherness is no longer located in the "bad" work and practice of a writer, but in the person, practice, and criticisms of a reader. The discourses which structure Otherness as constituted in the comments on the second post are, moreover, strongly racialized, as were others which were deployed throughout RaceFail 09, as I argue below.

The affordances of Web 2.0 technology in the creation of networked communities, combined with the older technology of hyperlinking, became extremely fraught during RaceFail 09. Some participants, particularly those who posted on LiveJournal and Dreamwidth and were accustomed to having their writings accessed only by existing circles on that forum, found the circulation of links to their posts intrusive and unwelcome.[46] Spaces designated as being for people of colour only were also – and still are – often not respected by Whites. People of colour in particular found that digital spaces which had once been safe for them were made highly contested – and at times dangerous and abusive – by the intrusion of aggressive questioners. Linking, while often presented and intended as a sign of engagement and respect,[47] also enabled the movement of negative affect directed outward toward the Other to move between communities. People of colour – and allies – found themselves having to defend their own spaces and ideas in ways that Whites largely did not.

The comments on Bear's initial post compared to Avalon's Willow's and Deepa D.'s demonstrate the key point that not all genre spaces are considered equal. While some commenters on Bear's post critiqued each other's statements, and others offered defensive accounts of their own ideas, and practices, there are only two critiques of the post in the comments. N. K. Jemisin wrote, "Yes on 98% of this, but one caveat," suggesting that writers should do research before asking people of colour for information, and emphasising that they should not assume all Black people have the same ideas or experiences; Bear amended the post. A second comes approximately 100 comments into the discussion, and is likewise embedded in a positive framework. It appear at the end of a contribution of several short para-graphs, begins "I am so with you on all of this," is followed with "maybe I'm just grouchy tonight," and comments on the blog post itself not Bear's fiction: "I couldn't help but think that you managed to turn your audience, or at least that 12-year-old kind, into exactly that: The Kid."[48]

Both Avalon's Willow and Deepa D., in contrast, were quickly attacked on their own blogs in terms that criticised their personal practice while also making very broad claims. The first comment on Avalon's Willow's post thanked her for writing it, but the second, written by a self-identified "white English male" attacked her position, taking a defensive tone: "The easiest thing for me, clearly, would be to not bother [to engage with people of colour] and therefore not take the risk of writing such characters. But that just perpetuates the exclusion and that's wrong too."[49] The "damned if I do, damned if I don't" trope was repeated time and time again throughout RaceFail 09 as a justification for White writers to not even attempt to be more inclusive in their writing. Deepa D.'s ideas, phrasing, and feelings were also very quickly critiqued in the comments section of her post. There are multiple factors in the different levels of respect evinced across these three posts, including that Bear is an established figure in SFF genre-culture com-pared to two fans who were relatively peripheral and insignificant to it. The discourses used to critique Avalon's Willow and Deepa D., however, were also racially loaded, as I explore in the following section.

Colour-Blind Racism and RaceFail 09

Bonilla-Silva developed his discursive frames based on interviews conducted in the context of the social and cultural context of the United States. In the current neoliberal global climate they are also applicable in more interna-tional contexts as well, although the majority of participants known to have been part of RaceFail 09 are based in the US. The four broad frames – abstract liberalism, minimization, cultural racism, and naturalization – support an ideology Bonilla-Silva terms colour-blind racism, which he argues replaced Jim Crow ideologies in the post-Civil Rights era. He says that it:

> explains contemporary racial inequality as the outcome of non-racial dynamics ... whites rationalize minorities' contemporary status as the product of market dynamics, naturally occurring phenomena, and blacks' imputed cultural limitations.[50]

The ideology enables Whites to absolve themselves as individuals, and the social and cultural institutions which maintain their privilege, of racism.

Abstract Liberalism

Abstract Liberalism consists of "using ideas associated with political ... [and] economic liberalism in abstract manners to explain racial matters."[51] In RaceFail 09 discussions, discourses of freedom, and restriction, of speech were frequently deployed. "Damned if we do and damned if we don't (We meaning the Caucasian folks)" summarizes the position of many participants in RaceFail 09 who identify themselves as White, often male writers and say they fear being called racist both for *not* writing characters that are not white and for writing them badly.[52] One commenter on "I Didn't Dream of Dragons" observed similar phenomena among fan-fiction writers: "Fans are scared to write black characters for fear of offending, so all the black characters simply disappear."[53] The idea is often expressed in ways that constructed White writers as powerless, for example: "I'm a white male, and this suggests that I'm not allowed to write anything but white males."[54] According to this discourse, as Deepa D. pointed out in a follow-up post, it is writers – many of whom identify themselves as White – who are shifted in the position of the oppressed where their freedom to write is curtailed.[55] The use of the language of freedom, particularly freedom of speech, is particularly potent in the United States, and resonates with one of the tenets of neoliberal thought.

The idea that writers can and should write about characters that come from different racial and cultural backgrounds to their own is almost universally held in SFF genre-culture, and is espoused in calls for the improvement of diversity in fictional worlds. [56] This includes a significant number of RaceFail 09 posts by people of colour.[57] Avalon's Willow critiqued not the act of a White author – Bear – writing characters of colour, but that she did so badly by using racist stereotypes, with the result that "I couldn't finish reading your book because I threw it across the room in disgust."[58] Negative responses and open critique are, according to the discursive constructs discussed in the previous paragraph, mechanisms of control which people of colour use to restrict the freedom of White writers. The caveat that representing characters of colour – and indeed any characters from minority and marginalized backgrounds – should be done with respect, and that doing so does not protect an author from criticism or entitle him or her to congratulations is overlooked, dismissed, and/or taken as a restriction according to this construct. The freedom to speak – write – un-censured is constructed as the freedom to write uncensored.

The concept of individual freedom underpins the idea that individual authors are the only true arbiters of who or what should appear in any given narrative, and that their decisions are not connected to social and cultural norms or to the habits of genre. The following comment was made in response to "I Didn't Dream of Dragons":

> If a character needs to be a certain ethnicity, then they are. Or if I see a character as a certain race or religion or whatever, and I envision them that way, then they are. The problem arises when you force characteristics on unnecessarily. I think this often stems from editorial suggestions/decisions.[59]

A comment on Mohanraj's first guest post on Scalzi's blog is another example:

> It's not your job to write fiction that flatters any particular group, due to current racial pressures and political correctness. Being sensitive to the race factor is one thing. Letting it dictate and control your characterization is probably a problem that will negatively impact your fiction overall.[60]

According to this manner of thinking, if characters of colour are to appear in imagined worlds, the process by which they do so must be organic, somehow detached from all social or political influence.

Bonilla-Silva argues that "a core tenet of liberal democracies is that government should intervene in economic and social matters as little as possible."[61] While the coercive force of "editorial suggestions/decisions" and "political correctness" are not linked to government or legislation, the rhetorical construct resonates strongly with resistance to, for example, affirmative action legislation. Neoliberalism's expression in the creative world argues for author/creator autonomy, which takes up Romantic and Modernist lines of thought that argued for the primacy of the artist. The notion that individual freedom, specifically the freedom of the author-as-artist to create the narrative and its world, is paramount above all other concerns is founded the principals of liberalism, extrapolated from the political sphere to the cultural.[62] The idea that an individual author is both capable of making and should be free to make decisions based entirely on their imagination is a concept that resonates extremely strongly with neoliberal ideas about individual freedom.

The figure of the author-as-artist is central to narratives which valorise fans' identity as coherent, authentic, and distinct from mere consumers of mass culture.[63] "Editorial decisions/suggestions" and "racial pressures and political correctness" are constructed in the quotes above as both external and extraneous to the artistic process of creation, as forces which will result in a work which has lower intrinsic artistic value even as it conforms with what are implied to be commercially-driven directives. Fans – or anyone else – who ask for better representation of characters of colour, or who critique a particular work, are constructed as inappropriately demanding, and, in the terms of Abstract Liberalism, encroaching on the (artistic) freedom of the author. They can thus be excluded from membership in a fan community. This type of discourse is often deployed in discussions which are *not* related overtly to race, however, its structure forms an established pattern onto which issues of race can be grafted.

Minimization

The second of Bonilla-Silva's broad frameworks is minimization, which "suggests that discrimination is no longer a central factor affecting minorities' life chances."[64] It took a range of forms in his study, including dismissing claims of discrimination as unfounded on the grounds that people from minorities might misinterpret situations or be overly sensitive.[65] Such claims were extremely common throughout RaceFail 09 in a very wide range of forums, particularly in debates about whether a given fictional work had been interpreted "correctly" by a reader or readers of colour. Bear's *Blood and Iron* was a common topic of discussion after Avalon's Willow criticised both book and author in her Open Letter post.[66] When Bear responded with an "Apology" post which said "you're right," the comments thread took a different tone.[67] The first was headed "Seems an overreaction," and began: "I have to say I find the open letter an overreaction. Over sensitivity to perceived racism tends to result in the nit picking of words and sentence structure. This open letter is full of just that."[68] An author, commenting on the same post, said "there is nothing I can do to present people from perceiving racism if they want to." A comment on another of Bear's posts said: "I read your book. It's not racist. If it gets interpreted that way, that's the eye of the beholder."[69] Yet another said: "you were wilfully misread and misinterpreted."[70] These types of statements were regularly directed at anyone who argued that any text included racist stereotypes or attitudes.[71] They locate fault in the person of colour, not in either the fictional work or the author who created it.

Fan communities all have, as Harry Jenkins argues, "particular interpretive conventions."[72] Some ways of reading a text, whatever medium it may be in, both as textual interpretation and mode and style of engagement, are correct according to those conventions and others are not. The "right" way of reading any given text is constructed through discussions – which may or may not also be struggles depending on those involved. Repeated statements that Avalon's Willow – and others involved in RaceFail 09 – misread and misinterpreted Bear's book in particular, and others that came into the discussion, racially charge this strategy for policing identity. "Incorrect" reading practices are explicitly linked to race in comments quoted above, in a discourse that effectively equates acceptable or genuine fandom with Whiteness by suggesting that the perceived failure to read correctly results from race.

Naturalization

This discursive frame, Bonilla-Silva argues, "allows whites to explain away racial phenomena by suggesting they are natural occurrences."[73]

Participants in his studies often used phrases like "natural" or "that's the way it is" to explain "events or actions that could otherwise be interpreted as racially motivated," including segregation in housing and schooling, as well as opposition to interracial marriage.[74] In the comments to Mohanraj's first guest-post on Scalzi's blog, one person wrote:

> The dominant culture in America is based on our European settlers, who generally have light skin tones (not saying that's good or bad, it just is) ... to get past our natural biases, we first need to understand what we HAVE those biases.

Key terms of this frame are used here – "it just is" and "natural" – in a post which argues that US society is "CULTURALLY BIASED, not racist," and that racism based on biology is largely a thing of the past.[75] The comment argues that overcoming "natural biases" is a positive and necessary thing for social progress, but nonetheless deploys some of the discursive frameworks which can be used to perpetuate colour-blind racism.

A similar sentiment can be discerned in RaceFail 09 discussions when participants argued that non-Western cultures were not often or well represented in speculative fiction because readers – and implicitly writers – were not interested in them. The comments were often put in cultural rather than directly racial terms, and thus intersect with the frame of Cultural Racism, discussed below. One person commented in response to "I Didn't Dream of Dragons," acknowledging that she or he was generalising, that:

> Most of US book readers and movies viewers have absolutely no curiosity or interest in worlds – I wouldn't say alien – but simply non-US cultures; they want to find their own values and frame of mind under fake exotic appearances. And of course those leanings are served, but also generated by political and economic powers.[76]

The post argues that this situation cannot be changed and that no attempt to do so is worth the effort: "I don't see any reason to fight the windmills ... Unless you are intending to change the very DNA of US culture."[77] The underlying belief that "this just how it is" resonates with Bonilla-Silva's framework very strongly, naturalizing Whiteness as dominant not only within US culture generally, but within SFF specifically.

Cultural Racism

Cultural Racism "relies on culturally based arguments ... to explain the standing of minorities in society."[78] Thus "minorities [supposed] lack of effort, loose family organization, and inappropriate values" might be raised to justify social and cultural inequalities. One long response to Deepa D.'s post exemplifies this by characterizing Indian culture negatively in order to justify the dominance of English-language Western publishing. The anonymous commenter wrote:

> Had India valued it's people, wanted to provide them with more books and opportunities, it have easily had a larger publishing industry, and done much more for them. Its elites view the majority of its fellow citizens as slaves, nothing more. That has nothing to do with the west.[79]

The same comment blames the Chinese government for the loss of US jobs in book production, then goes on to accuse Deepa D. of displacing a "citizen teacher" by working in the US. The tone is highly aggressive, even for a blogosphere phenomenon like RaceFail 09, even though it does not use overtly abusive language such as racial slurs. In another example, a commenter told Deepa D. that she was over-reacting, feeling the wrong emotions, and acting wrongly as a result of them:

> But why do you need to struggle? Why don't you just shrug and laugh as Europeans do when they are stereotypes and caricatured by North American (or more precisely US) fiction or script writers?[80]

The implication is that people from European cultures, as opposed to Deepa D.'s self-identified Indian background, would not have this "incorrect" response, generalising from the commenter's own beliefs about both cultures.[81]

Most cultural racism expressed during RaceFail 09 resembles the second comment more than the first, not because it is less aggressive but because it focuses on the emotions of people of colour and the ways they expressed them. A common discourse used in attempts to negate or dismiss the statements of people of colour was that they were excessively emotional and irrational. One person wrote in a comment on Bear's "apology" post: "If people can't plainly & accurately say what they think or feel w/o [without] tying themselves first in knots then there is no solid foundation on which to build bridges for understanding if not agreement."[82] A comment about people of colour and their views and statements on Bear's blog is representative of a much wider trend: "This is Sickening Absolutely Sickening to read. Walking on a tightrope over mindless, jabbering hordes."[83] These statements, although they vary in focus, are all criticisms of the tone in which people of colour – both those who identified as such and commenters who did not but were assumed to be because of the views they held – expressed themselves.

Characterizing people of colour – again especially but not only Black people – as "hordes" or mobs is a racist stereotype, however, one which is common to Fantasy worlds as discussed in chapter four, the collective responses of people of colour were termed "orcing."[84] Dismissing the tone of critical posts as excessively emotional and irrational, moreover, invokes racist stereotypes directly. It also deflects the initial critique and categorises the person or people making it as the "problem," as multiple RaceFail 09 participants argued.[85] The trope, in all its varied forms, expresses cultural racism by de-valuing people of colour, their experiences, and ideas, on the grounds of irrationality evidenced by their actions. It invokes racist stereotypes but retains deniability by focusing on actions – in this case, words – not overtly on biology. The distinction between failure to read "correctly" and to express the resulting "incorrect" feelings in a way that is deemed acceptable separates the minimization of the former from the cultural racism of the latter.

Attempts to control expression and modify behaviour which is seen to be inappropriate are, as Lucy Bennett argues, exercises in "subcultural power" which police normative identity in fan communities.[86] Expressing oneself "incorrectly" – excessively – is not always associated with race or cultural racism, although it is intimately linked to feeling "incorrectly" – again usually excessively. Matt Hills shows that historical "pathologizing stereotypes" of fans as excessively attached to or over-emotional about a given text are being used by fans against each other.[87] Although his work is on inter-fandom, the same tropes also occur in intra-fandom settings. As is the case for minimization, an existing discourse common to fan communities takes on new resonances when it is deployed in discussions of race.

After Effects

Richard Dyer rightly argues that Whiteness "secures its dominance by pretending not to be anything in particular," by being invisible and unremarkable because of its omnipresence.[88] The habitual Whiteness of SFF genre-culture is rendered visible through critiques of representation, and by people of colour asserting their own presence and perspectives. The resonances between colour-blind racism and discourses of fan identity demonstrate that the systemic racism of twenty-first-century Western societies – particularly but not exclusively that of the US – significantly influence the habits of SFF genre-culture. RaceFail 09 has arguably had ongoing effects precisely because these resonances were demonstrated; the normativity of Whiteness became hyper-visible through the thousands of discussion threads now grouped under the single label. The sheer scale and number of participants – across multiple communities and parts of SFF genre-culture – meant that neither habits of Whiteness nor the presence of people of colour could be as easily dismissed or ignored, while doing so – whether intentionally or not – is highly likely to be challenged.

One of the major affordances of digital communication technology is, as noted above, the creation of new communities. These, in turn, can enable people of colour to assert their presence in genre-culture. In just one example, a 2009 post on the LiveJournal community *Deadbrowalking* invited "POC/non-white" fans from around the globe to "give yourself a name check in this thread," because, as the original poster wrote, "I'm tired of people trying to render us invisible unless they have been given a memo about our existences."[89] The thread, titled "Wild Unicorn Herd Check In," responded to an assertion by the white SFF author Lois McMaster Bujold that "Readers of Color" had only come to SFF recently.[90] Reid analyses the kind of terms the 785 unique posters who name-checked identified themselves by, finding a significant range from the geographical to the hyphenated, intersectional, racial, and ethnic.[91] Their comments, as Reid observes, asserted not only their own existences, but sometimes those of their parents and grandparents among SFF audiences.[92] Small scale conversations, such as those discussed in chapter three, can still see fan communities constitute identity as White, but the presence and voices of people of colour within the broader genre-culture breaks the pattern of assumed and unchallenged Whiteness – as occurred on a massive scale during RaceFail 09.

In 2010, Jemisin wrote on her blog "RaceFail was a good thing. In fact, I think it was a *necessary* thing – not just for me and other writers/fans of color, but for the SFF field as a whole," because it "shocked the whole genre enough to make it pay attention."[93] Sparked by Jemisin's post, another blogger wrote, "As much as I'd like to simply attribute the changes to the discussions getting through to people, I think there's a second, more powerful force at hand. That during these discussions, there's been a lot of networking among POC – developing groups, organizing, and even publishing houses."[94] Mohanraj expressed a similar opinion almost five years later, saying "all I can say about long term effects is that what I'm seeing is a groundswell of conversation on these topics. I think it starts with RaceFail."[95] She also pointed to a variety of moves in SFF communities to foster the presence and voices of people of colour that have been developed in the years since RaceFail 09, although proving a direct connection with any given program, as she observed, is practically impossible.[96] Conversations, like those gathered under the RaceFail 09 umbrella, involve significant anti-racist work and make strong contributions to making SFF's habits of Whiteness visible, and breaking them. They also, as Mohanraj suggests, contribute significantly to efforts and organisations supporting the active presence of people of colour in SFF genre-culture.

CHANGING GENRE-CULTURE

Action seeking to challenge and change the habits of Whiteness of SFF genre-culture has been organized in online spaces for at least fifteen years,[97] and in offline venues as well. In 1999, inspired in part by Delany's important 1998 essay "Racism and Science Fiction,"[98] attendees of colour at the feminist convention Wiscon petitioned for greater attention to be paid to race, and met at the convention to plan future action. The formation of the Carl Brandon Society which works to "help build further awareness of race and ethnicity in speculative literature and other related fields" was a major result of their discussions.[99] The Carl Brandon Society exerts what Westfahl calls a "mechanism" of control,[100] by giving annual awards for speculative fiction works created by people of colour, and to works which engage with "issues of race and ethnicity."[101] It also gives financial support to help authors of colour attend the Clarion writers workshops,[102] and supports "Con or Bust," a program which "helps people of color/non-white people attend SFF conventions"[103] The Carl Brandon Society and Con or Bust are just two examples of the myriad ways people in SFF genre-culture are making organized efforts to change its habits, both of which are enabled by the affordances of digital communication and communities. Con or Bust, for example, is for the most part funded through an annual online auction.[104]

Crowd-funding websites and campaigns have become ubiquitous in genre spaces in recent years, and have helped increase the diversity of published voices by allowing audience members to contribute financially *before* publication. The anthology *Long Hidden: Speculative Fiction from the Margins of History* (2014) is one example of a project aimed at diversifying the authorial and textual voices of Fantasy that was successfully funded through Kickstarter. The key factor in the success of crowd-funding campaigns is translating affect into financial backing. "Fandom is an inherently emotional experience; digital technology can facilitate and channel that emotion into new avenues," including supporting the *creation* of desired works, as opposed to merely consuming them as in traditional capitalist models.[105] Hills shows that potential producers need to successfully engage the emotions of fans in order to gain their financial support.[106] Mohanraj, who has run two successful Kickstarter campaigns, identified three potential points at which affect might be translated to financial support in a genre setting: a concept or "idea that people want to get behind;" an existing "visible profile" for the project's creator(s); a personal connection – friendship – with them; and to fund a series that has already begun but will otherwise not be finished.[107] Established connections within the genre-culture are highly significant. Communities of readers interested in stories featuring protagonists of colour are crucial to publication and other crowd-funding projects.

Digital technologies have not only enabled fans to "adopt producer-like commercial functions," as Hills puts it,[108] but authors and other creators to publish their work in new ways which may arguably increase the diversity of voices and representation in SFF. Suzanne Dietzel argues of popular culture broadly that "the internet and computer technology have greatly contributed to the increased availability of black popular fiction," including through self-publishing.[109] While publishing houses profoundly shape the genre, the influence of self-publishing arguably has become significant in SFF in recent years. 2013 saw the first self-published work nominated for a Hugo award – Seanan McGuire's novelette "In Sea Salt Tears." Self-publishing is often seen as a way of improving the diversity of works available to the reading public, in terms of the kinds of writing and the representation of minority authors and characters.[110] Self-publishing has been a significant force in African American literature, including genre fiction, for decades, including before the advent of ebooks and print-on-demand publishing.[111] The situation is not straight forward however. Multiple factors, including access to technology, mean that the state of the playing field is far from level for authors from marginalized backgrounds, including but not limited to racial and ethnic minorities.[112]

The greater numbers and diversity of available works which results from digital publishing, including but not limited to self-publishing, "does not necessarily mean more diversity is consumed;"[113] simply making a narrative available does not guarantee audience members will find it, or read it if they do. Faced with an ocean full of possible choices, readers often rely on recommender systems, which range from commercial algorithms such as Amazon's "Customers Who Bought This Item Also Bought" bar at the bottom of every page, to crowd-sourced review sites like Goodreads, and social networks both online and offline. Systems like Amazon's can "exert a concentration bias,"[114] that is, they work against diversity in consumer choice by suggesting only works which are algorithmically "like" those in which a customer has already evinced interest.

The influence of social networking on diversity in the books that potential readers find has not, to date, been the topic of in-depth scholarly research; the small amount which does exist focuses on user behaviour and rightly observes that "it is impossible to know how … invisible or lurking readers have been influenced."[115] Nonetheless, anecdotal evidence strongly suggests that networked communication can play a significant role. Jemisin remarks, for example, that in order to find books written by authors or featuring characters of colour before the 1990s, "black readers had to rely on world-of-mouth – which, pre-internet, was actually kind of limiting."[116] The searchability of the internet enables even those readers who are not connected to communities who might share recommendations about diverse works to find information. Sites like Pinterest, Goodreads, and blogs provide opportunities for sharing and accessibility that are exponentially greater than any other method of communication.[117]

The scale on which communication can occur is also a significant factor. To take a single example among the myriad that could be mentioned: as I began drafting this chapter, World and British Fantasy Award–winning novelist Sofia Samatar tweeted a link to Kevin Rigathi's volume of Kenyan Fantasy available on *Will This be a Problem?*[118] Samatar at the time had around 3,200 Twitter followers. The simple act of tweeting a link exponentially increased the possible audience for the volume and the writers whose work appears in it. Rigathi said that the post about the volume had its "busiest day" on the day of Samatar's tweet, and that the following day, "the number of people who read the post and also went on to the volume was the highest."[119] Although the exact number of potential readers who first found and then read the post as a result of Samatar's tweet, there is no question from the interest it sparked and the spike in readership that followed it that a relatively small act like sharing a link can make a significant difference in visibility.[120]

CONCLUSION

In his essay "Racism and Science Fiction," Delany pointed to connections between representation and economic power, asserting that "until, say, black writers start to number thirteen, fifteen, twenty percent of the total," at which point "the competition [to the White genre establishment] might be perceived as having some economic heft, chances are we will have as much racism and prejudice here as in any other field."[121] Written just at the advent of Web 2.0, Delany's essay does not predict the burgeoning of communities and technologies which have enabled substantial diversification of the genre-culture. The most fundamental affordance of digital communication has been the ability of people of colour to assert their presence and have their voices heard in new ways within on- and offline communities, and SFF genre-culture as a whole. The circulation of affect and money – influence – within that highly complex network is changed by people and voices, particularly when they act collectively or with a common purpose to break its habits of Whiteness.

NOTES

1. The Hugos were first awarded in 1953, and have been annual since 1955; the Nebulas have been awarded since 1966; and the World Fantasy Awards since 1975.
2. Westfahl, "Who Governs Science Fiction?," 64.
3. See, for example, Baker-Whitelaw, "Hugos Give More Nods to Women, but Nominations Still Stir Controversy." A similar move, involving Beale and other authors and a "slate" of nominees, is troubling the SFF genre-culture in 2015 as this book is at proof stage.
4. He was expelled from the Science Fiction and Fantasy Writers of America after using that organization's Twitter feed to promote a blog post he wrote as Vox Day which viciously attacked Jemisin, including implied threats of violence. See "Beale Expelled from SFWA." This followed a campaign for his removal by a number of other authors including Jim C. Hines and Amal El-Mohtar. See, for example, El-Mohtar, "Calling for the Expulsion of Theodore Beale from SFWA."
5. In digital spaces, and in many offline ones as well, the boundaries between Science Fiction and Fantasy communities are so porous that they are functionally non-existent. Individual locations may be devoted to works which sit firmly in one genre or the other, but the genre-cultures are not separate. In this chapter, I discuss organizations, movements, events, and communities which bridge both genres, using "SFF" rather than Fantasy to refer to them. I do not explore those areas of the interlinked genre-cultures that are dedicated to Science Fiction, such as the magazine *Asimov's* or the Phillip K. Dick Awards.

6. Flew, *New Media*, 17.
7. Coppa, "A Brief History of Media Fandom," 54.
8. The two foundational works are Jenkins, *Fans, Bloggers, and Gamers: Exploring Participatory Culture*; Jenkins, *Convergence Culture: When Old and New Media Collide*. The *Journal of Transformative Works and Cultures* is devoted to digital media fandom. http://journal.transformative works.org/.
9. For example, Hills, "Veronica Mars, Fandom, and the 'Affective Economics' of Crowdfunding Poachers"; Pearson, "Fandom in the Digital Era"; Shefrin, "*Lord of the Rings, Star Wars*, and Participatory Fandom: Mapping New Congruencies Between the Internet and Media Entertainment Culture."
10. Bould and Vint, "There Is No Such Thing as Science Fiction," 48.
11. Zubernis and Larsen, *Fandom at the Crossroads: Celebration, Shame and Fan/ Producer Relationships*, 9.
12. I take a broad definition of "community" here, meaning any group – informal or formal – whose members share interests, specifically in some aspect of Fantasy or SFF more broadly.
13. Beer, "Making Friends with Jarvis Cocker: Music Culture in the Context of Web 2.0," 232.
14. Gelder, *Popular Fiction: the Logics and Practices of a Literary Field*, 23.
15. Zubernis and Larsen, *Fandom at the Crossroads*, 9.
16. Pearson, "Fandom in the Digital Era," 93.
17. Reid, "The Wild Unicorn Herd Check-in: the Politics of Race in Science Fiction Fandom," 228.
18. Dean, *Blog Theory: Feedback and Capture in the Circuits of Drive*, 95.
19. This is usually, although not always, positive. Some communities are focused on negative responses, the most well-known at the time of writing is Iswintercoming.org, and *A Song of Ice and Fire*-focused community, which exists largely to critique George R. R. Martin and was founded after criticisms of him were removed from *Westeros.org*.
20. The earliest known Science Fiction fanzine was published in 1930, while pulps such as *Weird Tales* featured letters pages from readers to communicate with each other as well as the editor. A 1936 letter to *Weird Tales*, moreover, proposed the creation of fan clubs in cities across the U.S.A.
21. Hills, "*Twilight* Fans Represented in Commercial Paratexts and Inter-Fandoms."
22. Bennett, "Discourses of Order and Rationality: Drooling R. E. M. Fans as 'Matter out of Place'"; Johnson, "Fan-tagonism: Factions, Institutions, and Constitutive Hegemonies of Fandom."
23. Hills, *Fan Cultures*, 27.
24. Bury, *Cyberspaces of Their Own: Female Fandoms Online*; Larbalastier, *The Battle of the Sexes in Science Fiction*; Merrick, *The Secret Feminist Cabal: A Cultural History of Science Fiction Feminisms*.
25. See also Young, "Race in Online Fantasy Fandom: Whiteness on Westeros. org," 742–743.
26. Ahmed, "Affective Economies."
27. Ahmed, "Affective Economies," 118.
28. Gatson and Reid, "Race and Ethnicity in Fandom," para. 3.3.
29. George R. R. Martin is the most high profile Livejournal user at the time of time of writing.

30. Gatson and Reid, "Race and Ethnicity in Fandom." Their count is based on a list created at the time by Rydra Wong, which is still available at Wong, "RaceFail 09." I have based my own research on this list as well.
31. Bonilla-Silva, *Racism Without Racists: Color-Blind Racism and the Persistence of Racial Inequality in the United States.*
32. I am deeply grateful for the work of my research assistants, Dr Kieryn McKay and Timothy Steains, who performed the initial qualitative analysis using NVIVO. Also to Lydia Saleh Rofail who collected material.
33. Reid, "The Wild Unicorn Herd Check-in," 228.
34. For example, Somerville, "A Themed Summary of RaceFail 09"; Tablesaw, "O HAI RACEFAILZ: Notes on Reading an Internet Conflict."
35. For example, Jemisin, "Why I Think RaceFail Was The Bestest Thing Evar for SFF."
36. Lake, "Another Shot at Thinking about the Other."
37. Bear, "Whatever You're Doing, You're Probably Wrong."
38. Deepa D., "I Didn't Dream of Dragons." The post was printed in *Foundation* as Dharmadhikari, "Surviving Fantasy through Post-Colonialism."
39. Avalon's Willow, "Open Letter: To Elizabeth Bear."
40. Personal interview via Skype, 28th January, 2015.
41. Scalzi, "The Internets Hate Scalzi!"
42. Mohanraj, "Mary Anne Mohanraj Gets You Up to Speed, Part I"; Mohanraj, "Mary Anne Mohanraj Gets You Up to Speed, Part II."
43. The post gathered almost 300 comments between 12th and 15th January.
44. Bear also linked to Deepa D.'s essay, and described it as "excellent."
45. Bear, "Real Magic Can Never Be Made by Offering Up Someone Else's Liver."
46. For example, Bales, "Me and RaceFail 2009 and the Ridiculous Fan History Wiki Page."
47. Bear's links to Avalon's Willow's and Deepa D.'s posts are examples.
48. Comment section in Bear, "Whatever You're Doing, You're Probably Wrong."
49. Comment section in Avalon's Willow, "Open Letter."
50. Bonilla-Silva, *Racism Without Racists*, 2.
51. Bonilla-Silva, *Racism Without Racists*, 28.
52. Comment section, Bear, "Whatever You're Doing, You're Probably Wrong."
53. Comment section, Deepa D., "I Didn't Dream of Dragons."
54. Comment on Bear, "Whatever You're Doing, You're Probably Wrong." Similar phrasing was used in the comments on Deepa D., "I Didn't Dream of Dragons."
55. Deepa D., "White People, Its Not All about You, but for This Post It Is."
56. See, for example, Gunn, "Racial Identity and Writing - Part 5."
57. For example, Mohanraj, "Mary Anne Mohanraj Gets You Up to Speed, Part II."
58. Avalon's Willow, "Open Letter."
59. Comment section, Deepa D., "I Didn't Dream of Dragons."
60. Comment on Mohanraj, "Mary Anne Mohanraj Gets You Up to Speed, Part I." Mohanraj wrote two guest posts on the blog during RaceFail 09 at Scalzi's invitation after he initially dismissed the various conversations which were ongoing and then issued an apology for that reaction. The second guest post is Mohanraj, "Mary Anne Mohanraj Gets You Up to Speed, Part II."
61. Bonilla-Silva, *Racism Without Racists*, 34.
62. See also my discussion of the rights of the author to make creative decisions and the exclusion of fans who 'misunderstand' the relationship between fan and author in Young, "Race in Online Fantasy Fandom," 741–743.

63. See chapter three, especially pages 78–79.
64. Bonilla-Silva, *Racism Without Racists*, 29.
65. Bonilla-Silva, *Racism Without Racists*, 44–45.
66. Avalon's Willow, "Open Letter."
67. Bear, "Real Magic Can Never Be Made by Offering Up Someone Else's Liver." A later post contradicted this statement: "I accepted criticism of my book that I knew to be untrue, that I knew to be based on a shallow and partial reading (a reading of the first chapter of a 160,000 word novel), because I felt it was important to serve as an example of how to engage dialogue on unconscious institutional racism." Bear, "Cease Fire."
68. Comment section, Bear, "Real Magic Can Never Be Made by Offering Up Someone Else's Liver."
69. Comment section, Ibid.
70. Comment section, Bear, "'I've Made a Lot of Mistakes …'."
71. See also the comment section of Deepa D., "I Didn't Dream of Dragons."
72. Jenkins, *Textual Poachers*, 89.
73. Bonilla-Silva, *Racism Without Racists*, 28.
74. Bonilla-Silva, *Racism Without Racists*, 37.
75. Comment on Mohanraj, "Mary Anne Mohanraj Gets You Up to Speed, Part I."
76. Comment on Deepa D., "I Didn't Dream of Dragons."
77. Comment on Ibid. Similar attitudes were displayed in comments on Mohanraj, "Mary Anne Mohanraj Gets You Up to Speed, Part I."
78. Bonilla-Silva, *Racism Without Racists*, 28.
79. Comment section Deepa D., "I Didn't Dream of Dragons."
80. Comment section, Ibid.
81. The comment also deploys the minimization frame discussed above.
82. Comment section, Bear, "'I've Made a Lot of Mistakes …'."
83. Comment section, Bear, "Real Magic Can Never Be Made by Offering Up Someone Else's Liver."
84. The post whether this first occurred has now been deleted, but is reported on widely, for example, Bradford, "RaceFail Amnesty Post"; Somerville, "A Themed Summary of RaceFail 09."
85. For example, Bradford, "Drowning in Apathy"; Tablesaw, "O HAI RACEFAILZ: Notes on Reading an Internet Conflict."
86. Bennett, "Discourses of Order and Rationality," 221.
87. Hills, "*Twilight* Fans Represented in Commercial Paratexts and Inter-Fandoms," 123. See also Young, "Race in Online Fantasy Fandom," 774.
88. Dyer, *White: Essays on Race and Culture*, 44.
89. Delux_vivens, "Wild Unicorn Herd Check In."
90. Comment by Lois McMaster Bujold on Fiction_theory, "You're Hurting My Head Again, Sf/f."
91. Reid, "The Wild Unicorn Herd Check-in," 231–239.
92. The second and third responses visible on the page at the time of writing say they are second generation fans, Delux_vivens, "Wild Unicorn Herd Check In." See also Reid, "The Wild Unicorn Herd Check-in," 227.
93. Jemisin, "Why I Think RaceFail Was The Bestest Thing Evar for SFF."
94. Bankuei, "From Geekdom to Freedom."
95. Interview.
96. Interview.

97. Reid, "The Wild Unicorn Herd Check-in," 228.

98. Delany, "Racism and Science Fiction."

99. "About the Carl Brandon Society."

100. Westfahl, "Who Governs Science Fiction?," 64.

101. "Carl Brandon Society Awards."

102. "The Octavia E. Butler Memorial Scholarship."

103. "About Con or Bust." The program began in response to RaceFail 09. Nepveu, "A Short History of Con or Bust," 1.

104. "Auction Information." Some conventions also donate memberships.

105. Booth, "Crowdfunding: A Spimatic Application of Digital Fandom," 162.

106. Hills, "Veronica Mars, Fandom, and the 'Affective Economics' of Crowdfunding Poachers." See also Booth, "Crowdfunding: a Spimatic Application of Digital Fandom."

107. Interview.

108. Hills, "*Veronica Mars*, Fandom, and the 'Affective Economics' of Crowdfunding Poachers," 194.

109. Dietzel, "The African American Novel and Popular Culture," 167.

110. See, for example, Bay, "Re-Writing Publishing: Fanfiction and Self-Publication in Urban Fantasy"; Zaid, *So Many Books: Reading and Publishing in an Age of Abundance*, 143.

111. Dietzel, "The African American Novel and Popular Culture," 166.

112. The so-called "digital divide" is potentially a factor here as people of colour are statistically less likely to have good internet access than Whites. Campos-Castillo, "Revisiting the First-Level Digital Divide in the United States: Gender and Race/Ethnicity Patterns, 2007–2012."

113. Farchy, Gansemer, and Patrou, "E-Book and Book Publishing," 358.

114. Hosanagar, "Blockbuster Culture's Next Rise and Fall: the Impact of Recommender Systems on Sales Diversity," 711.

115. Naik, "Finding Good Reads on Goodreads," 321.

116. Jemisin, "Don't Put My Book in the African American Section."

117. A few examples include Ahmed, "Ten Epic Fantasy / Sword & Sorcery Novels Set In 'Nonwestern' Worlds"; Various, "Favorite Non-Western SF/F Book Settings."

118. Rigathi, "Issue 1."

119. Kevin Rigathi, personal email, 18th December, 2014.

120. Samatar also tweeted about the Afrofuturism-themed issue of the pan-African collective *Jalada* earlier in the year. The editors had such an influx of interest immediately after that they extended the deadline for submissions. Sofia Samatar, email to the author, 18th December, 2014.

121. Delany, "Racism and Science Fiction."

Afterword

> *"The Magical Negro rested his red cane on his shoulder and leisurely stepped into the forest to see if he could find him some hobbits, castles, dragons, princesses, and all that other shit."*[1]

Exactly what the title character of Nnedi Okorafor's "The Magical Negro" has in mind when he walks into the forest in the final line of the story is uncertain. A stereotype who has just refused his conventional role as sacrifice and pushed the equally stereotypical White hero to his death, he might be intent on destruction of the other conventions as well or claiming his right to live among them as a free agent in Fantasyland; either way, it will be changed. There is a conservative – and often very vocal – element in any culture that views any change as inherently destructive. In SFF genre-culture that element is, if the results of the 2014 and the current troubles of the 2015 Hugo Awards are any indication, still significant. While the conservative slate of authors – which included the most vocal purveyor of racist abuse and White supremacist ideologies in the genre-cultures – did not win any awards, only one author who is not White did so. RaceFail 09, meanwhile, suggests that the idea of greater inclusiveness is more appealing than the process of change itself.

Two recent Kickstarter projects aimed at challenging pre-conceptions about what is "normal" on both Science Fiction and Fantasy by creating *Lightspeed* issues entirely written, edited, and illustrated by members of a particular marginalized group have been successfully funded: Women Destroy Science Fiction; and Queers Destroy Science Fiction. Both raised more than 1,000% of the $5,000 needed for the original project and created other magazine issues in different genres as a result: Fantasy and Horror for the former, Horror, Filk, and Fantasy for the latter. There has been, to date, no similar campaign for people of colour, or any specific cultural group whose members might be included under that broad term. This could be read as an indication that people of colour are now widely recognized as so much a part of the genre that their presence in it is not threatening. Given the strength of the habits discussed throughout this book, however, this seems highly improbable. The "Destroy" projects are a direct response to ongoing attacks on other marginalized groups, but similar projects seeking to address that of culturally and racially diverse peoples – such as the

Long Hidden volumes – are not framed in the same oppositional language. The policing of the emotions and tone of people of colour discussed in the previous chapter throws a troubling light on the difference.

In the course of writing this book I have encountered numerous expressions of surprise – varying from the neutral to the despairing – that Fantasy and Science Fiction, which necessarily imagined worlds that are not like our own, are not better at "doing" race, or at being inclusive of difference more generally. A key issue stems from J. R. R. Tolkien's axiom that an imagined world must be internally consistent; a Fantasy world can contain any impossibility as long as it obeys its own logic. The logics of race and racial difference are so deeply ingrained in Western society that it is extremely difficult, often even for members of marginalized racial groups, to imagine worlds that do not have those structures. This is not to suggest for a moment that it is impossible, but to observe that creating a new world that alters such a significant aspect of society and culture is no easy task no matter what one's identity. When the habits of the genre in which an imagined world is situated are those of Whiteness, it is even more difficult. As author Kate Elliott puts it, "the status quo does not need world building;"[2] change requires effort.

One of the reasons that the myth of biological race has persisted so long in Western society long after it was scientifically disproven is that it is constructed discursively and its discourses of human difference are built into both society and culture. Robert Wald Sussman argues that "only education about the history of the concept of racism will help us escape from these continuing cycles of ignorance, hatred, and fear."[3] For that education to be successful it cannot be *only* formal and scientific, but must also be received from the world around us, including popular culture, which has its own forms of pedagogy even if they are not enacted in formal classrooms. Breaking Fantasy's habits of Whiteness is one way to contribute to this project, by working from the microcosm of genre-culture to the macrocosm of popular culture and, ultimately, beyond.

NOTES

1. Okorafor, "The Magical Negro."
2. Elliott, "The Status Quo Does Not Need World Building."
3. Sussman, *The Myth of Race: The Troubling Persistence of an Unscientific Idea*, 307.

Bibliography

AAA. "American Anthropological Association Statement on 'Race.'" *American Anthropologist* 100, no. 3 (1998): 712–713.

Aaronovitch, Ben. *Foxglove Summer*. London: Gollancz, 2014.

———. *Rivers of London*. London: Gollancz, 2011.

Aarseth, Espen. "Genre Trouble," 2004. http://www.electronicbookreview.com/thread/firstperson/vigilant?mode=print.

"About Con or Bust." *Con or Bust*, 2014. http://con-or-bust.org/about/.

"About the Carl Brandon Society." *The Carl Brandon Society*, 2014. http://carlbrandon.org/about.html.

Abraham, Daniel. "'Concerning Historical Authenticity in Fantasy, or Truth Forgives You Nothing.'" *A Dribble of Ink*, 2012. http://aidanmoher.com/blog/2012/04/articles/concerning-historical-authenticity-in-fantasy-or-truth-forgives-you-nothing-by-daniel-abraham/.

Acrackedmoon. "The Tolkien Fanboy Fallacies – Yes, Tolkien Was a Racist, Sexist Bore: Deal with It." *Requires Only That You Hate*, 2012. http://requireshate.wordpress.com/2012/01/29/the-tolkien-fanboy-fallacies-yes-tolkien-was-a-racist-sexist-bore-deal-with-it/.

Ahmed, Saladin. "Is *Game of Thrones* Too White?" *Salon.com*, 2012. http://www.salon.com/2012/04/01/is_game_of_thrones_too_white/.

———. "Ten Epic Fantasy / Sword & Sorcery Novels Set In 'Nonwestern' Worlds." *Pinterest*, 2013. https://www.pinterest.com/saladinahmed/ten-epic-fantasy-sword-sorcery-novels-set-in-nonwe/.

Ahmed, Sara. "A Phenomenology of Whiteness." *Feminist Theory* 8, no. 2 (2007): 149–168.

———. "Affective Economies." *Social Text* 22, no. 279 (2004): 117–139.

———. *The Cultural Politics of Emotion*. New York: Routledge, 2004.

Alessio, Dominic. "From Body Snatchers to Mind Snatchers: Indigenous Science Fiction, Postcolonialism, and Aotearoa/New Zealand History." *Journal of Postcolonial Writing* 47, no. 3 (2011): 257–269.

———. "'Things Are Different Now'?: a Postcolonial Analysis of *Buffy the Vampire Slayer*." *The European Legacy* 6, no. 6 (2001): 731–740.

Amberstone, Celu. "Interview With First Nations Fantasy Author Daniel Heath Justice." *SF Canada*, 2008. http://www.sfcanada.ca/Spring 2008/Daniel Heath Justice.htm.

Anaesthetized. "The Othering of Orcs: a Post-Colonial Reading of Peter Jackson's *Lord of the Rings* Trilogy." *Anaesthetized*, 2009. http://imnotproper.blogspot.com.au/2009/05/othering-of-orcs-post-colonial-reading.html.

Applecliff, Shannon. "The Long Shadow of *D&D*." *Dnd.wizards.com*, 2014. http://dnd.wizards.com/articles/features/long-shadow-dd-0.

ArchstoneDistb. "*ORCS!* Trailer." *YouTube*, 2010. http://www.youtube.com/watch?v=Vs1_OyRwwpQ.

Ashcroft, Bill. *Postcolonial Transformation*. London: Routledge, 2001.

Atkin, Albert. *The Philosophy of Race*. Durham: Acumen, 2012.

Attebery, Brian. "Aboriginality in Science Fiction." *Science Fiction Studies* 32, no. 3 (2005): 385–404.

———. "Patricia Wrightson and Aboriginal Myth." *Extrapolation* 46, no. 3 (2005): 327–337.

———. *Stories about Stories: Fantasy and the Remaking of Myth*. Oxford: Oxford University Press, 2014.

———. *Strategies of Fantasy*. Bloomington: Indiana University Press, 1992.

———. *The Fantasy Tradition in American Literature*. Bloomington: Indiana University Press, 1980.

Atton, Chris. "Genre and the Cultural Politics of Territory: the Live Experience of Free Improvisation." *European Journal of Cultural Studies* 15, no. 4 (2012): 427–441.

"Auction Information." *Con or Bust*, 2014. http://con-or-bust.org/auction/.

Auger, Emily E. "*The Lord of the Rings* Interlace: the Adaptation to Film." *Mythlore* 30, no. 1/2 (2011): 143–163.

Augstein, Hannah Franziska. "Introduction." In *Race: The Origins of an Idea, 1760–1850*, edited by Hannah Franziska Augstein, ix–xxxiii. Bristol: Thoemmes Press, 1996.

AUSTLANG. "Frequently Asked Questions." *Australian Indigenous Languages Database*, 2014. http://austlang.aiatsis.gov.au/main.php.

Avalon's Willow. "Open Letter: To Elizabeth Bear." *Seeking Avalon*, 2009. http://seeking-avalon.blogspot.com/2009/01/open-letter-to-elizabeth-bear.html.

Baker-Whitelaw, Gavia. "Hugos Give More Nods to Women, but Nominations Still Stir Controversy." *The Daily Dot*, 2014. http://www.dailydot.com/geek/hugo-award-nominations-2014/.

Bales, E. L. "Me and RaceFail 2009 and the Ridiculous Fan History Wiki Page." *Dreamwidth (elbales)*, 2009. http://elbales.dreamwidth.org/254603.html.

Balfe, Myles. "Incredible Geographies? Orientalism and Genre Fantasy." *Social and Cultural Geography* 5, no. 1 (2004): 75–90.

Bankuei. "From Geekdom to Freedom." *Deeper in the Game*, 2010. https://bankuei.wordpress.com/2010/01/18/from-geekdom-to-freedom/.

Barkan, Elazar. *The Retreat of Scientific Racism: Changing Concepts of Race in Britain and the United States between World Wars*. Cambridge: Cambridge University Press, 1992.

Barton, Matt. *Dungeons and Desktops: the History of Computer Role-Playing Games*. Wellesley: A. K. Peters, 2008.

Bay, Jessica L. "Re-Writing Publishing: Fanfiction and Self-Publication in Urban Fantasy." University of Lethbridge, 2014.

"Beale Expelled from SFWA." *Locus Online*, 2013. http://www.locusmag.com/News/2013/08/beale-expelled-from-sfwa/.

Bear, Elizabeth. "Cease Fire." *Throw Another Bear in the Canoe*, 2009. http://matociquala.livejournal.com/1582583.html.

———. "'I've Made a Lot of Mistakes …'." *Throw Another Bear in the Canoe*, 2009. http://matociquala.livejournal.com/2009/03/06/.

———. "Real Magic Can Never Be Made by Offering Up Someone Else's Liver." *Throw Another Bear in the Canoe*, 2009. http://matociquala.livejournal. com/1544999.html.

———. "Whatever You're Doing, You're Probably Wrong." *Throw Another Bear in the Canoe*, 2009. http://matociquala.livejournal.com/1544111. html?ffoformat==l=light.

Bearick, Anderson. "Why Is the Only Good Orc a Dead Orc? The Dark Face of Racism Examined in Tolkien's World." *Modern Fiction Studies* 50, no. 4 (2004): 861–874.

Beasley, Edward. *The Victorian Reinvention of Race: New Racisms and the Problem of Grouping in the Human Sciences.* New York: Routledge, 2010.

Beck, Ulrich. "Critical Theory of World Risk Society: a Cosmopolitan Vision." *Constellations* 16, no. 1 (2009): 3–22.

———. *World Risk Society.* New York: Wiley-Blackwell, 1999.

Beer, David. "Making Friends with Jarvis Cocker: Music Culture in the Context of Web 2.0." *Cultural Sociology* 2, no. 2 (2008): 222–241.

Bell, John. "A Charles R. Saunders Interview." *African American Review* 18, no. 2 (1984): 90–92.

Benefiel, Candace R. "Shadow of a Dark Muse: Reprint History of Original Fiction from *Weird Tales* 1928–1939." *Extrapolation* 49, no. 3 (2008): 450–465.

Bennett, Lucy. "Discourses of Order and Rationality: Drooling R. E. M. Fans as 'Matter Out of Place.'" *Continuum: Journal of Media & Cultural Studies* 27, no. 2 (2013): 37–41.

Bennett, Tony. *Making Culture, Changing Society: the Perspective of "Culture" Studies.* London: Routledge, 2013.

Bennett, Tony, F. Dodsworth, G. Noble, M. Poovey, and M. Watkins. "Habit and Habituation: Governance and the Social." *Body & Society* 19, no. 2–3 (2013): 3–29.

Bernstein, Rachael. "*The Sims Medieval* Updated Q&A – the Hazards of Medieval Life." *Gamespot.com*, 2011. http://au.gamespot.com/the-sims-medieval/previews/the-sims-medieval-updated-qanda-the-hazards-of-medieval-life-6297455/.

Beukes, Lauren. *Broken Monsters.* London: HarperCollins, 2014.

Bhabha, Homi. *The Location of Culture.* London, UK: Routledge, Psychology Press, 1994.

Biddick, Katherine. *The Shock of Medievalism.* London, UK: Duke University Press, 1998.

Billingr, C.R. "The Hobbit Race is Based on the European Race. Please Stop PC in the Media." *YouTube*, 2010. http://www.youtube.com/watch?v=JluoKFp9_-A.

Blizzard. "Orc." *World of Warcraft*, 2015. http://us.battle.net/wow/en/game/race/orc.

Boardman, John. "Letter." In *The Best of Xero*, edited by Richard Lupoff and Pat Lupoff, 238. San Francisco: Tachyon Press, 2004.

Bonilla-Silva, Eduardo. *Racism Without Racists: Color-Blind Racism and the Persistence of Racial Inequality in the United States.* 3rd ed. New York: Rowman & Littlefield, 2010.

Booth, Paul. "Crowdfunding: a Spimatic Application of Digital Fandom." *New Media & Society* 17 (2015): 149–166.

Bould, Mark, and Sherryl Vint. "There Is No Such Thing as Science Fiction." In *Reading Science Fiction*, edited by M. Gunn, J., Barr, M. S. and Candelaria, 43–51. London, UK: Palgrave Macmillan, 2009.

Bourdieu, Pierre. "Habitus." In *Habitus: A Sense of Place*, edited by Jean Hillier and Emma Rooksby, 27–34. Aldershot: Ashgate, 2002.

———. *The Field of Cultural Production.* Polity Press, 1993.

Bowyer, Clifford B. *The Impending Storm. The Imperium Saga.* Holliston, MA: Silver Leaf, 2004.

Boyle, Elizabeth. "Vanishing Bodies: 'Race' and Technology in Nalo Hopkinson's *Midnight Robber.*" *African Identities* 7, no. 2 (2009): 177–191.

Boym, Svetlana. *The Future of Nostalgia.* New York: Basic Books, 2001.

Brackman, Rebecca. "'Dwarves are Not Heroes': Antisemitism and the Dwarves in J. R. R. Tolkien's Writings." *Mythlore* 28, no. 3/4 (2010): 85–106.

Bradford, Clare. *Reading Race: Aboriginality in Australian Children's Literature.* Melbourne: Melbourne University Press, 2001.

Bradford, K. Tempest. "Drowning in Apathy." *K. Tempest Bradford: Between Boundaries,* 2009. http://tempest.fluidartist.com/drowning-in-apathy/.

———. "RaceFail Amnesty Post." *K. Tempest Bradford: Between Boundaries,* 2009. http://tempest.fluidartist.com/racefail-amnesty-post/.

Braham, Persephone. "The Monstrous Caribbean." In *The Ashgate Research Companion to Monsters and the Monstrous,* edited by Asa Simon Mittman and Peter J. Dendle, 17–47. Farnham: Ashgate, 2013.

Broaddus, Maurice. "Putting the Urban in Urban Fantasy." *http://mauricebroaddus.com,* 2012. http://mauricebroaddus.com/uncategorized/putting-the-urban-in-urban-fantasy/.

Brooker, Will. *Hunting the Dark Knight: Twenty-First Century Batman.* London: I . B. Tauris, 2012.

Brookey, Robert Alan, and Paul Booth. "Restricted Play: Synergy and the Limits of Interactivity in *The Lord of the Rings: The Return of the King* Video Game." *Games and Culture* 1, no. 3 (2006): 214–230.

Burgess, Melinda C. R., Karen E. Dill, S. Paul Stermer, Stephen R. Burgess, and Brian P. Brown. "Playing With Prejudice: The Prevalence and Consequences of Racial Stereotypes in Video Games." *Media Psychology* 14, no. 3 (2011): 289–311.

Burke, Rusty. "De Camp vs. Howard: Rewriting Conan." In *The Fantastic Worlds of Robert E. Howard,* edited by James van Hise, 45–54. Yucca Valley: James van Hise, 2001.

———. "The Robert E. Howard Bookshelf." *Robert E. Howard United Press Association,* 1998. http://www.rehupa.com/OLDWEB/bookshelf.htm.

Bury, R. *Cyberspaces of Their Own: Female Fandoms Online.* New York: Peter Lang, 2005.

Campbell, Peter Odell. "Intersectionality Bites: Metaphors of Race and Sexuality in HBO's *True Blood.*" In *Monster Culture in the Twenty-First Century: a Reader,* edited by Marina Levina and Diem-My T. Bui, 99–114. London: Bloomsbury, 2013.

Campos-Castillo, C. "Revisiting the First-Level Digital Divide in the United States: Gender and Race/Ethnicity Patterns, 2007–2012." *Social Science Computer Review* (2014): 1–17.

Carino, Joji, Naomi Kipuri, Neva Collings, Duane Champagne, Mayrna Cunningham, Dalee Sambo Dorough, and Mililani Trask. *State of the World's Indigenous Peoples.* New York: Secretariat of the United Nations Permanent Forum on Indigenous Issues, 2010.

"Carl Brandon Society Awards." *The Carl Brandon Society,* 2014. http://carlbrandon.org/awards.html.

Carroll, Siobhan. "Place and National Identity in Neil Gaiman's *American Gods*." *Extrapolation* 53, no. 3 (2012): 307–326

Carter, Angela. "Introduction." In *Angela Carter's Book of Fairy Tales*, xi–xxiv. London: Virago, 2005.

Cavatore, Alessio. *Warhammer: The Game of Fantasy Battles*. Nottingham, UK: Games Workshop Ltd, 2006.

Chambliss, Julian C, and William L Svitavsky. "From Pulp Hero to Superhero: Culture, Race, and Identity in American Popular Culture, 1900–1940." *Studies in American Culture* 30, no. 1 (2008): 1–33.

Chance, Jane, ed. *Tolkien the Medievalist*. Lexington: Routledge, Taylor & Francis, 2004.

Chance, Jane, and Alfred K. Siewers, eds. *Tolkien's Modern Middle Ages*. New York: Palgrave Macmillan, 2005.

Chism, Christine. "Middle-Earth, the Middle Ages, and the Aryan Nation: Myth and History in World War II." In *Tolkien the Medievalist*, edited by Jane Chance, 63–92. London, UK: Routledge, 2003.

Chrisman, Laura. *Postcolonial Contraventions: Cultural Readings of Race, Imperialism, and Trannationalism*. Manchester: Manchester University Press, 2003.

Clute, John, and John Grant. *The Encyclopedia of Fantasy*. London, UK: Orbit, 1997.

Cohen, Jeffrey Jerome. "Monster Culture (Seven Theses)." In *Monster Theory: Reading Culture*, edited by Jeffrey Jerome Cohen, 3–25. Minneapolis: University of Minnesota Press, 1996.

———. "Undead (A Zombie Oriented Ontology)." *Journal of the Fantastic in the Arts* 23, no. 3 (2012): 397–412.

Collins-Gearing, Brooke. "Imagining Indigenality in Romance and Fantasy Fiction for Children." *Papers: Explorations into Children's Literature* 13, no. 3 (2003): 32–42.

"Complete Product List." *Dragonlance Nexus*, 2014. http://www.dlnexus.com/products/list.aspx.

"Conan Comics from Dark Horse." *Stormfront.org: White Pride World Wide*, 2007. http://www.stormfront.org/forum/t351874/.

"Conan the Barbarian (2011)." *Rotten Tomatoes*, 2014. http://www.rottentomatoes.com/m/conan_the_barbarian_2011/.

Connors, Bill, and Gary Thomas, eds. *Advanced Dungeons and Dragons Monstrous Compendium Volume One*. 2nd ed. Lake Geneva, WI: TSR Inc, 1989.

Cook, Monte, Jonathon Tweet, and Skip Williams. *Dungeons & Dragons: Monster Manual*. 3.0 ed. Renton, WA: Wizards of the Coast, 2000.

———. *Dungeons & Dragons: Monster Manual*. 3.5 ed. Benton: Wizards of the Coast, 2003.

———. *Dungeons & Dragons: Player's Handbook*. 3.0 ed. Renton, WA: Wizards of the Coast, 2000.

Coppa, Francesca. "A Brief History of Media Fandom." In *Fan Fiction and Fan Communities in the Age of the Internet*, edited by Karen Hellekson and Kristina Busse, 41–59. Jefferson: McFarland, 2006.

Council of Conservative Citizens. "Marvel Studios Declares War on Norse Mythology." *Council of Conservative Citizens*. St Louis: Author, 2011. http://cofcc.org/2011/04/marval-studios-declares-war-on-norse-mythology/.

Crawford, Jeremy, ed. *Monster Manual*. 5.0 ed. Renton: Wizards of the Coast, 2014.

Csicsery-Ronay, Istvan. "Science Fiction and Empire." *Science Fiction Studies* 30, no. 2 (2003): 231–245.

Cuppycake. "Bioware on Racial Diversity in *Dragon:Age II*." *The Border House*, 2011. http://borderhouseblog.com/?p=3784.

de Bodard, Aliette. "The Big Idea: Aliette de Bodard." *Whatever*, 2010. http://whatever.scalzi.com/2010/10/27/the-big-idea-aliette-de-bodard/.

de Bodard, Aliette. "The Universe of Xuya." Aliette de Bodard. 2015. http://alietedebodard.com/bibliography/the-universe-of-xuya/.

de Camp, Lyon Sprague. "Editing Howard." In *The Blade of Conan*, edited by Lyon Sprague de Camp. Ace, 1979.

———. "Howard and the Races." In *The Blade of Conan*, edited by Lyon Sprague de Camp, 127–129. Ace, 1979.

———. "Kush." In *The Conan Grimoire*, edited by Lyon Sprague de Camp and Scithers George H., 183–190. Mirage Press, 1972.

———. *Literary Swordsmen and Sorcerers: The Makers of Heroic Fantasy*. Sauk City: Arkham House, 1976.

———, ed. *Swords and Sorcery*. New York: Pyramid Books, 1963.

de Gobineau, Arthur. *The Inequality of Human Races*. Edited by Adrian Collins. New York: Howard Fertig, 1967.

de Saussure, Ferdinand. *Course in General Linguistics*. Edited by Perry Meisel and Haun Saussy. New York: Columbia University Press, 2011.

de Vries, Kelly. "Game of Thrones as History." *Foreign Affairs*. New York, March 2012. http://www.foreignaffairs.com/articles/137363/kelly-devries/game-of-thrones-as-history.Dean, Jodi. *Blog Theory: Feedback and Capture in the Circuits of Drive*. Cambridge: Polity, 2010.

Deepa D. "I Didn't Dream of Dragons." *Kabhi Kabhi Mere Dil Mein, Yeh Khayal Aata Hai …*, 2009. http://deepad.dreamwidth.org/29371.html.

———. "White People, Its Not All about You, but for This Post It Is." *Kabhi Kabhi Mere Dil Mein, Yeh Khayal Aata Hai …*, 2009. http://deepad.dreamwidth.org/29598.html.

Delany, Samuel R. *Neveryóna*. Ebook. London: Orion, 2011.

———. "Racism and Science Fiction." *The New York Review of Science Fiction* no. 120 (1998). http://www.nyrsf.com/racism-and-science-fiction-.html.

Deleuze, Giles. *Difference and Repetition*. London, UK: Continuum, 2004.

Delux_vivens. "Wild Unicorn Herd Check In." *Deadbrowalking (Livejournal)*, 2009. http://deadbrowalking.livejournal.com/357066.html.

Dharmadhikari, Deepa. "Surviving Fantasy through Post-Colonialism." *Foundation* 38 (2009): 15–20.

Dietrich, David R. "Avatars of Whiteness: Racial Expression in Video Game Characters." *Sociological Inquiry* 83, no. 1 (2013): 82–105.

Dietzel, Suzanne B. "The African American Novel and Popular Culture." In *The Cambridge Companion to the African American Novel*, edited by Maryemma Graham, 156–170. Cambridge: Cambridge University Press, 2004.

Dillon, Grace. "Imagining Indigenous Futurisms." In *Walking the Clouds: An Anthology of Indigenous Science Fictions*, edited by Grace Dillon, 1–12. Tucson: University of Arizona Press, 2012.

———, "Diaspora Narrative in Battlestar Galactica." *Science Fiction Film and Television* 5, no. 1 (2012): 1–21.

———, ed. *Walking the Clouds: an Anthology of Indigenous Science Fiction*. University of Arizona Press, 2012.

Dinshaw, Carolyn. *How Soon Is Now? Medieval Texts, Amateur Readers, and the Queerness of Time*. Durham: Duke University Press, 2012.

Ditomasso, Lorenzo. "Robert E. Howard's Hyborian Tales and the Question of Race in Fantastic Literature." *Extrapolation* 37, no. 2 (1996): 150–170.

Douglas, De Witt. *Astrofuturism: Science, Race, and Visions of Utopia in Space*. Philadelphia: University of Pennsylvania Press, 2003.

Doyle, Sady. "Enter Ye Myne Mystic World of Gayng-Raype: What the 'R' Stands for in 'George R. R. Martin.'" *Tiger Beatdown*, 2011. http://tigerbeatdown. com/2011/08/26/enter-ye-myne-mystic-world-of-gayng-raype-what-the-r-stands-for-in-george-r-r-martin/.

Dragon Age: Origins. Canada: Bioware, 2009.

Drake, David. "Storytellers: A Guided Ramble into Sword and Sorcery Fiction." In *The Sword and Sorcery Anthology*, edited by David G. Hartwell and Jacob Weisman, 7–11. San Francisco: Tachyon, 2012.

Drout, Michael D. C. "A Mythology for Anglo-Saxon England." In *Tolkien and the Invention of Myth*, edited by Jane Chance, 229–247. Lexington: The University Press of Kentucky, 2004.

Du Coudray, Chantal Bourgault. *The Curse of the Werewolf: Fantasy, Horror and the Beast Within*. London, New York: I. B. Tauris & Co., 2006.

Duke, Shaun. "Gritty Fantasy: Why Do I Love It So?" *The World in the Satin Bag*, 2012. http://wisb.blogspot.com.au/2012/06/gritty-fantasy-why-do-i-love-it-so.html.

Dunn, K. M., N. Klocker, and T. Salabay. "Contemporary Racism and Islamaphobia in Australia: Racializing Religion." *Ethnicities* 7, no. 4 (11, 2007): 564–589.

Dyer, Richard. *White: Essays on Race and Culture*. London, New York: Routledge, 1997.

Eckhrdt, Florian. "Racism in *Age of Conan*'s Hyborian Age." *Destructoid*, 2007. http://www.destructoid.com/racism-in-age-of-conan-s-hyborian-age-36626. phtml.

Eddings, David. *Magician's Gambit*. M. Rpt. London: Corgi Books, 1992.

———. *Pawn of Prophecy*. Rpt. Morebank, Australia: Corgi, 1993.

Eddings, David, and Leigh Eddings. *Belgarath the Sorcerer*. London: Voyager, 1995.

Edwards, Paul. "The Lesser Key of Solomon." *Sleepy Hollow*. Fox. USA. October 7, 2013.

Ekman, Stefan. *Here Be Dragons: Exploring Fantasy Maps and Settings*. Middletown: Wesleyan University Press, 2013.

Elliott, Andrew B. R. *Remaking the Middle Ages: the Methods of Cinema and History in Portraying the Medieval World*. Jefferson: McFarland, 2011.

Elliott, Kate. "The Status Quo Does Not Need World Building." *Livejournal (kateelliott)*, 2013. http://kateelliott.livejournal.com/233135.html.

El-Mohtar, Amal. "Calling for the Expulsion of Theodore Beale from SFWA." *Amal El-Mohtar*, 2013. http://amalelmohtar.com/2013/06/13/calling-for-the-expulsion-of-theodore-beale-from-sfwa/.

Enteen, Jillana. "'On the Receiving End of the Colonization': Nalo Hopkinson's 'Nansi Web." *Science Fiction Studies* 34, no. 2 (2014): 262–282.

Erikson, Steven. "Not Your Grandmother's Epic Fantasy: a Fantasy Author's Thoughts upon Reading *The Cambridge Companion to Fantasy Literature*." *The New York Review of Science Fiction* 24, no. 9 (2012): 1, 4–5.

Faircloth, Kelly. "Why the Turn Towards Gritty Realism in Epic Fantasy? Authors Sound Off!" *i09*, 2011. http://io9.com/5850891/why-the-turn-towards-gritty-realism-in-epic-fantasy-authors-sound-off.

Fanon, Frantz. *The Wretched of the Earth*. Edited by Constance Farrington. New York: Grove Press, 1963.

Farchy, Joelle, Mathilde Gansemer, and Jessica Patrou. "E-Book and Book Publishing." In *Handbook on the Digital Creative Economy*, edited by Ruth Towse and Christian Handke, 353–364. Cheltenham: Edward Elgar, 2014.

Feist, Raymond E. *Magician*. Revised. London: HarperCollins, 1997.

Ferber, Abby L. "The Construction of Black Masculinity: White Supremacy Now and Then." *Journal of Sport & Social Issues* 31, no. 1 (2007): 11–24.

Fiction_theory. "You're Hurting My Head Again, Sf/f." *Dreamwidth (fiction_ theory)*, 2009. http://fiction-theory.livejournal.com/116708.html?thread=296164# t296164.

Fimi, Dimitra. *Tolkien, Race, and Cultural History*. London: Palgrave Macmillan, 2009.

Finke, Laurie A., and Martin B. Shichtman. "Inner-City Chivalry in Gil Junger's *Black Knight*: a South Central Yankee in King Leo's Court." In *Race, Class, and Gender in "Medieval" Cinema*, edited by Lynn Ramey and Tison Pugh, 107–122. Basingstoke: Palgrave Macmillan, 2007.

Finn, Mark. "'I Had No Idea He Was a Racist Douchebag.'" *Finn's Wake*, 2013. http://marktheaginghipster.blogspot.com.au/2013/05/i-had-no-idea-he-was-racist-douchebag.html.

———. "Southwestern Discomfit: An Analysis of Gary Romeo's Controversial Article on Robert E. Howard and Racism." *REHupa*, 2011. http://www.rehupa.com/OLDWEB/SouthwesternDiscomfit.htm.

Firchow, Peter E. "The Politics of Fantasy: *The Hobbit* and Fascism." *The Midwest Quarterly* 50, no. 1 (2008): 8, 15–31.

Flew, Terry. *New Media*. 3rd ed. Oxford: Oxford University Press, 2008.

Flood, Alison. "World Fantasy Awards Pressed to Drop HP Lovecraft Trophy in Racism Row." *The Guardian*, 2014. http://www.theguardian.com/books/2014/sep/17/world-fantasy-awards-hp-lovecraft-racism-row-statuette.

Ford, Judy Ann. "The White City: *The Lord of the Rings* as an Early Medieval Myth of the Restoration of the Roman Empire." *Tolkien Studies* 2, no. 1 (2005): 53–73.

Fox, Rose, and Daniel Jose Older. "Introduction." In *Long Hidden: Speculative Fiction from the Margins of History*, edited by Rose Fox and Daniel Jose Older, i–ii. Framlingham: Crossed Genres Publications, 2014.

Funcom. "Locations." *Age of Conan*. http://www.ageofconan.com/world/locations/khitai.

Gaider, David. "David Gaider Speaks to Save Game on the New Comic *Dragon Age: The Silent Grove #1*." *Save Game*, 2012. http://savegameonline.com/interviews/david-gaider-speaks-to-save-game-on-the-new-comic-dragon-age-the-silent-grove-1.

Galloway, Alexander R. "'Starcraft,' or Balance." *Grey Room, Inc.* 28 (2007): 86–107.

Gander, Matt. "*Of Orcs and Men* – the Meanest, Greenest RPG You've Never Played." *Games Asylum*, 2013. http://www.gamesasylum.com/2013/07/30/of-orcs-and-men-the-meanest-greenest-rpg-youve-never-played/.

Garcia, Louis, and David Gaider. "David Gaider Answers *Dragon Age 2* Questions at PAX." *GamesBeat*, 2010. http://venturebeat.com/2010/09/04/david-gaider-answers-dragon-age-2-questions-at-pax/.

Garstad, Benjamin. "'Death to the Masters!': The Role of Slave Revolt in the Fiction of Robert E. Howard." *Slavery & Abolition: a Journal of Slave and Post-Slave Studies* 31, no. 2 (2010): 233–256.

Gatson, Sarah N., and Robin Anne Reid. "Race and Ethnicity in Fandom." *Transformative Works and Cultures* 8 (2011). http://journal.transformativeworks.org/index.php/twc/article/view/392/252.

Geary, Patrick. *The Myth of Nations: the Medieval Origins of Europe.* Princeton: Princeton University Press, 2002.

Gelder, Ken. *Popular Fiction: the Logics and Practices of a Literary Field.* London: Routledge, 2004.

Gentle, Mary. *Grunts!* London: Gollancz, 2013.

———. "Smarter Than Root Vegetables: an Introduction to *Grunts!*" In *Grunts!*, np. Kindle. London: Gollancz, 2013.

Gershman, Michael. "A New Man." USA.: Fox, 2000.

Gill, Candra K. " 'Cuz the Black Chick Always Gets It First: Dynamics of Race in *Buffy the Vampire Slayer.*" In *Gender Relations in Global Perspectives: Essential Readings*, edited by Nancy Cook, 243–252. Toronto: Canadian Scholars Press, 2007.

Glazier, Jocelyn, and Jung-A Seo. "Multicultural Literature and Discussion and Mirror and Window?" *Journal of Adolescent and Adult Literacy* 48, no. 8 (2005): 688–700.

Goff, Phillip Atiba, Jennifer L. Eberhardt, Melissa J. Williams, and Matthew Christian Jackson. "Not Yet Human: Implicit Knowledge, Historical Dehumanization, and Contemporary Consequences." *Journal of Personality and Social Psychology* 94, no. 2 (2008): 292–306.

Gray, Kishonna L. "Intersecting Oppressions and Online Communities: Examining the Experiences of Women of Color in Xbox Live." *Information, Communication and Society* 15, no. 3 (2012): 37–41.

Grimm, Jacob, and Wilhelm Grimm. *The Original Folks and Fairy Tales of the Brothers Grimm: The Complete First Edition.* Edited by Jack Zipes. Princeton: Princeton University Press, 2015.

Grin, Leo. "The Bankrupt Nihilism of Our Fallen Fantasists." *Breitbart.com*, 2011. http://www.breitbart.com/Big-Hollywood/2011/02/12/The-Bankrupt-Nihilism-of-Our-Fallen-Fantasists.

Gunn, Eileen. "Racial Identity and Writing – Part 5." In *Writing and Racial Identity: The Wicons Chronicles, Volume 5*, edited by Nisi Shawl, 125–131. Seattle: Aqueduct Press, 2011.

Gunthera1, and Ann Lemay. "A Glimpse into BioWare: an Interview with Ann Lemay." *The Border House*, 2012. http://borderhouseblog.com/?p=9227.

Gygax, Gary. *Advanced Dungeons & Dragons Monster Manual.* 4th ed. Random House, 1979.

Haase, Donald. "German Fairy Tales and America's Culture Wars: From Grimm's *Kinder- Und Hausmarchen* to William Bennett's *Book of Virtues.*" *German Politics and Society* 13, no. 3 (1995): 17–25.

———. "Yours, Mine, or Ours? Perrault, the Brothers Grimm, and the Ownership of Fairy Tales." *Mervailles & Contes* 7, no. 2 (1993): 383–402.

Hahn, Thomas. "The Difference the Middle Ages Makes: Color and Race before the Modern World." *Journal of Medieval and Early Modern Studies* 31, no. 1 (2001): 1–38.

Halberstam, Judith. "Technologies of Monstrosity: Bram Stoker's *Dracula*." *Victorian Studies* 36, no. 3 (1993): 333–352.

Haley, Guy. "Fantasy Family Tree." *SFX*, 2011.

Hall, Mark. "Crash Go the Civilizations: Some Notes on Robert E. Howard's Use of History and Anthropology." *The Dark Man: the Journal of Robert E. Howard Studies* 2, no. 2 (2006): 27–37.

Halliwell, Richard, Byran Ansell, and Rick Priestly. *Warhammer: Battle Bestiary*. 2nd ed. Games Workshop Ltd, 1984.

Haraway, Donna. "The Promises of Monsters: a Regenerative Politics for Inappropriate/d Others." In *Cultural Studies*, edited by Lawrence Grossberg, Cary Nelson, and Paula A. Treichler, 295–337. New York: Routledge, 1992.

Hartwell, David G. "The Making of the American Fantasy Genre." In *The Secret History of Fantasy*, edited by Peter S. Beagle, 367–379. San Francisco: Tachyon, 2010.

Haslanger, Sally. "Language, Politics, and 'The Folk': Looking for 'The Meaning' of 'Race.'" *The Monist* 93, no. 2 (2010): 169–187.

Headrick, Daniel R. *The Tools of Empire. Technology and European Imperialism in the Nineteenth Century*. Oxford: Oxford University Press, 1981.

Heard, Bruce. *The Orcs of Thar*. Lake Geneva, WI: TSR Inc, 1988.

Heitz, Markus. *The Dwarves*. London: Hachette, 2010.

Heng, Geraldine. "The Invention of Race in the European Middle Ages I: Race Studies, Modernity, and the Middle Ages." *Literature Compass* 8, no. 5 (2011): 315–331.

———. "The Invention of Race in the European Middle Ages II: Locations of Medieval Race." *Literature Compass* 8, no. 5 (2011): 275–293.

Herman, Paul. "The Copyright and Ownership Status of the Works and Words of Robert E. Howard." *www.robert-E-Howard.org*, 2007. http://www.robert-e-howard.org/anotherthought4rerevised.html.

Herron, Don. "Robert E. Howard's Library." In *The Dark Barbarian: The Writings of Robert E. Howard*, edited by Don Herron, 183–200. Westport, CT: Greenwood Press, 1984.

Higgin, Tanner. "Blackless Fantasy." *Games and Culture* 4, no. 1 (2009): 3–26.

Hills, Matt. *Fan Cultures*. New York: Routledge, 2002.

———. "*Twilight* Fans Represented in Commercial Paratexts and Inter-Fandoms." In *Genre, Reception and Adaptation in the* Twilight *Series*, edited by Anne Morey, 113–129. Farnham: Ashgate, 2012.

———. "*Veronica Mars*, Fandom, and the 'Affective Economics' of Crowd-funding Poachers." *New Media & Society* 17 (2014): 183–197. doi:10.1177/1461444814558909.

Hinckley, D. "Conan the Oxymoron: the Civilized Savage of Robert E. Howard and Frank Frazetta." *Contributions to the Study of Science-Fiction and Fantasy* 98 (2002): 141–151.

Hoagland, Ericka, and Reema Sarwal, eds. *Science Fiction, Imperialism and the Third World*. Jefferson: McFarland, 2010.

Hodgman, John, and George R. R. Martin. "John Hodgman Interviews George R.R. Martin." *Public Radio International*, 2011. http://www.pri.org/stories/arts-entertainment/books/john-hodgman-interviews-george-r-r-martin6041.html.

Hogset, Oystein. "The Adaptation of *The Lord of the Rings*: a Critical Commentary." In *Translating Tolkien: Text and Film*, edited by Thomas Honegger, 165–177. Zurich: Walking Tree, 2004.

Holmes, Morgan. "Imaro and Me." *REHupa*, 2010. http://www.rehupa. com/?p=1384.

———. "Lin Carter: The Inept Pasticheur." In *The Fantastic Worlds of Robert E. Howard*, edited by James van Hise, 161–166. Yucca Valley: James van Hise, 2001.

hooks, bell. *Black Looks: Race and Representation*. Boston: South End Press, 1992.

———. *Writing Beyond Race: Living Theory and Practice*. New York: Routledge, 2013.

Hopkinson, Nalo. "A Reluctant Ambassador from the Planet of Midnight. " *Journal of the Fantastic in the Arts* 21, no. 3 (2010): 339–350.

———. "Maybe They're Phasing Us In: Re-Mapping Fantasy Tropes in the Face of Gender, Race, and Sexuality." *Journal of the Fantastic in the Arts* 18, no. 1 (2007): 99–105.

———. *Sister Mine*. New York: Grand Cental Publishing, 2013.

Hopkinson, Nalo, and Uppinder Meehan, eds. *So Long Been Dreaming: Postcolonial Science Fiction and Fantasy*. Vancouver: Arsenal Pulp Press, 2004.

Horsman, Reginald. *Race and Manifest Destiny: the Origins of American Racial Anglo-Saxonism*. Cambridge, MA: Harvard University Press, 1986.

Hosanagar, Daniel Fleder Kartik. "Blockbuster Culture's Next Rise and Fall: the Impact of Recommender Systems on Sales Diversity." *Management Science* 55, no. 5 (2009): 697–712.

Howard, Robert Ervin. "Shadows in Zamboula." *Weird Tales* 26, no. 5 (1935): 530–551.

———. *The Coming of Conan the Cimmerian*. Edited by Patrice Louinet. New York: Random House, 2002.

———. *The Hour of the Dragon*. ebook edit. Gutenberg.net, 2013.

Hughey, Matthew. "The (dis)similarities of White Racial Identities: the Conceptual Framework of 'Hegemonic Whiteness.'" *Ethnic and Racial Studies* 33, no. 8 (September 2010): 1289–1309.

Hughey, Matthew W. "The White Savior Film and Reviewers' Reception." *Symbolic Interaction* 33, no. 3 (2010): 475–496.

Hunnewell, Sumner Gary. *Tolkien Fandom Review from Its Beginnings to 1964*. 2nd ed. Arnold: The New England Tolkien Society, 2010.

Hunt, Darnell. *Hollywood Diversity Brief: Spotlight on Cable Televison*. Los Angeles, 2013. http://www.bunchecenter.ucla.edu/wp-content/uploads/2013/10/Hollywood-Diversity-Brief-Spotlight-10-2013.pdf.

Huysmans, Jef. *The Politics of Insecurity: Fear, Migration and Asylum in the EU*. Abingdon: Routledge, 2006.

Idlewilder. "Painting With Grey: the Development and Popularity of 'Gritty Fantasy.'" *Fantasy Faction*, 2012. http://fantasy-faction.com/2012/painting-with-grey-the-development-and-popularity-of-gritty-fantasy.

Irvine, Alexander C. "Urban Fantasy." In *The Cambridge Companion to Fantasy Literature*, edited by Edward James and Farah Mendlesohn, 200–213. Cambridge: Cambridge University Press, 2012.

Irving, Washington. *The Legend of Sleepy Hollow*. Ebook. Project Gutenberg, 2012. http://www.gutenberg.org/files/41/41-h/41-h.htm.

Isaacs, Neil D. "On the Possibilities of Writing Tolkien Criticism." In *Tolkien and the Critics*, edited by Neil D. Isaacs and Rose Zimbardo, 1–11. Notre Dame: University Notre Dame Press, 1968.

Jackson, Rosemary. *Fantasy: The Literature of Subversion*. London: Methuen & Co, 1981.

Jacobson, Matthew Frye. *Roots Too: White Ethnic Revival in Post-Civil Rights America*. Cambridge, MA: Harvard University Press, 2006.

———. *Whiteness of a Different Color: European Immigrants and the Alchemy of Race*. Cambridge, MA: Harvard University Press, 1998.

James, Edward. "Tolkien, Lewis and the Explosion of Genre Fantasy." In *The Cambridge Companion to Fantasy Literature*, edited by Edward James and Farah Mendlesohn, 62–78. Cambridge: Cambridge University Press, 2012.

Jameson, Frederic. "Radical Fantasy." *Historical Materialism* 10, no. 4 (2002): 273–280.

Jemisin, N. K. "Your Groundbreaking Is Not My Groundbreaking." *Epiphany 2.0*, 2014. http://nkjemisin.com/2014/11/your-groundbreaking-is-not-my-ground-breaking/.

———. "Considering Colonialism." *Epiphany 2.0*, 2011. http://nkjemisin.com/2011/08/considering-colonialism/.

———. *The Kingdom of Gods*. London: Orbit, 2011.

———. *The Broken Kingdoms*. London: Orbit, 2010.

———. "Don't Put My Book in the African American Section." *Epiphany 2.0*, 2010. http://nkjemisin.com/2010/05/dont-put-my-book-in-the-african-american-section/.

———. *The Hundred Thousand Kingdoms*. London: Orbit, 2010.

———. "Identity Should Always Be Part of the Gameplay." *Epiphany 2.0*, 2012. http://nkjemisin.com/2012/08/identity-should-always-be-part-of-the-gameplay/.

———. "Why I Think RaceFail Was The Bestest Thing Evar for SFF." *Epiphany 2.0*, 2010. http://nkjemisin.com/2010/01/why-i-think-racefail-was-the-bestest-thing-evar-for-sff/.

Jenkins, Henry. *Convergence Culture: When Old and New Media Collide*. New York: New York University Press, 2006.

———. *Fans, Bloggers, and Gamers: Exploring Participatory Culture*. New York University Press, 2006.

———. *Textual Poachers*. London: Routledge, 1992.

Jernigan, Zachary. "Writing About Race in Science Fiction and Fantasy (Part 2 of a Roundtable Interview)." *SF Signal*, 2012. http://www.sfsignal.com/archives/2012/06/guest-post-writing-about-race-in-science-fiction-and-fantasy-part-2-of-a-roundtable-interview/.

Johnson, Derek. "Fan-Tagonism: Factions, Institutions, and Constitutive Hegemonies of Fandom." In *Fandom: Identities and Communities in a Mediated World*, 285–300. New York University Press, 2007.

Jon. "World According To Jon: Are Hobbits Racist? In SUPER-HIGH-." *YouTube*, 2010. http://www.youtube.com/watch?v=2Zk7Ep-C6Rs.

Jones, Dan. "*Game of Thrones* Season Three: How the Show Is (Re)Making History." *Speakeasy - The Wall Street Journal*, 2013. http://blogs.wsj.com/speakeasy/2013/03/31/how-game-of-thrones-is-remaking-history/.

Jordan, Robert. *The Eye of the World*. Ebook. London: Hachette Digital, 2009.

Joshi, Khyati Y. "The Racialization of Hinduism, Islam, and Sikhism in the United States." *Equity & Excellence in Education* 39, no. 3 (2006): 211–226.

Joshi, S. T. "Barbarism vs. Civilization: Robert E. Howard and H. P. Lovecraft in Their Correspondence." *Studies in the Fantastic* 1 (2008): 95–124.

Justice, Daniel Heath. *The Way of Thorn and Thunder*. Kindle. Albuquerque: University of Minnesota Press, 2011.

Kabachnik, Peter. "Place Invaders: Constructing the Nomadic Threat in England." *The Geographical Review* 100, no. 1 (2010): 90–108.

Kamenetsky, Christa. "Folktale and Ideology in the Third Reich." *The Journal of American Folklore* 90, no. 356 (1977): 168–178.

Kane, Brad, and David Gaider. "The Writing Of BioWare's *Dragon Age II*: David Gaider Speaks." *Gamasutra*, 2011. http://www.gamasutra.com/view/feature/134812/the_writing_of_biowares_dragon_.php.

Keizer, Arlene R. "'Obsidian Mine': The Psychic Aftermath of Slavery." *American Literary History* 24, no. 4 (2012): 686–701.

Kelly, Phil. *Codex Orks*. Lenton: Games Workshop, 2010.

Kim, Sue. "Beyond Black and White: Race and Postmodernism in *The Lord of the Rings* Films." *Modern Fiction Studies* 50, no. 4 (2004): 877–907.

King, J. Robert. "Characters, Places and Things in the *Dragonlance* Novels." In *The Universes of Margaret Weis and Tracy Hickman: Realms of Dragons*, edited by Margaret Weis and Tracy Hickman, 93–166. New York: HarperPrism, 1999.

Kirkland, Ewan. "The Caucasian Persuasion of *Buffy the Vampire Slayer*." *Slayage: The Online Journal of Buffy Studies* 17 (2005): n.p. http://www.slayageonline.com/essays/slayage17/Kirkland.htm.

Knaus, Christopher. "More White Supremacy? *The Lord of the Rings* as Pro-American Imperialism." *Multicultural Perspectives* 7, no. 4 (2005): 54–58.

Kupperman, Karen Ordahl. "Angells in America." In *Writing Race Across the Atlantic World*, edited by P Beidler and G Taylor, 27–50. Basingstoke: Palgrave Macmillan, 2005.

Kwaymullina, Ambelin. "Edges, Centres, and Futures: Reflections on Being an Indigenous Speculative Fiction Writer." *Kill Your Darlings* 18 (2014): 18–33.

———. "Guest of Honour Speech, from Continuum X." *Andromeda Spaceways Inflight Magazine*, 2014. http://www.andromedaspaceways.com/ambelinkwaymullinagohspeech_continuumx/.

Lake, Jay. "Another Shot at Thinking about the Other." *Lakeshore*, 2009. http://jaylake.livejournal.com/1692287.html.

Lampert, Lisa. "Race, Periodicity, and the (Neo-) Middle Ages." *Modern Language Quarterly* 65, no. 3 (2004): 391–421.

Langer, Jessica. *Postcolonialism and Science Fiction*. Houndmills: Palgrave Macmillan, 2011.

———. "The Familiar and the Foreign: Playing (Post)Colonialism in *World of Warcraft*." In *Digital Culture, Play, and Identity: A World of Warcraft Reader*, edited by Hilde G Corneliussen and Jell Walker Rettberg, 87–108. London: MIT Press, 2008.

Larbalastier, Justine. *The Battle of the Sexes in Science Fiction*. Middletown, CT: Wesleyan University Press, 2002.

Latham, R. G. *The Germania of Tacitus with Ethnological Dissertations and Notes*. London: Taylor, Watson and Maberley, 1851.

Latour, Bruno. *Reassembling the Social*. Oxford: Oxford University Press, 2005.

Lavender, Isiah, ed. *Black and Brown Planets: The Politics of Race in Science Fiction*. Jackson: University of Mississippi Press, 2014.

———. *Race in American Science Fiction*. Bloomington: Indiana University Press, 2011.

Le Guin, Ursula K. "A Whitewashed Earthsea." *Slate*, 2004. http://www.slate.com/articles/arts/culturebox/2004/12/a_whitewashed_earthsea.html.

———. *A Wizard of Earthsea*. Reprint. Boston: Houghton Harcourt Mifflin, 2012.

———. *Cheek by Jowl*. Ebook. Seattle: Aqueduct Press, 2009.

Leiber, Fritz. "Fafhrd and the Grey Mouser Have Their Say." *The Dragon*, June 1976. http://www.noosfere.com/heberg/nehwon/htm/fr/resume.asp?code=614.

Lentin, Alana. "Post-Race, Post Politics: The Paradoxical Rise of Culture after Multiculturalism." *Ethnic and Racial Studies* (March 22, 2012): 1–19. doi:10.10 80/01419870.2012.664278.

Leonard, David. "'Live in Your World, Play in Ours': Race, Video Games, and Consuming the Other." *SIMILE: Studies In Media & Information Literacy Education* 3, no. 4 (2003): 1–9.

Leonard, Elisabeth Anne. *"Into Darkness Peering": Race and Color in the Fantastic.* Edited by Elisabeth Anne Leonard. *Into Darkness Peering: Race and Color in the Fantastic.* Westport, CT: Greenwood, 1997.

Lewis, C. S. "The Dethronement of Power." In *Tolkien and the Critics*, edited by Neil D. Isaacs and Rosemary Zimbardo, 12–16. Notre Dame: University of Notre Dame Press, 1968.

Lieberman, Robert. "Something Wicked This Fae Comes." *Lost Girl*. USA: Showcase, 2011.

Livingston, Michael, and John William Sutton. "Reinventing the Hero: Gardner's *Grendel* and the Shifting Face of Beowulf in Popular Culture." *Studies in Popular Culture* 29, no. 1 (2006): 1–16.

Loomba, Ania. *Colonialism/Postcolonialism.* 2nd ed. London: Routledge, 2005.

Lopez, L. K. "Fan-Activists and the Politics of Race in *The Last Airbender*." *International Journal of Cultural Studies* (2011). doi:10.1177/1367877911422862.

"LOTR Southern Humans." *Stormfront.org: White Pride World Wide.* West Palm Beach: Jelsoft, 2011. http://www.stormfront.org/forum/t820580/.

"LOTR: Racist?" *SFF Chronicles.* SFF Chronicles Network, 2007. http://www.sffchronicles.co.uk/forum/1129-lotr-racist-8.html.

Lott, Tommy Lee. *The Invention of Race.* Malden: Blackwell, 1999.

Louinet, Patrice. "Robert E. Howard, Founding Father of Modern Fantasy for the First Time Again." *Contemporary French and Francophone Studies* 15, no. 2 (2011): 163–170.

Loza, Susana. "Playing Alien in Post-Racial Times." In *Monster Culture in the Twenty-First Century: A Reader*, edited by Marina Levina and Diem-My T. Bun, 54–72. London, 2013.

MacCallum-Stewart, Esther. "'The Street Smarts of a Cartoon Princess.' New Roles for Women in Games." *Digital Creativity* 20, no. 4 (2009): 225–237.

MacDougall, Hugh A. *Racial Myth in English History: Trojans, Teutons, and Anglo-Saxons.* Montreal: Harvest House Press of New England, 1982.

Manlove, Colin. *The Impulse of Fantasy Literature.* Kent: Kent State University Press, 1983.

Marshall, David W. "Neomedievalism, Identification, and the Haze of Medievalism." *Studies in Medievalism* 20 (2011): 21–34.

Martin, George R. R. "Great Times at the Jean Cocteau." *Not a Blog*, 2014.

Martin, George R.R., Elio M. Garcia, and Linda Antonsson. *The World of Ice and Fire.* London: HarperCollins, 2014.

Mäyrä, Frans. "From the Demonic Tradition to Art-Evil in Digital Games: Monstrous Pleasures in *The Lord of the Rings Online*." In *Ringbearers The Lord of the Rings Online as Intertextual Narrative*, edited by Tanya Krzywinska, Esther MacCallum-Stewart, and Justin Parsler, 111–135. Manchester: Manchester University Press, 2011.

McAlister, Elizabeth. "Slaves, Cannibals, and Infected Hyper-Whites: the Race and Religion of Zombies." *Anthropological Quarterly* 85, no. 2 (2012): 457–486.

McLeod, John. *Postcolonial London: Rewriting the Metropolis*. London: Routledge, 2004.

Mearls, Mike. *D&D Player's Handbook*. Renton, WA: Wizards of the Coast, 2014.

Mearls, Mike, Stephen Schubert, and James Wyatt. *Dungeons & Dragons: Monster Manual*. 4th ed. Benton: Wizards of the Coast, 2008.

Meer, Nasar. "Racialization and Religion: Race, Culture and Difference in the Study of Antisemitism and Islamophobia." *Ethnic and Racial Studies* 36, no. 3 (2013): 385–398.

Mendlesohn, Farah. *Rhetorics of Fantasy*. Middletown, CT: Wesleyan University Press, 2008.

Mendlesohn, Farah, and Edward James. *A Short History of Fantasy*. Kobo ebook. London: Middlesex University Press, 2009.

———. "Introduction." In *The Cambridge Companion to Fantasy Literature*, edited by Farah Mendlesohn and Edward James, 1–4. Cambridge: Cambridge University Press, 2012.

Merrick, Helen. *The Secret Feminist Cabal: A Cultural History of Science Fiction Feminisms*. Seattle: Aqueduct Press, 2009.

Mié, Ankhesen. "So, I'm Watching 'Merlin,' Right …" *At The Bar*, 2010. http://www.ankhesen-mie.net/2010/07/so-im-watching-merlin-right.html.

Miller, Laura. "JUST WRITE IT !: Onward and Upward with the Arts." *The New Yorker*. New York, April 2011.

———. "Just Write It: A Fantasy Author and His Impatient Fans." *The New Yorker*, 2011. http://www.newyorker.com/reporting/2011/04/11/110411fa_fact_miller?currentPage=all.

———. "The Real-Life Inspirations for 'Game of Thrones.'" *Salon*, 2012. http://www.salon.com/2012/04/04/the_real_life_inspirations_for_game_of_thrones/.

Mitter, Partha. *Much Maligned Monsters: a History of European Reactions to Indian Art*. Oxford: Clarendon Press, 1977.

Mohanraj, Mary Anne. "Mary Anne Mohanraj Gets You Up to Speed, Part I." *Whatever!*, 2009. http://whatever.scalzi.com/2009/03/12/mary-ann-mohanraj-gets-you-up-to-speed-part-i/.

———. "Mary Anne Mohanraj Gets You Up to Speed, Part II." *Whatever*, 2009. http://whatever.scalzi.com/2009/03/13/mary-anne-mohanraj-gets-you-up-to-speed-part-ii/.

Monson, M. J. "Race-Based Fantasy Realm: Essentialism in the *World of Warcraft*." *Games and Culture* 7, no. 1 (2012): 48–71.

"N.K. Jemisin: Rites of Passage." *Locus Online Perspectives*, 2010. http://www.locusmag.com/Perspectives/2010/08/n-k-jemisin-rites-of-passage/.

Naik, Richard. "Breaking the Immersion - *Skyrim*'s Racism Lacks Authenticity." *GameCritics.com*, 2011. http://www.gamecritics.com/richard-naik/breaking-the-immersion-skyrims-racism-lacks-authenticity.

Naik, Yesha. "Finding Good Reads on Goodreads." *Reference & User Services Quarterly* 51, no. 4 (June 1, 2012): 319–323. doi:10.5860/rusq.51n4.319.

Nakamura, Lisa. "Don't Hate the Player, Hate the Game: the Racialization of Labor in *World of Warcraft*." *Critical Studies in Media Communication* 26, no. 2 (2009): 128–144.

———. "'It's a Nigger in Here! Kill the Nigger!': User-Generated Media Campaigns Against Racism, Sexism, and H omophobia in Digital Games." In *The*

International Encyclopedia of Media Studies: Volume IV Media Studies Futures, edited by Kelly Gates. Vol. VI. Digital. Maldon: Blackwell, 2013.

———. "Race In/For Cyberspace: Identity Tourism and Racial Passing on the Internet." In *Reading Digital Culture*, edited by D. Trend, 226–235. New York: Wiley Blackwell, 2001.

Nama, Adilifu. *Black Space: Imagining Race in Science Fiction Film*. Austin: University of Texas Press, 2008.

———. *Super Black: American Pop Culture and Black Superheroes*. Austin: University of Texas Press, 2011.

NB. "Demographics of Adult Gamers." *ZD Net*, 2009. http://www.zdnet.com/blog/itfacts/demographics-of-adult-gamers/15694.

NBC. "About *Grimm* & Cast Bios." *www.mbc.com*, 2015. http://www.nbc.com/grimm/about.

Nelson, Angela M. "Studying Black Comic Strips: Popular Art and Discourses of Race." In *Black Comics: Politics of Race and Representation*, edited by Sheena C. Howard and Ronald L. Jackson, 97–110. New York: Bloomsbury, 2013.

Nepveu, Kate. "A Short History of Con or Bust." In *Writing and Racial Identity: The Wicons Chronicles, Volume 5*, edited by Nisi Shawl, 1–4. Seattle: Aqueduct Press, 2011.

"New 'Conan' Star Never Saw Arnold's 'Conan.'" *Access Hollywood*, 2011. http://www.today.com/id/43883441/ns/today-entertainment/#.VGxCaGfEx8E.

Newton, Mark. "Science Fiction, Fantasy & Minorities." *The Huffington Post*, 2011. http://www.huffingtonpost.co.uk/mark-newton/science-fiction-fantasy-minorities_b_931078.html.

Nicholls, Stan. "An Interview with Stan Nicholls on *Orcs*." *Orbit Books.net*, 2012. http://www.orbitbooks.net/interview/stan-nicholls/.

———. *Orcs*. London: Gollancz, 2004.

———. *Orcs: Bad Blood*. London: Gollancz, 2013.

Nichols, Ian. "A Comparison of the Ideology of Robert E. Howard's Conan Tales and J. R. R. Tolkien's *The Lord of the Rings*." *The Dark Man: The Journal of Robert E. Howard Studies* 4, no. 1 (2009): 35–78.

Nispel, Marcus. *Conan the Barbarian*. Nu Image, 2011.

Novik, Naomi. *Crucible of Gold*. London: HarperCollins, 2012.

———. *Throne of Jade*. HarperCollins, 2007.

———. *Tongues of Serpents*. London: HarperCollins, 2009.

Oberhelman, David D. "'Coming to America': Fantasy and Native America Explored, an Introduction." In *The Intersection of Fantasy and Native America: From H.P. Lovecraft to Leslie Marmon Silko*, edited by David D. Oberhelman and Amy H. Sturgis, iii–vii. Altadena, CA: The Mythopoeic Press, 2009.

———. "Review of Daniel Heath Justice *The Way of Thorn and Thunder*." *Sail* 25, no. 3 (2013).

Okorafor, Nnedi. "Lovecraft's Racism The World Fantasy Award Statuette, with Comments from China Miéville." *Nnedi's Wahala Zone Blog*, 2012. http://nnedi.blogspot.com.au/#!/2011/12/lovecrafts-racism-world-fantasy-award.html.

———. "The Magical Negro." In *Kabu Kabu*. ebook. Prime Books, 2013.

———. "Writers of Color." In *The Cambridge Companion to Fantasy Literature*, edited by Edward James and Farah Mendlesohn, 179–189. Cambridge: Cambridge University Press, 2012.

Older, Daniel José. *Half-Resurrection Blues*. New York: Roc, 2015.

Ono, Kent A. *Contemporary Media Culture and the Remnants of a Colonial Past.* New York: Peter Lang, 2009.

———. "To Be a Vampire on *Buffy the Vampire Slayer*: Race and (Other) Socially Marginalizing Positions on Horror TV." In *Fantasy Girls: Gender in the New Universe of Science Fiction and Fantasy Television*, edited by Elyce Rae Helford. 163–186. Lanham, MD: Rowman & Littlefield, 2000.

"Over 300,000 Players Join *Age of Conan: Unchained* in First Month." *Funcom.com*, 2011. http://www.funcom.com/news/over_300000_players_join_age_of_conan_unchained_in_first_month.

Pace, Tyler. "Can an Orc Catch a Cab in a Stormwind? Cybertype Preference in the *World of Warcraft* Character Creation Interface." In *Conference on Human Factors in Computing Systems Extended Abstracts*, 2011: 2493–2502. Florence, Italy: Academia.net, 2008.

Packer, Joseph. "What Makes an Orc? Racial Cosmos and Emergent Narrative in *World of Warcraft.*" *Games and Culture* 9, no. 2 (December 26, 2014): 83–101.

Packwood, Damon. "Hispanics and Blacks Missing in Gaming Industry." *New America Media*, 2011. http://newamericamedia.org/2011/09/gamer-to-game-makers-wheres-the-diversity.php.

Painter, Nell Irvin. *The History of White People.* New York: Norton, 2010.

Pearson, Roberta. "Fandom in the Digital Era." *Popular Communication* 8, no. 1 (2010): 84–95.

Petzold, Dieter. "'Oo, Those Awful Orcs!': Tolkien's Villains as Protagonists in Recent Fantasy Novels." *Inklings- Jarbuch* 28 (2010): 76–95.

Phi, Thien-bao Thuc. "Game over: Asian Americans and Video Game Representation." *Transformative Works and Cultures* 2 (2009). http://journal.transformativeworks.org/index.php/twc/article/view/84/89.

Pillai, Nicolas. "'What Am I Looking At, Mulder?': Licensed Comics and the Freedoms and Transmedia Storytelling." *Science Fiction Film & Television* 6, no. 1 (2013): 101–117.

"Plot Summary, Conan the Barbarian (2011)." *iTunes Store*, 2011.

Poniewozik, James. "GRRM Interview Part 2: Fantasy and History." *Time*, 2011. http://entertainment.time.com/2011/04/18/grrm-interview-part-2-fantasy-and-history/.

———. "Review of Game of Thrones, 'Winter Is Coming.'" *Time.com*, 2011. http://entertainment.time.com/2011/04/18/game-of-thrones-watch-its-all-in-the-execution/.

Poole, W. Scott. *Monsters in America: Our Historical Obsession with the Hideous and the Haunted.* Kindle. Waco, TX: Baylor University Press, 2011.

Poor, N. "Digital Elves as a Racial Other in Video Games: Acknowledgment and Avoidance." *Games and Culture* 7, no. 5 (2012): 375–396.

Pratchett, Terry. "Guardian Book Club: Terry Pratchett on *Unseen Academicals.*" *The Guardian.* December 12, 2009. http://www.guardian.co.uk/books/2009/dec/12/guardian-book-club-terry-pratchett.

———. *Unseen Academicals.* London: Doubleday, 2009.

Priestly, Rick. *Warhammer Armies: Orcs and Goblins.* 4th ed. Nottingham, UK: Games Workshop Ltd, 1996.

Priestly, Rick, Richard Halliwell, and Bryan Ansell. *Warhammer Fantasy Battle.* Nottingham. UK: Games Workshop Ltd, 1991.

Pucik, David, and David Gaider. "Interview with *Dragon Age: Origins* Lead Writer, David Gaider." *Tor.com*, 2009. http://www.tor.com/blogs/2009/08/interview-with-ligdragon-age-originslig-lead-writer-david-gaider.

Quinnae. "No More Excuses: 'It's the Middle Ages, Yo!'" *The Border House*, 2011. http://borderhouseblog.com/?p=4957.

"Race." *AoCWiki, the Age of Conan Wiki*, 2014. http://aoc.wikia.com/wiki/Race.

Racebending. "Racebending.com." *Racebending.com*, 2013. http://www.racebending.com/v3/about/.

Radish, Christina, and George R. R. Martin. "George R. R. Martin Interview, *Game of Thrones*." *Collider*, 2011. http://collider.com/george-r-r-martin-interview-game-of-thrones/86337/.

Ramraj, Ruby S. "Nalo Hopkinson's Colonial and Dystopic Worlds in *Midnight Robber*." In *The Influence of Imagination: Essays on Science Fiction and Fantasy as Agents of Social Change*, edited by Lee Easton and Randy Schroeder, 131–138. Jefferson: McFarland, 2008.

Randall, Neil, and Kathleen Murphy. "*The Lord of the Rings Online*: Issues in the Adaptation of MMOPRGs." In *Dungeons, Dragons, and Digital Denizens: The Digital Role-Playing Game*, edited by Gerald A. Voorhies, Joshua Call, and Kaite Whitlock, 113–131. New York: Continuum, 2012.

Ransom, A. J. "Warping Time: Alternate Histories, Historical Fantasy, and the Postmodern Uchronie Quebecoise." *Extrapolation: A Journal of Science Fiction and Fantasy* 51, no. 2 (2010): 258–280.

Rastogi, Nina. "Is *Games of Thrones* Racist?" *Browbeat: Slate's Culture Blog*, 2011. http://www.slate.com/content/slate/blogs/browbeat/2011/04/20/is_game_of_thrones_racist.html.

Redding, Maureen T. "Invisibility/Hypervisibility: the Paradox of Normative Whiteness." In *Privilege: A Reader*, edited by Michael S. Kimmer and Abby L. Ferber, 233–255, 2010.

Redfern, Nick. "Genre Trends at the US Box Office, 1991 to 2010." *European Journal of American Culture* 31, no. 2 (2012): 145–167.

Redmond, Sean. "The Whiteness of the Rings." In *The Persistence of Whiteness: Race and Contemporary Hollywood Cinema*, edited by Daniel Bernardi, 91–101. London: Routledge, 2008.

Reid, Robin Anne. "The Wild Unicorn Herd Check-in: the Politics of Race in Science Fiction Fandom." In *Black and Brown Planets: The Politics of Race in Science Fiction*, edited by Isiah Lavender, 225–240. Jackson: University of Mississippi Press, 2014.

Reynolds, James, and Fiona Stewart. "*Lord of the Rings* Labelled Racist." *The Scotsman*. December 14, 2002. http://www.scotsman.com/lifestyle/film/lord-of-the-rings-labelled-racist-1-632928.

Rieder, John. *Colonialism and the Emergence of Science Fiction*. Middletown, CT: Wesleyan University Press, 2008.

Rigathi, Kevin. "Issue 1." *Will This Be a Problem?*, 2014. http://willthisbeaproblem.com/issue-1/.

Riper, A. Bowdoin van. *Science in Popular Culture*. Westport, CT: Greenwood Press, 2002.

Ritter, Christopher John. "Why the Humans Are White: Fantasy, Modernity, and the Rhetorics of Racism in *World of Warcraft*," 2010.

Rivers, Tamara. *The Guardian of Hope*. Oklahoma: Tate, 2009.

Roberts, Celeste. "Go Back in Time with *The Sims Medieval*." *Examiner.com*, 2011. http://www.examiner.com/article/go-back-time-with-the-sims-medieval.

Roberts, Tansy Rayner. "Historically Authentic Sexism in Fantasy. Let's Unpack That." *Tor.com*, 2012. http://www.tor.com/blogs/2012/12/historically-authentic-sexism-in-fantasy-lets-unpack-that.

Robinson, Carol L., and Pamela Clements, eds. *Neomedievalism in the Media: Essays on Film, Television, and Electronic Games*. Lewiston: Edwin Mellen, 2012.

Romeo, Gary. "Southern Discomfort: Was Howard A Racist?" *REHupa*, 2002. http://www.rehupa.com/OLDWEB/romeo_southern.htm.

Rosebury, Brian. "Race in Tolkien Films." In *J. R. R. Tolkien Encyclopedia: Scholarship and Critical Assessment*, edited by Michael D C Drout, 557. London: Routledge, 2007.

Rowland, Thomas D., and Amanda C. Barton. "Outside Oneself in *World of Warcraft*: Gamers' Perception of the Racial Self-Other." *Transformative Works and Cultures* 8 (2010). doi:10.3983/twc.v8i0.258.

Russell, Anna. "Margaret Atwood Chooses 'A Wizard of Earthsea.'" *The Wall Street Journal*, 2014. http://online.wsj.com/articles/wsj-book-club-margaret-atwood-chooses-a-wizard-of-earthsea-1413493430.

Rutledge, Gregory E. "Futurist Fiction & Fantasy : the 'Racial' Establishment Author(s)." *Callaloo* 24, no. 1 (2001): 236–252.

Saldivar, R. "Historical Fantasy, Speculative Realism, and Postrace Aesthetics in Contemporary American Fiction." *American Literary History* 23, no. 3 (August 2, 2011): 574–599. doi:10.1093/alh/ajr026.

Salter, Jessica. "The Fantasy King." *The Age*. 2013.

Salvatore, R L. *The Orc King*. Renton: Wizards of the Coast, 2008.

Sanford, Jason. "Robert E. Howard Was a Racist. Deal with It." *Jason Stanford*, 2010. http://www.jasonsanford.com/jason/2010/09/robert-howard-racist.html.

Saunders, Charles R. *Imaro*. San Francisco: Night Shade, 2006.

———. "Revisiting 'Die, Black Dog!'" *Charles R. Saunders*, 2011. http://reindeermo tel.com/CHARLES/charles_blog42_dieblackdog.html.

———. "Revisiting Imaro." In *Imaro*, 5–12. San Francisco: Night Shade, 2006.

———. "What Is Africa to Me?" *The Chicago Fantasy Newsletter*. Chicago, 1980.

Scalzi, John. "The Internets Hate Scalzi!" *Whatever*, 2009. http://whatever.scalzi.com/2009/03/10/the-internets-hate-scalzi/.

Scheurer, Timothy E., and Pam Scheurer. "The Far Side of the World: Naomi Novik and the Blended Genre of Dragon Fantasy and the Sea Adventure." *The Journal of Popular Culture* 45, no. 3 (2012): 572–591.

Schneer, Jonathon. *London 1900: The Imperial Metropolis*. New Haven: Yale University Press, 1999.

Sernett, Matthew. "Racism in Fantasy." *Matt Sernett: Writer. World Builder. Game Designer*, 2010. http://sernett.com/world-building/racism-in-fantasy/.

Sernett, Matthew. "Human Frailty." In *Races and Classes*, edited by Michele Carter, 20–21. Renton: Wizards of the Coast, 2007.

Serwer, Adam. "*Games of Thrones*: When Fantasy Looks Like Reality." *The Atlantic*, 2011. http://www.theatlantic.com/entertainment/archive/2011/04/game-of-thrones-when-fantasy-looks-like-reality/237196/.

Shanks, Jeffrey. "History, Horror, and Heroic Fantasy: Robert E. Howard and the Creation of the Sword and Sorcery Genre." In *Critical Insights: Pulp Fiction of the '20s and '30s*, edited by Gary Hoppenstand, 3–18. Ipswich, MA: Grey House Publishing, 2013.

Shawl, Nisi. "Appropriate Cultural Appropriation." *International Review of Science Fiction*, 2004. http://www.irosf.com/q/zine/article/10087.

Shefrin, Elana. "*Lord of the Rings*, *Star Wars*, and Participatory Fandom: Mapping New Congruencies Between the Internet and Media Entertainment Culture." *Critical Studies in Media Communication* 21, no. 3 (2004): 261–281.

Shippey, T. A. *J. R. R. Tolkien: Author of the Century*. London: HarperCollins, 2001.
———. *The Road to Middle Earth*. London: HarperCollins, 1982.
Shiu, Anthony Sze-Fai. "What Yellowface Hides: Video Games, Whiteness, and the American Racial Order." *Journal of Popular Culture* 39, no. 1 (2006): 109–125.
Shohat, Ella, and Robert Stam. *Unthinking Eurocentrism: Multiculturalism and the Media*. New York: Routledge, 1997.
Shovlin, Paul. "Canaan Lies Beyond the Black River: Howard's Dark Rhetoric of the Contact Zone." In *Conan Meets the Academy: Multidisciplinary Essays on the Enduring Barbarian*, edited by Jonas Prida, 91–102. Jefferson: McFarland, 2012.
Singer, Marc. "'Black Skins' and White Masks : Comic Books and the Secret of Race." *African American Review* 36, no. 1 (2002): 107–119.
Smith, Craig. "Motion Comics: Modes of Adaptation and the Issue of Authenticity." *Animation Practice, Process and Production* 1, no. 2 (2011): 357–378.
Smith, Justin E. H. "'Curious Kinks of the Human Mind': Cognition, Natural History, and the Concept of Race." *Perspectives on Science* 20, no. 4 (2012): 504–529.
Smith-Akel, Catherine. "A Historical Dissection Of *A Game Of Thrones* Part I." *MTV Geek*, 2011. http://geek-news.mtv.com/2011/04/15/a-historical-dissection-of-a-game-of-thrones-part-i/.
Solomon, David. "Bad Moon Rising." *Grimm*. NBC, USA. August 27, 2012.
———. "Danse Macabre." *Grimm*. NBC, USA. December 8, 2011.
Somerville, Ann. "A Themed Summary of RaceFail '09." *Fiction by Ann Somerville*, 2009. http://logophilos.net/articles/a-themed-summary-of-racefail-'09-in-large-friendly-letters-for-those-who-think-race-discussions-are-hard/.
Spivak, Gayatri Chakravorty. "Can the Subaltern Speak?" In *Marxism and the Interpretation of Culture*, edited by C. Nelson and L. Grossberg, 271–313. Basingstoke: MacMillan, 1988.
Stanfill, Mel. "Doing Fandom, (Mis)Doing Whiteness: Heteronormativity, Racialization, and the Discursive Construction of Fandom." *Transformative Works and Cultures Special Issue: Race and Ethnicity in Fandom: Theory* 8 (2011). doi:10.3983/twc.v8i0.256.
Stanzler, Wendey. "Mama." *Sleepy Hollow*. Fox, USA. November 17, 2014.
Stillinger, Jack. *Multiple Authorship and the Myth of Solitary Genius*. Oxford: Oxford University Press, 1991.
Stout, Amy. "The Novels of Margaret Weis and Tracy Hickman." In *The Universes of Margaret Weis and Tracy Hickman: Realms of Dragons*, edited by Margaret Weis and Tracy Hickman, 1–15. New York: HarperPrism, 1999.
Straubhaar, Sandra Ballif. "Myth, Late Roman History, and Multiculturalism in Tolkien's Middle-Earth." In *Tolkien and the Invention of Myth*, edited by Jane Chance, 101–117. Lexington: The University Press of Kentucky, 2004.
Strickland, Debra Higgs. "Monstrosity and Race in the Late Middle Ages." In *The Ashgate Research Companion to Monsters and the Monstrous*, edited by Asa Simon Mittman and Peter J. Dendle, 365–386. Farnham: Ashgate, 2013.
Sturgis, Amy H. "Meeting at the Intersection: The Challenges Before Us." In *The Intersection of Fantasy and Native America: From H.P. Lovecraft to Leslie Marmon Silko*, edited by David D. Oberhelman and Amy H. Sturgis, 11–22. Altadena, CA: The Mythopoeic Press, 2009.
Sturgis, Amy H., and David D. Oberhelman, eds. *The Intersection of Fantasy and Native America: From H. P. Lovecraft to Leslie Marmon Silko*. Altadena, CA: Mythopoeic Press, 2009.

Sussman, Robert Wald. *The Myth of Race: the Troubling Persistence of an Unscientific Idea*. Cambridge, MA: Harvard University Press, 2014.

Suvin, Darko. *Metamorphoses of Science Fiction*. New Haven: Yale University Press, 1979.

Swinfen, Ann. *In Defence of Fantasy: a Study of the Genre in English and American Literature since 1945*. London: Routledge, 1984.

Tablesaw. "O HAI RACEFAILZ: Notes on Reading an Internet Conflict." *LiveJournal (Tablesaw)*. Live Journal, 2009. http://tablesaw.livejournal.com/404850.html.

Talley, Robert T. "Let Us Now Praise Famous Orcs: Simple Humanity in Tolkien's Inhuman Creatures." *Mythlore* 29, no. 1/2 (2010): 17–28.

"The Octavia E. Butler Memorial Scholarship." *www.carlbrandon.org*, 2014. http://www.carlbrandon.org/butlerscholarship/.

Thomas, Douglas. "KPK, Inc: Race, Nation, and Emergent Culture in Online Games." In *Learning Race and Ethnicity: Youth and Digital Media*, edited by Anna Everett, 155–174. Cambridge, MA: MIT Press, 2008.

Thompson, Kristin. *The Frodo Franchise: The Lord of the Rings and Modern Hollywood*. Berkeley: University of California Press, 2007.

Tolkien, J R R. "Orcs." In *Morgoth's Ring*, edited by Christopher Tolkien, 416–423. London: HarperCollins, 1994.

———. *The Fellowship of the Ring*. London: HarperCollins, 2007.

———. *The Letters of J. R. R. Tolkien*. Edited by Humphrey Carpenter. Kindle. HarperCollins, 2012.

———. *The Return of the King*. London: HarperCollins, 2007.

———. *The Silmarillion*. London: George Allen & Unwin, 1977.

———. *The Two Towers*. London: HarperCollins, 2007.

"Tortage." *AoCWiki, the Age of Conan Wiki*, 2014. http://aoc.wikia.com/wiki/Tortage.

Toynbee, Jason. *Making Popular Music: Musicians, Creativity and Institutions*. London: Hodder Headline, 2000.

Tresca, Michael J. *The Evolution of Fantasy Role-Playing Games*. Jefferson: McFarland, 2011.

Trilling, Renée R. "Medievalism and Its Discontents." *Postmedieval* 2, no. 2 (2011): 216–224.

Tucker, Jeffrey Allen. *A Sense of Wonder: Samuel R. Delany, Race, Identity, and Difference*. Middletown: Wesleyan University Press, 2004.

TV Tropes. "Fantasy Counterpart Culture." *TV Tropes*. http://tvtropes.org/pmwiki/pmwiki.php/Main/FantasyCounterpartCulture.

Unknown. "'Game' Changers: The 10 Biggest Changes Between 'Game of Thrones' and the Books." *Rolling Stone*, 2012. http://www.rollingstone.com/movies/lists/game-changers-the-10-biggest-changes-between-game-of-thrones-and-the-books-20120515/party-on-qarth-19691231.

Utz, Richard. "A Moveable Feast: Repositionings of 'The Medieval' in Medieval Studies, Medievalism, and Neomedievalism." In *Neomedievalism in the Media*, edited by Carol L. Robinson and Pamela Clements, i–v. Lewiston: Edwin Mellen, 2012.

VanDyke, Chris. "Race in *Dungeons & Dragons*." *Race in D&D*, 2008. http://raceindnd.wordpress.com/2008/11/18/nerd-nite-presentation-november-18th-2008/.

Various. "Customer Discussions: Jim Butcher Drama." *Amazon.com*, 2011. http://www.amazon.com/Jim-Butcher-drama/forum/Fx1FI5BSDM1LWIS/Tx3DKU5E06SXCUY/1?asin=0425241130.

———. "*DA3*: Color-Blind Casting." *Bioware Social Network*, 2012. http://social.bioware.com/forums..topic=716201/forum/1/topic/315/index/11928927/1.

———. "Dark Fantasy and Political Correctness?" *Bioware Social Network*, 2009. http://social.bioware.com/forum/1/topic/47/index/47149/1.

———. "Diversity in Thedas …" *Bioware Social Network*, 2009. http://social.bioware.com/forum/1/topic/9/index/1198792/1.

———. "Elven Alienage = Jewish Ghetto?" *Bioware Social Network*, 2009. http://social.bioware.com/forum/1/topic/9/index/642539/5.

———. "Fantasy Novels in Non-Medevial Settings?" *MobileRead*, 2012. http://www.mobileread.com/forums/showthread.php?t=179309.

———. "Fantasy Racism." *Giant in the Playground: Forum*, 2011. http://www.giantitp.com/forums/showthread.php?t=188043.

———. "Favorite Non-Western SF/F Book Settings." *Goodreads*, 2013. http://www.goodreads.com/topic/show/1628773-favorite-non-western-sf-f-book-settings.

———. "More Asian People in *DA*." *Bioware Social Network*, 2011. http://social.bioware.com/%253Cbr/%253Ehttp:/social.bioware.com/forum/1/topic/141/index/7695163/4.

———. "Non-Western Mythology Based Fantasy Novels …" *Giant in the Playground: Forum*, 2012. http://webcache.googleusercontent.com/search?q=cache:6b-gPL3JyqoJ:www.giantitp.com/forums/showthread.php?t=257464+&cd=16&hl=en&ct=clnk&gl=uk.

———. "Political Correctness and *WoW* – Where Do You Stand." *MMO Champion*, 2012. http://www.mmo-champion.com/threads/1117517-Political-correctness-and-WoW-Where-do-you-stand/page4.

———. "Race in *Game of Thrones*: a Request to Not Repeat the Folly of Xaro." *A Forum of Ice and Fire*, 2012. http://asoiaf.westeros.org/index.php/topic/75299-race-in-game-of-thrones-a-request-to-not-repeat-the-folly-of-xaro/.

———. "Racism in Middle Earth." *Reddit*, 2014. http://www.reddit.com/r/tolkienfans/comments/20f25g/racism_in_middle_earth/.

———. "Why No Asian Race?" *A Forum of Ice and Fire*, 2012. http://asoiaf.westeros.org/index.php/topic/76902-why-no-asian-race/.

Vetock, Jeremy. *Orcs & Goblins*. Lenton: Games Workshop, 2010.

Wade, Juliette. "Beyond the Same-Old Fantasy Culture: Nine Authors Worth Reading." *TalkToYoUniverse*, 2013. http://talktoyouniverse.blogspot.com.au/2013/04/beyond-same-old-fantasy-culture-nine.html?showComment=1365442087790&m=1.

Wallin, Mark Rowan. "Myths, Monsters and Marlets: Ethos, Identification, and the Video Game Adaptations of *The Lord of the Rings*." *Game Studies* 7, no. 1 (2007). http://gamestudies.org/0701/articles/wallin.

Washburn, Kathleen. "*The Way of Thorn and Thunder: The Kynship Chronicles* by Daniel Heath Justice." *The American Indian Quarterly* 37, no. 4 (2013): 400–403. doi:10.1353/aiq.2013.0051.

Weis, Margaret, and Tracy Hickman. *Legends I: Time of the Twins*. TSR Inc, 1986.

Weiss, Allen S. "Ten Theses on Monsters and Monstrosity." *TDR: The Drama Review* 48, no. 1 (2004): 124–125.

Wendig, Chuck. "The Pasty White Person Is King." *The Escapist*, 2010. http://www.escapistmagazine.com/articles/view/issues/issue_269/8042-The-Pasty-White-Person-Is-King.

Werber, Niels. "Geo- and Biopolitics of Middle-Earth: a German Reading of Tolkien's *The Lord of the Rings*." *New Literary History* 36, no. 2 (2005): 227–246.

Werner, Peter. "Tarantella." *Grimm*. NBC, U.S.A. February 10, 2011.

Westfahl, Gary. "Who Governs Science Fiction?" *Extrapolation* 41, no. 1 (2000): 63–72.

Whedon, Joss. "Chosen." *Buffy the Vampire Slayer*. UPN, USA. May 20, 2003.

Whitmarsh, Ian, and David S. Jones, eds. *What's the Use of Race?: Modern Governance and the Biology of Difference*. Cambridge, MA: MIT Press, 2010.

Wiggins, Troy L. "*Dragon Age*: Inquisitioning While Black," 2014. https://afrofantasy.wordpress.com/2014/11/23/black-dragon-age-inquisition/.

Wilcox, Rhonda V. "Let It Simmer': Tone in 'Pangs.'" *Slayage: The Journal of the Whedon Studies Association* 9, no. 1 (2011). http://slayageonline.com/essays/slayage33/Wilcox.pdf.

Wilkins, Kim. "'Cutting off the Head of the King': Sovereignty, Feudalism, Fantasy." *Australian Literary Studies* 26, no. 3 (2011): 133–147.

Willsey, Kristiana. "New Fairy Tales Are Old Again: *Grimm* and the Brothers Grimm." In *Channeling Wonder: Fairy Tales on Television*, edited by Pauline Greenhill and Jill Terry Rudy, 210–228. Detroit: Wayne State University Press, 2014.

Wilson, G. Willow. *Alif the Unseen*. London: Corvus Books, 2012.

Winegar, Astrid. "Aspects of Orientalism in J.R.R. Tolkien's *The Lord of the Rings*." *The Grey Book* 1 (2005): 1–10.

Wirth-Nesher, Hana. *City Codes: Reading the Modern Urban Novel*. Cambridge: Cambridge University Press, 1996.

Wiseman, Len. "Pilot." *Sleepy Hollow*. Fox, USA. September 16, 2013.

Wolf, Mark J. P. *Building Imaginary Worlds: the Theory and History of Subcreaton*. New York: Routledge, 2012.

Wolfe, Gary K. *Evaporating Genres: Essays on Fantastic Literature*. Middletown: Wesleyan University Press, 2011.

Wong, Rydra. "RaceFail '09," 2009. http://rydra-wong.livejournal.com/146697.html.

Wood, Brian. *Conan the Barbarian: The Song of Bêlit Part 2*. Digital. Dark Horse, 2013.

———. *Conan: Queen of the Black Coast*. Milwuakee: Dark Horse, 2013.

Workman, Leslie J. "Editorial." *Studies in Medievalism* 1, no. 1 (1979): 1–3.

Worley, Alec. *Empires of the Imagination: A Critical Survey of Fantasy Cinema from Georges Melies to* The Lord of the Rings. Jefferson: McFarland, 2005.

Wynne-Jones, Diana. *A Tough Guide to Fantasyland*. Vista, 1996.

Young, Helen. "Approaches to Medievalism: a Consideration of Taxonomy and Methodology Through Fantasy Fiction." *Parergon* 27, no. 1 (2010): 163–179.

———. "Critiques of Colonialism in Robin Hobb's *Soldier Son* Trilogy." *Extrapolation* 55, no. 1 (2014): 33–20.

———. "Diversity and Difference: Cosmopolitanism and *The Lord of the Rings*." *Journal of the Fantastic in the Arts* 21, no. 3 (2010): 351–365.

———. "'It's the Middle Ages, Yo!': Race, Neo/medievalism, and the World of *Dragon Age*." *The Year's Work in Medievalism* 27 (2012). http://ejournals.library.gatech.edu/medievalism/index.php/studies/article/view/11/29.

———. "Place and Time: Medievalism and Making Race." *The Year's Work in Medievalism* 28 (2013). https://sites.google.com/site/theyearsworkinmedievalism/all-issues/28-2013.

———. "Race in Online Fantasy Fandom: Whiteness on Westeros.org." *Continuum: Journal of Media & Cultural Studies* 28, no. 5 (2014): 737–747.

———. "Racial Logics, Franchising, and Video Game Genres: *The Lord of the Rings.*" *Games and Culture* (2015): 1–22. doi:10.1177/1555412014568448.

———. "Whiteness and Time: the Once, Present, and Future Race." *Studies in Medievalism* 24 (2015): 39–49.

Young, Robert J. C. *The Idea of English Ethnicity.* Maldon, MA: Blackwell, 2008.

Zaid, Gabriel. *So Many Books: Reading and Publishing in an Age of Abundance.* Edited by Natasha Zimmer. Paul Dry Books, 2003.

Zubernis, Lynn, and Katherine Larsen. *Fandom at the Crossroads: Celebration, Shame and Fan/Producer Relationships.* Newcastle Upon Tyne: Cambridge Scholars Press, 2012.

Index